INDIGO
BAR HARBOR

ACADIA
THE COMPLETE GUIDE

4th Edition

©2016 DESTINATION PRESS & ITS LICENSORS

ISBN: 978-1-940754-02-4

Written & Photographed
by James Kaiser

This book would not have been possible without the help of many generous people.

Special thanks to Wanda Moran, Ginny Reams, Brooke Childrey, and the entire staff at Acadia National Park, professors Bill Carpenter and Helen Hess at COA, Mindy Viechnicki at Allied Whale, Rebecca Cole-Will at the Abbe Museum, and Erika Latty at Unity College. Special thanks also to Andrea Rincon, Rick Crowe, Whitney Crowe, Kevin Crowe, every other Crowe, Steve Foley, Cathy McDonald, Dan Shubert, Scott Petticord, Abby Johnston, Matt Tracy, Alyssa and Seth, Josia and Maria, and Lacey Sinclair. As always, a very special thanks to my family & friends, who have always supported me. Even when they shouldn't have.

All information in this guide has been exhaustively researched, but names, phone numbers, and other details do change. If you encounter a change or mistake while using this guide, please send an email to changes@jameskaiser.com. Your input will help improve future editions of this guide. Special thanks to eagle-eyed readers Mark Goldstein, who spotted typos/errors in past editions!

Legal Disclaimer: Although every attempt has been made to ensure the accuracy of information contained within this guide, the author and publisher do not assume and disclaim any liability to any party for any loss or damage caused by errors or omissions. Information has been obtained from sources believed to be reliable, but its accuracy and completeness are not guaranteed. All maps in this guide are based on official USGS data, but serious hikers should supplement their outings with detailed hiking maps. If the rigors and threats of nature are in any way beyond your capabilities, do not attempt any hike in this guide. Many photos in this book depict people in precarious situations. Do not assume that any situations depicted in this book are safe in any way.

Additional Photography & Image Credits

National Park Service: 98, 99, 105, 120, 125; Abbe Museum: 100, 101;
Bangor Daily News: 126; Bar Harbor Historical Society: 118, 122, 123;
North Wind Picture Archives: 77, 78, 109, 116, 119; Kim Strauss: 27;
USGS: 71; Wildlife Stock: 86–97; Hinckley Company: 260; Allied Whale: 113
Printed in China

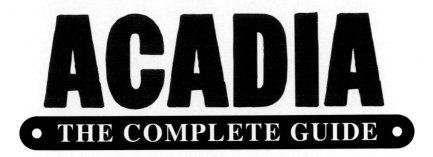

ACADIA

• THE COMPLETE GUIDE •

4th Edition

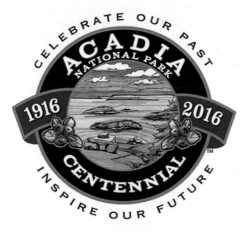

Five percent of this book's profits will be
donated to Friends of Acadia

friendsofacadia.org

MIX
Paper from
responsible sources
FSC® C005748
FSC
www.fsc.org

JAMES KAISER

CONGRATULATIONS!

IF YOU'VE PURCHASED this book, you're going to Mount Desert Island. Perhaps you're already here. If so, you're in one of the most amazing places in the world—a gorgeous island filled with granite mountains that rise above the sea. An island so beautiful that nearly half of it has been permanently protected as Acadia National Park. A place where you can hike in the morning, sea kayak in the afternoon, and sit down to a gourmet meal at night.

So who am I and why should you listen to me? My name is James Kaiser, and I was born and raised near Mount Desert Island. I spent my childhood summers hiking and biking in Acadia National Park and my college summers working in Bar Harbor. Although my work as a travel writer and photographer has carried me away from Mount Desert Island, I return as often as possible. It's my favorite place in the world. I know the park, I know the towns, I know the locals—I know the secrets! And I'm going to show you the best that Mount Desert Island has to offer.

You could easily spend a month exploring Mount Desert Island and not run out of things to do. But if you're like most people, you've only got a few days. Make those few days count! With a limited amount of time, you've got to plan your trip wisely. This book puts the best of Mount Desert Island and Acadia National Park at your fingertips, helping you maximize your time for an unforgettable vacation. Whether you're here to hike, here to sight-see, or just here to eat and hang out, *Acadia: The Complete Guide* is the only guide you'll need.

Now let me show you the best that Mount Desert Island and Acadia National Park have to offer!

CONTENTS

ADVENTURES p.21

Hiking, biking, sea kayaking, rock climbing, sailing—Acadia has it all. The only question is what not to do!

BASICS p.28

Everything you need to know to plan an amazing trip, from seasonal weather patterns and local transportation, to the island's best lobster and beer.

GEOLOGY p.55

Over the past 500 million years, Acadia has been home to colliding continents, erupting volcanoes, massive glaciers, and countless other splendid catastrophes.

ECOLOGY & WILDLIFE p.61

Lying at the boundary of two major ecological zones, Mount Desert Island is home to a stunning range of plants and animals. The pristine waters offshore are also filled with hundreds of amazing creatures, from starfish to humpback whales.

HISTORY p.99

Originally home to Wabanaki Indians, Mount Desert Island was settled by white colonists in the 1700s. Artists arrived in the mid-1800s, and by the end of the century Bar Harbor was one of America's most exclusive resort. In 1919 wealthy summer visitors spearheaded the creation of Acadia National Park—the first national park east of the Mississippi.

ACADIA NATIONAL PARK p.131

Nearly half of Mount Desert Island has been protected as Acadia National Park. The Park Loop Road is Acadia's most popular attraction, and the park's hiking trails and carriage roads are world-class. Acadia also includes Schoodic Peninsula on the mainland and half of Isle au Haut, a small, rugged island 15 miles southwest.

ISLAND TOWNS p.223

From bustling tourist towns to traditional fishing villages, there's something for everyone here. The eastern half of the island is home to Bar Harbor, the island's unofficial capital, and the exclusive summer colonies of Northeast Harbor and Seal Harbor. The western "quiet" side of the island sees far fewer tourists, but it's home to some of the island's best attractions.

OFFSHORE ISLANDS p.269

Over a dozen smaller islands lie offshore Mount Desert Island, and several are accessible by ferry. Day tripping to small islands with year-round fishing communities is a fascinating experience. Physically cut off from the mainland, these islands are home to some of the most rugged and remote communities in America.

ACADIA TOP 5

TOP 5 SIGHTS

Cadillac Mountain, 174
Bass Harbor Lighthouse, 266
Jordan Pond House, 162
Sand Beach, 148
Bar Island, 226

TOP 5 ADVENTURES

Hiking, 17
Biking, 21
Sea Kayaking, 19
Rock Climbing, 23
Scenic Flights, 232

TOP 5 HIKES

Precipice, 180
Beehive, 178
Penobscot Mountain, 186
Acadia Mountain, 190
Sargent Mountain, 188

TOP 5 PLACES TO SWIM

Echo Lake Beach, 257
Echo Lake Ledges, 257
Long Pond, 235
Seal Harbor Beach, 241
Sand Beach, 148

HIGHLIGHTS

TOP 5 RESTAURANTS

Burning Tree, 235
Mâche, 235
Red Sky, 259
Fiddler's Green, 259
XYZ, 259

TOP 5 PLACES FOR LOBSTER

Thurston's, 265
Beal's, 259
Trenton Bridge, 221
C-Ray, 221
Islesford Dock, 272

TOP 5 BOAT TRIPS

Diver Ed, 26
Bar Harbor Whale Watch, 26
R.L. Gott, 27
Margaret Todd, 27
Alice E., 27

TOP 5 RAINY DAY ACTIVITIES

Mount Desert Oceanarium, 219
Abbe Museum, 229
Dorr Museum, 229
Criterion Theater, 233
Reel Pizza, 233

INTRODUCTION

TWO-THIRDS OF the way up the craggy coast of Maine lies Mount Desert Island, home to granite mountains, picture-perfect harbors, and Acadia National Park. Mount Desert Island is the crown jewel of coastal New England—the only place on the East Coast where the mountains literally meet the sea. Those mountains, rounded and smoothed by Ice Age glaciers, form one of the most distinctive profiles in the world. From the sea they look like a string of giant ice cream scoops rising out of the water. Cadillac Mountain, the island's tallest peak, is 1,530 feet—the highest point on the eastern seaboard north of Rio de Janeiro.

Nestled between the island's 24 mountain peaks are forests, lakes, meadows, marshes and Somes Sound, a narrow inlet that nearly cuts the island in two. Roughly half of Mount Desert Island has been set aside as Acadia National Park. At just 46,000 acres, Acadia is one of the smallest national parks in America, but it's also one of the most popular, luring roughly 3 million visitors a year. Acadia's most famous attraction is the Park Loop Road. This 27-mile road runs along the island's dramatic eastern shore before cutting through the forest, passing two pristine lakes, then twisting and turning to the top of Cadillac Mountain.

Acadia also boasts 125 miles of stunning hiking trails and 45 miles of carriage roads perfect for biking or horseback riding. In addition to land on Mount Desert Island, the park also includes Schoodic Peninsula and half of Isle au Haut, a remote island 14 miles southwest of Mount Desert Island.

About half a dozen coastal villages dot the shores of Mount Desert Island. Some, like Bar Harbor, are built around tourism. Others, like Bass Harbor, carry on as quiet fishing hamlets, much as they always have. There are also wealthy summer towns like Seal Harbor and Northeast Harbor, plus historic villages like Somesville, the island's oldest town. Several offshore islands are also accessible by ferry, making them great for day tripping.

In the days before Columbus, Mount Desert Island was the seasonal home of the Wabanaki Indians. Hardy coastal settlers arrived in the late 1700s. Artists and tourists discovered the island in the mid-1800s, and by the end of the century Bar Harbor was one of America's most exclusive summer resorts. By the 1930s, however, the glamour of the island had started to fade, and in 1947 a massive fire burned down many of Bar Harbor's once-grand mansions. Following the fire, the island rebuilt and reestablished itself as a major tourist mecca. Today it attracts a diverse mix of summer visitors—outdoor junkies, fanny-packed retirees, college students, hippies and billionaires—proving there's something for everyone here.

Physically beautiful, ecologically diverse, and culturally unique, Mount Desert Island is one of the most fascinating islands in the world.

Cranberry Isles & MDI

Bass Harbor

Penobscot Mountain

HIKING

ACADIA NATIONAL PARK is a hiker's paradise. There are roughly 125 miles of trails in Acadia, ranging from gentle strolls through spruce-pine forest to sheer ascents up nearly vertical cliffs. Over a dozen mountain peaks are accessible via hiking trails, offering some of the dramatic views on the East Coast.

If Acadia's trails were just crumbling dirt paths, they would still be amazing. But here on Mount Desert Island—home to hundreds of rich, civic-minded summer residents—the trails have been spruced up beyond belief. In 1999 the non-profit Friends of Acadia and Acadia National Park launched *Acadia Trails Forever*, a $13 million project to fully restore the entire trail system. Today Acadia's trails are in fantastic shape. Nearly every trail is well-marked and easy-to-follow, with cairns (stone piles) and blue blazes on trees and rocks leading the way. Many trails also feature stone steps that gracefully lead you up otherwise challenging terrain. This is rich man's hiking—open to the public. If you visit Acadia without going on at least one hike, you should return to the mainland ashamed.

This book provides maps and trail info for eight terrific hiking trails (p.178). My favorites are the Precipice, Penobscot Mountain and Acadia Mountain. In Acadia National Park hikes are rated easy, moderate, strenuous or ladder (strenuous with some climbing on iron ladders or rungs). If you're looking for easy hikes, check out the Shorepath or Bar Island in Bar Harbor (p.223), Thuya Garden in Northeast Harbor (p.243), or Ship Harbor and Wonderland in Bass Harbor (p.263). And if your thirst for hiking exceeds that of the average visitor, pick up a copy of Tom St. Germain's *A Walk In The Park*, available at stores throughout the island.

Also note that the Island Explorer Shuttle (p.30) is a fantastic resource for hikers. By removing the hassle of parking, the Island Explorer opens up new realms of hiking possibilities. In the pre-Island Explorer days, you had to loop back to wherever you parked your car. Now you can take full advantage of Acadia's extensive trail network, starting in one place and finishing someplace completely different. (Long live the Island Explorer!)

Hiking Rules: Overnight backpacking is not allowed in Acadia National Park. Bicycles and horses are not allowed on any hiking trails, all pets must be kept on a leash no greater than six feet in length at all times. Also note that swimming is prohibited in lakes or ponds that are posted as public water supplies.

Porcupine Islands

SEA KAYAKING

THE CRAGGY COAST of Maine is famous for great sea kayaking, and everything kayakers love about Maine—deserted islands, calm bays, pristine water, abundant wildlife—can be found around Mount Desert Island. Not surprisingly, sea kayaking is one of Acadia's most popular adventures.

The waters around Mount Desert Island present some unique challenges. Frigid water, craggy shorelines, fishing boats, dense fog, unpredictable weather, 12-foot tides, swift currents—these are just some of the things you might encounter. With a trained guide, you're in good hands. Without a trained guide, you can get in trouble, fast. Fortunately, Mount Desert Island has some of the best sea kayak guides in Maine, so everyone, including beginners, can get out on the water. The outfitters below are all recommended. Rates generally run $40–$50 for a 2–4 hour tour.

AQUATERRA ADVENTURES

Launching directly from the Bar Harbor Pier, Aquaterra Adventures specializes in half-day trips around the Porcupine Islands. Their Family Discovery trip is geared to young children. (Bar Harbor, 207-288-0007, aquaterra-adventures.com)

COASTAL KAYAKING TOURS

Coastal Kayaking offers half-day and full-day tours, plus sunset paddles and multi-day trips. (Bar Harbor, 207-288-9605, acadiafun.com)

NATIONAL PARK SEA KAYAKING

This eco-oriented outfitter offers tours on the quiet western shores of MDI, which is calmer than Frenchman Bay and has terrific wildlife. (Bar Harbor, 207-288-0342, acadiakayak.com)

MAINE STATE SEA KAYAK

Based in Southwest Harbor, Maine State Sea Kayak (a sister company of National Park Sea Kayaking) also specializes in tours of western MDI. (Southwest Harbor, 207-244-9500, mainestateseakayak.com)

Carriage Roads

BIKING

IF YOU LOVE biking, there's plenty to love about Acadia National Park. Although the park's mountains and hiking trails are off-limits to mountain bikers, there are plenty of on-road options in and around the park, including paved roads that skirt the coastline and carriage roads that explore the island's forests.

Acadia's carriage roads are a 57-mile network of gravel roads, built by John D. Rockefeller, Jr. between 1913 and 1940. The roads were originally designed for horse-drawn carriages, but today the gravel roads are perfect for mountain bikes. The carriage road system stretches from Bar Harbor to Seal Harbor, meandering through beautiful forests, passing a dozen lakes and ponds, and crossing a series of 17 dramatic stone bridges. The overall experience feels like stepping into a New England fairy tale. Not surprisingly, Acadia's carriage roads are one of the park's most popular attractions.

Most of the carriage roads follow a gentle grade. They were designed, after all, for relaxing carriage rides. But there are some hilly sections throughout the system that offer a good workout. The best entry points for the carriage roads near Bar Harbor are Eagle Lake and Duck Brook Bridge. From late June through September, the popular Bicycle Express shuttle runs every 30 minutes between the Bar Harbor Village Green and Eagle Lake. Farther south, you can hop on the carriage roads at Bubble Pond, the Jordan Pond House, or at one of two stops along Route 198 north of Northeast Harbor. For more info on the carriage roads see page 195.

If you're more interested in cycling on paved roads, check out the famous 27-mile Park Loop Road (p.133), which passes by some of Acadia's top attractions. During the busy summer months, however, you'll contend with traffic, tour buses and plenty of gawking tourists. More relaxing rides are found on the western side of the island, particularly Route 102A and Route 102 between Bass Harbor and Pretty Marsh.

There are also some great off-island cycling options. The six-mile loop on Schoodic Peninsula (p.205) offers beautiful ocean scenery with far fewer tourists than the Park Loop Road. There's also great biking on Swan's Island (p.279), a 7,000-acre island six miles south of Mount Desert Island that's accessible via a ferry from Bass Harbor. Swan's Island has over a dozen miles of paved roads that pass by working harbors and quaint fishing villages. And because it only has about 350 year-round residents, there's very little traffic on Swan's Island.

Bicycle rentals are available in both Bar Harbor (p.223) and Southwest Harbor (p.255).

Otter Cliffs

ROCK CLIMBING

Acadia's bold mountains and stunning coastal scenery make it one of the most unique climbing destinations on the East Coast. There's lots of great rock climbing from Georgia to Maine, but only in Acadia can you scale sheer cliffs that rise out of the sea. Spend a day climbing above crashing waves while sailboats and lobsterboats pass by just offshore, and you'll understand why thousands of climbers flock to Acadia in the summer and fall.

If you've never rock climbed before, Acadia is a great place to learn. There are plenty of beginner climbs, and two outfitters in Bar Harbor offer private lessons and guided climbs. Rates at both outfitters are similar. Private lessons run about $150 per half day, $260 per full day. Group rates are much cheaper. If you're an experienced rock climber, be sure to pick up a copy of *Acadia: A Climber's Guide*, by Jeff Butterfield, or *Rock Climbs of Acadia* by Grant Simmons.

The most famous and popular climbing spot on the island is Otter Cliffs (p.154). These vertical cliffs rise straight out of the ocean, offering stunning views of the rocky shore along Ocean Drive. Climbs at Otter Cliffs range in difficulty from 5.4 to 5.12. Due to its fame, popularity and accessibility, Otter Cliffs is often crowded in the summer months. But there are plenty of other climbs on the island that offer equally stunning views with few, if any, crowds. South Wall, a multi-pitch climb on Champlain Mountain, rises hundreds of feet above sea level and offers terrific views of Frenchman Bay. There are also some challenging climbs on Great Head (next to Sand Beach) and on South Bubble at the north end of Jordan Pond.

Rock Climbing Outfitters

ACADIA MOUNTAIN GUIDES

Based out of Alpenglow Adventure Sports on 228 Main Street, AMG offers a wide range of climbing lessons and a well-stocked retail store.
(207-288-8186, acadiamountainguides.com)

ATLANTIC CLIMBING SCHOOL

Atlantic Climbing School offers everything from pure beginner courses to guiding and advanced skills.
(207-288-2521, climbacadia.com)

Sailing on the Alice. E

SAILING & BOAT TOURS

THE BEAUTIFUL, ISLAND-STREWN coast of Maine is one of America's premier boating destinations, and the waters around Mount Desert Island offer some of the best boating in Maine. Fortunately, you don't need to own a boat or know anything about boating to spend some time on the water. There are over a dozen boat tours departing from Mount Desert Island, featuring everything from mellow day sails to whale watching on jet-powered catamarans.

I love boats, and I've never been on a boat tour that I didn't enjoy. If nothing else, the views of Mount Desert Island from the water are spectacular. That said, some boat tours are definitely better than others. Listed on the following pages are my favorite tours. If none of them strikes your fancy, there are plenty of additional tours that depart from Bar Harbor (p.223), Northeast Harbor (p.243) and Southwest Harbor (p.255).

The most popular tours are on motorboats, which cover more distance in less time than sailboats. Motorboat tours include whale watching, nature tours, lobstering demonstrations, deep sea fishing, lighthouse tours and day trips to small offshore islands.

Sailboat tours, by contrast, tend to focus more on the sailing experience and the scenery than any specific activity. If you just want to spend a relaxing day on the water, sailboats are the way to go. The question is big or small? Small sailboats offer a more intimate experience where you'll get to know your captain and fellow passengers. (Most small sailboats also offer private charters.) At the other end of the spectrum, big sailboats offer a smoother ride, a better value, and the unique experience of watching trained crew hoist massive sails—a rare sight these days, but an important part of daily life in Maine a century ago. In my opinion, the only drawback of big sailboats is the cattle-call feel that can come from boarding a boat with dozens of other passengers.

Finally, if you're more interested in hands-on boating, head to Southwest Harbor, the unofficial boat building capital of the island. In Southwest Harbor you can charter boats or, if your pockets are deep enough, buy them. Also worth mentioning is the Wooden Boat School (thewoodenboatschool.com), a famous sailing and boat-building school located west of Mount Desert Island in the town of Brooklin, on the mainland.

ACADIA'S BEST BOAT TRIPS

Starfish Enterprise

I can't recommend this "Dive-In Theater" trip highly enough! The supremely entertaining Diver Ed (A Downeast version of Jacques Cousteau) and his knowledgeable wife "Captain Evil" show visitors Maine's fascinating underwater world from the 51-foot Starfish Enterprise. After putting on a dry suit, Diver Ed jumps overboard with an HD video camera and seeks out strange and fascinating creatures on the seafloor. The live images are then projected onboard, showing crabs, starfish, lobsters, and other ocean critters in their natural habitat. Ed then resurfaces with the animals for a highly entertaining show-and-tell. If you're visiting with kids, this will probably be the highlight of their trip. Adults $40, seniors $35, kids $30. (207-288-3483, divered.com)

Friendship V

This jet-powered, 112-foot aluminum catamaran whisks passengers 25–30 miles offshore in search of whales. Humpback, finback and minke whales sightings are common. The Gulf of Maine is one of the world's premier whale habitats, and the sight of these gentle giants is breathtaking. You'll also be treated to stunning offshore views of Mount Desert Island and potential porpoise, seal, and seabird sightings. I like the morning trip, which combines whale watching with a trip to Petit Manan Island, which is home to puffins and Maine's second tallest lighthouse (p.113). The *Friendship V* is closely affiliated with Allied Whale (p.86), so whale watching trips are enjoyable *and* they help a great cause. Adults $60, kids $25. (207-288-2386, barharborwhales.com)

R.L. Gott

For nearly two decades Captain Kim Strauss has been offering narrated cruises through the gorgeous islands just south of Bass Harbor. If you're interested in wildlife, coastal Maine history, lobstering or idyllic scenery, a tour on the 40-foot *R.L. Gott* can't be

beat. Captain Strauss has been plying the waters of Blue Hill Bay since he was two months old, and he's a wealth of local knowledge. Two trips are offered: a 3.5-hour lunch cruise ($30 adults, $15 kids) that includes a stop on Frenchboro Island (p.277) and a two-hour afternoon trip ($25 adults, $15 kids) focused on wildlife. (207-244-5785, bassharborcruises.com)

Margaret Todd

This 151-foot schooner offers two-hour cruises around Frenchman Bay and the Porcupine Islands. The *Margaret Todd* is the only four-masted schooner to work New England's waters in over 50 years, and she sails

three times daily (10 am, 2 pm, sunset). All trips depart from the Bar Harbor Inn pier, where tickets are also available. Adults $40, children $30. (207-288-4585 , downeastwindjammer.com)

Alice E.

This gorgeous 42-foot sailboat, built in 1899, is the oldest known Friendship Sloop still sailing today. (In the days before diesel engines, Friendship Sloops were the original Maine lobsterboat). The *Alice E.*'s affable captain, Karl Brunner, had this historic vessel exquisitely restored, and today it sails from Southwest Harbor on trips around Somes Sound and the Cranberry Isles— two of the most scenic waterways in the region. Two-hour sails are $50 per passenger. Reservations required. (207-266-5210, sailacadia.com)

Mount Desert Island
BASICS

Getting to Mount Desert Island

You don't need a boat to get to Mount Desert Island (which is only an island by about 50 feet at low tide). The Trenton Bridge connects the island to the mainland via Route 1A. How you get to the Trenton Bridge is up to you.

BY CAR

Driving is the most popular way to get to Mount Desert Island. From southern Maine there are two options: the fast route and the scenic route. The fast route follows I-95 north to Bangor, heads east on I-395 to Route 1A, and follows Route 1A to Mount Desert Island (about a 3-hour drive from Portland). The scenic route starts in Portland and follows Route 1 up the coast of Maine to Ellsworth. From there you'll connect with Route 1A to Mount Desert Island. Between Portland and Ellsworth, you'll pass through Rockland, Camden and other beautiful coastal towns. The scenic route takes about 5–6 hours from Portland (not counting weekend traffic).

BY PLANE

The Hancock County/Bar Harbor Airport (bhbairport.com) is located in the town of Trenton on the mainland, 12 miles from downtown Bar Harbor. In the summer US Airways runs daily flights between Boston and Bar Harbor. From late June through August the Island Explorer Shuttle (p.30) runs free shuttles between the Bar Harbor Airport and downtown Bar Harbor. Taxis and rental cars are available year-round. The next closest airports are Bangor International Airport, located in Bangor, Maine (1.5-hour drive from MDI) and Portland International Jetport, located in Portland, Maine (3-hour drive from MDI).

BY BUS

Greyhound and Concord Coach offer daily service to Bangor. From June–October, the Bar Harbor Shuttle (207-479-5911, barharborbangorshuttle.com) offers daily service from Bangor to Bar Harbor (advance reservations required). Limited year-round service from Bangor to Bar Harbor is available from Downeast Transportation (207-667-5796 , downeasttrans.org).

BY BOAT

Over 100 cruise ships call to port in Bar Harbor each year. Most arrive in September and October on fall foliage cruises.

Mount Desert Island At a Glance

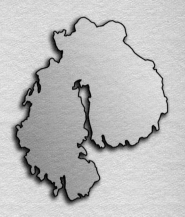

Area: 108 Square Miles

Length: 16 miles

Width: 10 miles

Mountain Peaks: 26

Lakes and Ponds: 28

Average Tides: 8–12 feet

Population: 10,500

Year-round Residences: 5,000

Summer Residences: 2,100

Avg. Annual Rainfall: 48 inches

Avg. Annual Snowfall: 61 inches

Avg. Annual Fish and Lobster Harvest: 6 Million Pounds

Total Assessed Value of Private Property on MDI: $4.6 Billion

Latitude: 44.3° N, Longitude: 68.3° W

If you headed due east from MDI, you'd hit Bordeaux, France; Bologna, Italy; the Gobi Desert, China; and Mongolia.

If you headed due south from MDI, you'd hit Caracas, Venezuela; La Paz, Bolivia; and Mendoza, Argentina.

Pronouncing Mount "Desert" Island

Is it "Desert" (as in the Sahara) or "Dessert" (as in ice cream)? Strangely, Mainers say both, and the island's linguist roots offer little clarification. The island was named in 1604 by the French explorer Samuel Champlain, who dubbed it *L'Isle des Monts-déserts* ("Island of Barren Mountains"). The "desert" (Sahara) camp claims they are justified by the "Barren" description. The granite peaks, they argue, are barren like a desert. Meanwhile, the "dessert" (ice cream) camp claims the French pronunciation of *desert* sounds more like "dessert." In addition, Champlain was saying the peaks were "deserted" which sounds more like "dessert." Where do I stand? I grew up saying "dessert," which I learned from my mother, a fifth generation Mainer. And far be it for me to argue with mom.

Getting Around Mount Desert Island

BY CAR

Driving around Mount Desert Island is easy. There are only a handful of major roads, and because you're on an island it's nearly impossible to get lost. The only hassle is parking, which is often in short supply in July and August, especially on the Park Loop Road.

ISLAND EXPLORER SHUTTLE

The best way to get around the island these days is the free Island Explorer shuttle. These propane-powered buses were experimentally introduced in 1999 to reduce traffic and air pollution. The experiment was wildly successful, and today the Island Explorer runs seven routes linking hotels, inns and campgrounds with popular destinations throughout the island. (An eighth shuttle route circles Schoodic Peninsula on the mainland.) Shuttles run from late June through mid-October, but service is scaled back after Labor Day. Island Explorer maps and timetables are available at any visitor center and on the Island Explorer Web site (exploreacadia.com). In addition to helping the environment, riding the Island Explorer removes the hassle of parking. Unless you're going somewhere the Island Explorer doesn't go (the top of Cadillac Mountain, for example), it's often easier and more convenient to take the Island Explorer.

TAXI COMPANIES

Acadia Cab (207-288-8294), **At Your Service Taxi** (207-288-9222), **MDI Taxi & Touring Company** (207-288-3333)

Visitor Information

THOMPSON ISLAND VISITOR CENTER

This small visitor center, located on tiny Thompson Island near the northern tip of MDI, is a great place to ask questions, pick up free publications, and inquire about last-minute lodging. Open 8am–6pm, mid-May to mid-October.

HULLS COVE VISITOR CENTER

Acadia National Park's main visitor center is also the start of the Park Loop Road and a minor hub for the Island Explorer. See page 138.

ACADIA INFORMATION CENTER

This information center on Route 3 in Trenton offers free brochures, interactive displays and a knowledgeable staff. (800-358-8550, acadiainfo.com).

Hotels & Lodging

There are dozens of places to stay on Mount Desert Island, and listing them all would take dozens of pages. Rather than waste all that paper (when all you need is one room), I've posted all lodging information at jameskaiser.com.

The vast majority of lodging is found in Bar Harbor, but Northeast Harbor and Southwest Harbor also have some great options. No matter where you end up, the island is small, and you won't be too far from anything. If you find hotels on the island expensive, check out off-island towns such as Trenton or Ellsworth.

Camping

Acadia National Park operates four campgrounds (below). There are also about a dozen private campgrounds just outside the park. Visit jameskaiser.com for complete camping info, including campground photos.

BLACKWOODS CAMPGROUND

Acadia's most popular campground is located between Bar Harbor and Seal Harbor on the eastern side of Mount Desert Island. Over 300 campsites. Open year-round. Reservations recommended May–Oct. Cost: $30 per night May–Oct, $10 per night Nov–April.

SEAWALL CAMPGROUND

This remote 200-site campground is located near the southwestern tip of Mount Desert Island. Some people love the quiet location; others find it too far away from the popular attractions on the eastern half of the island. Open Memorial Day weekend through September. Reservations recommended June–August. Cost: $30 per night drive-in sites, $22 per night walk-in sites.

DUCK HARBOR CAMPGROUND

Located on remote Isle au Haut (p.213), Duck Harbor Campground is my favorite campground in the park. It offers a terrific combination of peace, quiet and natural beauty. There are five primitive campsites, each with a three-sided, lean-to shelter. Duck Harbor is open May 15 to October 15. Campsites are only available by advance reservation. Cost: $25 special use permit fee.

SCHOODIC WOODS CAMPGROUND

This brand new campground opened in 2015. It features 94 campsites near Schoodic Peninsula (p.205), about three miles southeast of Winter Harbor. There are 8.5 miles of bike paths near the campground, plus a hiking trail to the top of Schoodic Head. Cost: $22 walk-in tent sites, $30 drive up tent/small RV, $36 RV with electric only sites, $40 RV with electric and water. Open late May to Columbus Day.

Weather & When to Go

"If you don't like the weather in Maine, wait a minute. It'll change." It's a cliché, but it's also true. The weather in Maine, especially along the coast, is *highly* unpredictable. It varies from day to day, month to month, and year to year. There's simply no rhyme or reason to it—as any local weatherman will attest. (Tough job, Maine weatherman.)

My favorite source of forecasts and weather info is the National Weather Service (weather.gov). But in my experience, even their forecasts are only partially reliable. Most are based on regional forecasts, and there's tremendous variability within the region. In my highly non-scientific study of local forecasts, I've found that 24-hour reports are right about 70% of the time, 48-hour reports are right about 50% of the time, and 36-hour reports are right about 30% of the time. Any report over 36 hours is pretty much useless.

That said, when the weather is good in Acadia, it's incredible—sunny, warm, with a cool ocean breeze. And even when it's bad—foggy, rainy, snowy—the coast has a beautiful mystique. Also keep in mind that, in terms of annual precipitation, coastal Maine is ranked second in America only to the Pacific Northwest. It can rain any time of the year on short notice, so pack accordingly.

SPRING

Spring (aka Mud Season) definitely has its pros and cons. Melting ice and snow keep things soggy in the early spring, but by late spring the island has often dried out and temperatures can be divine. Spring is also bug season. Biting bugs are most active between mid-May and mid-June when running water provides optimum breeding conditions. But bug numbers very much depend on how rainy it has been (p.41). Spring is also when local businesses come out of their long winter hibernation. Hotels and shops start opening in late April, and by Memorial Day most of the island is open for business. Peak tourist season doesn't arrive until Fourth of July, at which point everything is open for business.

SUMMER

Sunny summer days bring perfect temperatures to Mount Desert Island: high 70s with a cool ocean breeze. But summer can also bring thick fog that blankets the island for hours, or sometimes days. Sunny or not, July is when things get busy on Mount Desert Island—booked hotels, waiting lists at restaurants, crowded parking lots. (This is all relative, of course. By Maine standards it's crazy, but New Yorkers will probably appreciate the peace and quiet.) August is even busier than July, with families trying to cram in one last vacation before school starts, and Mainers trying to enjoy one last blast of summer before fall. Then, just when things seem like they can't get any crazier, Labor Day hits and peak season suddenly ends.

FALL

Fall is one of the best times to visit Mount Desert Island. The weather is crisp, the crowds are light, and the foliage is spectacular. Weather in early September is generally divine, but temperatures start dropping by the end of the month. Fall is also the busiest season for cruise ships, which dock in Bar Harbor and disgorge thousands of passengers onto the town's narrow streets. But there's usually a lull in visitation in mid-September between peak summer season and "leaf peeping" season. Fall foliage generally peaks between October 13–22, but the dates vary from year to year. (Check out mainefoliage.com for current conditions.) By late October, temperatures start dropping, tourists start departing en masse, and locals start hunkering down. By early November, many storefront windows in Bar Harbor are covered in plywood, and the island enters its long winter visitation.

WINTER

Winter is a cold, desolate season on Mount Desert Island. New England has some of the longest winters in the United States, although the ocean does warm things up a bit on the coast. Average snowfall on Mount Desert Island is 61 inches, but the snow that falls often melts quickly. When the snow sticks, Acadia's carriage roads are fantastic for cross country skiing, and snowmobiling is allowed on the Park Loop Road. Although most hotels, restaurants, museums and attractions are closed in winter, there are a few hardy restaurants and hotels that stay open year-round.

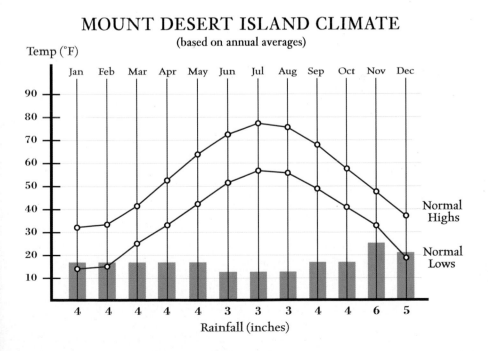

MOUNT DESERT ISLAND CLIMATE
(based on annual averages)

ACADIA WEATHER

Weather in coastal Maine is, in a word, unpredictable. Although summers on the coast are generally sunny and divine, conditions can quickly change. What started out as a sunny day can end in rain, fog or (in very rare cases) snow! It turns out that weather patterns in Maine—and all of New England for that matter—are more variable and more extreme than almost any other place the United States. As Mark Twain once said, "I reverently believe that the Maker who made us all makes everything in New England but the weather. I don't know who makes that, but I think it must be some raw apprentices in the weather-clerk's factory."

Maine is located at roughly 45° N latitude, exactly halfway between the Equator and the North Pole. This puts Maine in the middle battleground between the hot, humid air of the tropics and the cold, dry air of the Arctic. Storms in these middle latitudes follow fairly predictable paths called storm tracks, and almost all storm tracks in the United States have the potential to pass through Maine.

In addition to regular storms, Maine must also contend with hurricane season, which officially runs from June through November. Most hurricanes make landfall in the Southeast and dissipate long before reaching Maine. Those hurricanes that make it to Maine generally arrive in August, September or October, and most are Category 2 or less by the time they arrive.

Temperatures in Maine can vary dramatically throughout the year, but temperatures along the coast are moderated by the ocean. During the dog days of summer, when inland Maine is hot and humid, the Gulf of Maine's cold water keeps temperatures mild. And in the dead of winter, when inland Maine often suffers sub-zero temperatures, the ocean's relative warmth boosts temperatures along the coast.

Long-term weather trends in Maine are also influenced by a weather system known as the North Atlantic Oscillation (NAO). The NAO results from the interaction between a semi-permanent low pressure system over Iceland (the Icelandic Low) and a semi-permanent high pressure system over Bermuda (the Bermuda High). The interactions between these two systems have the power to alter storm tracks across the North Atlantic. When the pressure difference between these two systems is high, the NAO is in positive mode, resulting in relatively milder temperatures and decreased storm activity in Maine. When the pressure difference between the Icelandic Low and the Bermuda High is low, the NAO is in negative mode, which often brings cold temperatures and increased storm activity to Maine. NAO modes are long-term trends that can last for decades. The present NAO mode has been mostly positive since the late 1970s.

Reading the Wind

Maine weather can change in an instant, but you can still get a sense of what lies ahead by doing what sailors have done for hundreds of years: reading the wind.

During the summer, western winds generally bring sunny days. Winds that blow from the southwest bring warm, dry air, while winds that blow from the northwest bring cool, dry air, sweeping away moisture and creating spectacular visibility.

Winds that blow from the east are far less desirable. Southeasterly winds often bring overcast days with the possibility of drizzle and fog. And if the wind starts blowing from the northeast, batten down the hatches—a dreaded nor'easter could be on the way.

Although most common in the winter, nor'easters can happen any time of year. They form when cold, arctic air blowing down from Canada collides with warm, tropical air moving up the East Coast. The collision creates a counterclockwise spinning cyclone similar to a hurricane. As the cyclone moves offshore, winds arrive from the northeast—hence the term "nor'easter." When nor'easters form offshore, they can bring gale force winds, extreme surf, and massive amounts of rain, sleet or snow. Remember *The Perfect Storm*? That was an offshore nor'easter. Onshore nor'easters are much less catastrophic; many behave like regular storms.

"Nor'easter" or "No-theaster"?

Today everyone calls them nor'easters. But old salts claim the original word, spoken by true Mainers, was "no-theaster." Back then, the distinction was critical in life-or-death situations, because "nor'east" might be mistaken for "nor'west," especially when wind, waves, and Maine accents were taken into account.

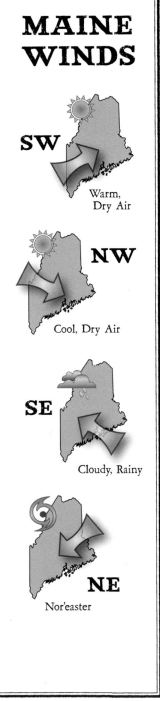

MAINE WINDS

SW
Warm, Dry Air

NW
Cool, Dry Air

SE
Cloudy, Rainy

NE
Nor'easter

Coastal Fog

Fog is a fact of life in Downeast Maine, which typically sees 55 or more foggy days each year. (Locals sometimes refer to August as "Fogust.") Fog is essentially a cloud that forms at ground level when moist air cools to the dew point. Along the coast there are two common types of fog: evaporation fog and advection fog. Evaporation fog, also known as "sea smoke," forms in the winter when frigid air flows over the ocean. As ocean water evaporates into the frigid air, the air saturates and condenses. Sea smoke is light and thin and generally burns off by late morning. Advection fog, on the other hand, forms when warm and cold air interact. This happens in the summer when cool, moist air from the ocean blows over the heated land. It also happens offshore when warm, moist air from the Gulf Stream comes into contact with cold air in the Gulf of Maine. This is the classic pea-soup fog, and it can blow in from the ocean and linger along the coast for days. As one Maine sea captain put it in the 1800s, "You'll find fogs all the world over, but the Gulf Stream fog beats 'em all. It will heave in sooner, stay longer, and become thicker, and go away quicker than any fog I ever met in my voyaging."

One Perfect Day on Mount Desert Island

- Sunrise on Cadillac Mountain (p.174)
- Breakfast at Cafe This Way (p.235) or Two Cats (p.235)
- Midmorning walk on the Bar Harbor Shorepath (p.225)
- Late-morning drive along the Park Loop Road (p.133)
- Lunch at the Jordan Pond House (p.162)
- Afternoon Nature Cruise on the R.L. Gott (p.27)
- Sunset at Bass Harbor Lighthouse (p.266)
- Dinner at Thurston's Lobster Pound (p.265)

One Perfect Day for the Outdoor Lover

- Sunrise on Cadillac Mountain (p.174)
- Blueberry Pancakes at Jordan's Restaurant (p.237)
- Morning hike on the Precipice (p.180)
- If the Precipice is closed, hike Penobscot Mountain (p.186)
- Lunch at Side Street Cafe (p.228)
- Afternoon Sea Kayaking (p.19)
- Sunset on Cadillac Mountain (p.174)
- Dinner at Rosalie's Pizza ($) (p.236) or Mâche ($$$) (p.235)
- Bar Harbor Real Ale at the Lompoc Cafe (p.237)

Rainy Day Options

Rainy days are a fact of life in Maine. Fortunately, there are plenty of indoor activities on Mount Desert Island.

MUSEUMS

Abbe Museum (p.229)

Bar Harbor Historical Society (p.229)

Bar Harbor Oceanarium (p.219)

George B. Dorr Natural History Museum (p.229)

Great Harbor Maritime Museum (p.246)

MDI Historical Society (p.253)

Old School House & Museum (p.246)

Petite Plaisance (p.247)

Seal Cove Auto Museum (p.253)

Wendell Gilley Museum (p.257)

MOVIES & ENTERTAINMENT

Criterion Theater (p.233)

Reel Pizza (p.233)

ImprovAcadia (p.228)

Atlantic Brewing Company Tour (p.52)

What is Downeast Maine?

Downeast Maine refers to the state's northeast coastal region lying between Penobscot Bay and Canada. The term "Downeast" is derived from sailing terminology. Because the region's prevailing winds blow from the west, and because the coast of Maine trends northeast, ships sailing from Boston to Maine would sail downwind to travel east. Hence the term "Downeast." On a similar note, ships sailing from Maine to Boston sail upwind, which explains why some Mainers still say they're going "up to Boston."

Downeast Maine

Seasonal Festivals & Events

After emerging from its winter slumber, Mount Desert Island celebrates with festivals in the spring, summer and fall. Check local newspapers and publications for exact festival dates.

LEGACY OF THE ARTS FESTIVAL (June)

This week-long festival, held every year in late June, features exhibits, workshops and an art show on the Village Green. (legacyartsfestival.com)

FOURTH OF JULY

The biggest celebration of the year in Bar Harbor is filled with small town charm. Events include a pancake breakfast, morning parade, afternoon lobster bake, "lobster races" where live lobsters race each other in specially designed saltwater tanks, and evening fireworks at the town pier.

BAR HARBOR TOWN BAND (July, August)

The Bar Harbor Town Band offers free concerts on Mondays and Thursdays at 8pm on the Village Green.

HARBOR HOUSE FLAMINGO FESTIVAL (July)

Southwest Harbor's annual plastic pink flamingo-themed festival is a sight to behold. Don Featherstone, the inventor of the pink plastic flamingo, presides over a parade, which is followed by food and music events.

BAR HARBOR MUSIC FESTIVAL (July)

Since 1967 the Bar Harbor Music Festival has been organizing weekend concerts featuring classical, jazz and pop. Times and locations vary, so call or check the schedule online. (207-288-5744, barharbormusicfestival.org)

NATIVE AMERICAN FESTIVAL (July)

This annual festival, co-sponsored by the Abbe Museum, is held the first Saturday after the Fourth of July at the College of the Atlantic. It features Native American basketry, beadwork, drumming and dancing.

OPEN GARDEN DAY (July)

Every other year, members of the Mount Desert Garden Club showcase their private gardens in late July. (gcmdgardenday.com)

LOBSTERBOAT RACES (July, August)

Lobsterboat races—Maine's version of NASCAR—are a summer tradition. The closest races are held in Bass Harbor (p.263) in early July and Winter Harbor (p.207) in early August.

ACADIA NIGHT SKY FESTIVAL (September)

The dark skies of Downeast Maine are delightfully free of urban light pollution, making it one of the East Coast's top stargazing destinations. The Acadia Night Sky Festival celebrates the regions dark skies with a variety of astronomy programs. (nightskyfestival.org)

GARLIC FESTIVAL (September)

In late September food lovers unite for a celebration of food, beer, wine and garlic at Smuggler's Den Campground. (nostrano.com)

OKTOBERFEST (October)

Every October nearly two dozen Maine breweries descend on Southwest Harbor for the town's annual Oktoberfest celebration at Smuggler's Den Campground. (acadiaoktoberfest.com)

MDI MARATHON (October)

The island's annual marathon always draws a crowd. (mdimarathon.org)

Local Publications

Mount Desert Island's weekly newspaper, *The Islander* (mdislander.com), focuses on local news and includes plenty of info geared towards visitors. It's worth picking up a copy just for the weekly calendar of events that lists upcoming festivals, concerts, lectures and more.

Acadia National Park publishes a seasonal newspaper, which includes tide charts, sunrise/sunset times and a calendar of free ranger programs. A separate guide for the Island Explorer shuttle lists routes and schedules.

There are also several free advertiser-supported publications on the island. As long as you take their commercial recommendations with a grain of salt, they can also offer some good local info.

Finally, if you're interested in coastal Maine news, look for a copy of *The Working Waterfront* (workingwaterfront.com). This excellent free monthly paper, published by the Island Institute (p.44), focuses on fishing, fishermen, and Maine island life.

Bugs

Mosquitoes and tiny biting midges (aka "no-see-ums") are the most common bugs encountered on Mount Desert Island. The number of biting bugs varies each year depending on how much rain falls—more rain, more bugs—but bugs are most common in the spring and early summer. If you plan on hiking, biking or walking through the woods, it's always a good idea to bring bug spray with DEET. If you do find yourself covered with red, itchy bug bites, buy some hydrocortisone cream (1%) and apply it to the bites.

Astronomy in Acadia

Today nearly two-thirds of Americans live where they can't see the stars due to "light pollution" (manmade light). But here in Acadia National Park, which boasts some of the darkest skies in the U.S., the Milky Way still blazes across the sky at night. If you're not looking up at the stars, you're literally missing half the show. Don't know much about astronomy? Check out the free ranger program "Stars Over Sand Beach" (Acadia's free newspaper lists dates and times). And if you visit in September, be sure to check out the Acadia Night Sky Festival (acadianightskyfestival.com), a multi-day event that features workshops, speakers and plenty of telescopes aimed at those spectacular stars.

Charitable Organizations

Acadia was the first national park created entirely from privately donated land, and that spirit of giving continues today. The following organizations all offer fantastic ways to give back to Acadia, helping to protect the spectacular landscape for future generations.

FRIENDS OF ACADIA

This wonderful non-profit, founded in 1986, works with the National Park Service to help preserve and protect Acadia National Park. Friends of Acadia has raised millions of dollars to maintain Acadia's hiking trails and carriage roads in perpetuity, and it was a driving force behind the Island Explorer shuttle system. Friends of Acadia also organizes volunteer programs and lobbying efforts on behalf of the park. (friendsofacadia.org)

ALLIED WHALE

This marine mammal research center, affiliated with Bar Harbor's College of the Atlantic, conducts conservation research on marine mammal populations and their habitats. Founded in 1972, it has been at the forefront of whale research for decades. More information on page X. (coa.edu/allied-whale)

MAINE COAST HERITAGE TRUST

Founded in 1970, the Maine Coast Heritage Trust was a pioneer in using conservation easements to put permanent development restrictions on private land (often in exchange for tax breaks). To date it has protected over 130,000 acres in Maine, including more than 275 entire islands and 3,000 acres on Mount Desert Island. (mcht.org)

ISLAND INSTITUTE

This community development organization, founded in 1983, focuses on preserving the ecological and cultural heritage of Maine's 15 year-round island communities. Five of those islands—Islesford, Great Cranberry Island, Frenchboro, Swan's Island and Isle au Haut—lie within sight of Mount Desert Island. (islandinstitute.org)

NATURE CONSERVANCY

This global non-profit, founded in 1956 by a group that included Rachel Carson (author of *Silent Spring*), helps protect natural places around the world, including over one million acres in Maine. Several islands near Mount Desert Island are protected by the Nature Conservancy, including Great Duck Island and Placentia Island. (nature.org)

Blueberry Bushes, Fall

LOCAL FOOD

Maine Lobster

Maine is home to the tastiest lobster on the planet, so don't even think about visiting without sampling the state's quintessential crustacean. In addition to being delicious, lobster meat is extremely healthy. It's virtually fat free, has less cholesterol than chicken or beef, and it's packed full of vitamins A, B12, E and Omega-3 fatty acids.

Lobster has been a local delicacy for thousands of years. Native tribes cooked lobster by placing layers of seaweed over hot embers, then piling lobsters, mussels and clams on top. European colonists copied this technique, which came to be known as a lobster bake.

For the most part, however, early settlers thought of lobster as cheap food that was inferior to fish. Many people claim there was once a law that stated prisoners would not be fed lobster more than twice a week. (Scholars who have investigated this law can find no evidence of its existence.) Then, sometime in the 1800s, diners in Boston and New York developed a taste for fresh lobster. This led to the invention of the lobster smack, a sailboat designed specifically to transport live lobster, which kicked off the commercialization of the lobster industry. Before long popular dishes like Lobster Newburg and Lobster Thermidor had catapulted the once-lowly crustacean to the height of sophistication.

There are plenty of restaurants that serve expensive lobster dinners on Mount Desert Island, but the freshest, best lobster is generally found at rough-around-the-edges lobster shacks where salt water tanks are often built right into the counter. Don't be fooled by appearances. These raggedy seafood shrines are as good as it gets. My favorite places for lobster are Thurston's (p.265), Beal's (p.259), Abel's (p.247) and the Trenton Bridge Lobster Pound (p.221).

To learn about the natural history of lobsters, see p.74.

Soft Shell Clams

Commonly called "steamers," soft shell clams (*Mya arenaria*) are the famous "steamed clams" served throughout Maine.

They are harvested from tidal mudflats, where they live 6–10 inches under the surface, extending long black siphons ("necks") to the surface to filter nutrients from the water at high tide. When steamed, the thin white shells open to reveal soft, tender meat. To eat a steamer, scoop out the innards and peel off the tough, rubbery exterior covering the neck and outer edges. Next, dip the meat in clam broth, which removes any remaining grit. Finally, dip the clam in butter, pop into your mouth and enjoy. (Although purists insist on butter, I love steamers dipped in extra virgin olive oil.) Try the steamers at C-Ray (p.221), where owner Joshua is one of three licensed clammers on Mount Desert Island. You can rest assured his clams are always fresh.

Hard Shell Clams

Most East Coast hard shell clams are the same species, *Mercenaria mercenaria*, but they have different names depending on their size. Littlenecks (named for Little Neck Bay, New York) are less than 2 inches across. Cherrystones (named for Cherrystone Creek, Virginia) are about 2.5 inches across. And quahogs (pronounced *coe*-hogs—a word likely derived from the native word

Cherrystone

"poquauhock") measure 3 inches or more across. Clam meat gets tougher with size. Littlenecks are often used in pasta dishes, cherrystones are enjoyed raw on the half shell, and quahogs are chopped up for clam chowder. Sadly, most clam chowder served on Mount Desert Island is not made from scratch—it's ordered in bulk from large food distributors and arrives in plastic bags. Try the homemade clam chowder at the Fish House (p.237) or Peekytoe (p.236). (Maine clam chowder starts with a milky, brothy base—a stark contrast to the clear clam chowders found in southern New England.) If you'd like to try raw cherrystones, head to—where else?—Cherrystones (185 Main Street, Bar Harbor).

Littlenecks

Oysters

Oysters have complex flavors heavily influenced by their local habitat. They are filter feeders that remove plankton and nutrients from the water—a single oyster can filter up to 50 gallons per day—and over time they concentrate the various flavors of their surroundings. Oyster farmers refer to this unique taste as *meroir*—a play on the French word *terroir*, which describes how local soil influences the flavor of wine. Maine's pristine inlets and bays are ideal for oyster cultivation, and over the past decade oyster farming has flourished. Although Maine oysters need at least three years to reach market size (compared to one year in warmer climates), they possess a depth of texture and flavor prized by top chefs. Oysters grown near Acadia include Waukeag Neck, Top Notch and Tauton Bay. Try the oysters at Peekytoe (p.236), which caries a number of local varieties.

Mussels

Although the mussels native to Maine, *Mytilus edulis*, are commonly called "blue" mussels, the shells are mostly black with bands of iridescent blue. The most popular way to cook these beautiful bivalves is to steam them with white wine, garlic and parsley. When the shells open, they release a briny liquid, creating a delicious broth that you can scoop up with discarded shells or soak up with crusty bread. Mussels are simple to cook, so go ahead and order them at any decent restaurant.

Pickled Wrinkles

These large carnivorous sea snails are the escargot of Downeast Maine. Traditionally harvested during lean times, these protein-packed snacks are preserved through pickling. Unlike periwinkles, which are found in the intertidal zone (p.68), wrinkles (aka whelks) are found in deeper water below the tide line. Lobstermen often find them in their traps. The best place to try wrinkles is the Pickled Wrinkle (p.207) near Schoodic Peninsula. You can also find packaged wrinkles in some local markets.

Scallops

There are three kinds of
scallops on the East Coast.
Sea scallops are the most
common, with shells that grow up
to 12 inches across. Bay scallops and calico
scallops grow 2–3 inches across. Scallops live on the ocean floor, and their beautiful shells (made famous by the Shell Oil logo) have over 100 tiny bight blue
"eyes" that help them detect predators. Unlike most bivalves scallops can swim
short distances by clapping their shells, propelling them away from predators such as starfish. Scallops are commonly harvested by dredging—towing
heavy metal nets across the ocean floor. The scallop meat prized by cooks is
the adductor muscle that holds the shells together. This meat is often soaked in
the preservative sodium tripolyphosphate to increase bulk and give it a shiny
white appearance. Although they look nice in the supermarket, such "wet" scallops are considered inferior to the "dry" scallops that have not been soaked in
chemicals. Dry scallops are often hand harvested by divers, which is more labor
intensive than dredging but far less destructive to the marine ecosystem. Try
the scallops at the Burning Tree (p.235).

Fiddleheads

The coiled tips of young ostrich ferns (*Matteuccia
struthiopteris*) are considered a delicacy in Maine and
eastern Canada. When boiled or steamed they have a
texture similar to asparagus with a woodsy aftertaste.
European settlers learned to eat fiddleheads from native
tribes, who foraged for them in the spring to use as food
and medicine. Ostrich ferns grow in clusters along the banks
of rivers, streams and marshes. Overharvesting can destroy a
patch, however, so foragers are *very* secretive about their favorite
locations. Foragers must be able to distinguish fiddleheads from
similar looking braken ferns, which are toxic. Fiddleheads must be
gathered when young—adult ferns are toxic—and raw fiddleheads
are also toxic. If you don't poison yourself trying to eat a fiddlehead,
you'll savor a tasty wild vegetable packed with antioxidants, omega-3s,
omega-6s and vitamin D. No matter the season, you can buy pickled
fiddleheads at the Atlantic Brewing Company (p.52).

Popovers

These puffy pastries are the unofficial baked treat of Acadia and Mount Desert Island. The basic batter is the essence of simplicity: flour, eggs, milk, salt. When baked in a popover pan, the batter "pops" over the top, thus inspiring the name. Popovers are normally served with butter and jam. In effect, they are an Americanized version of English Yorkshire pudding. Popovers and tea have been the signature dish at the Jordan Pond House (p.162) for over a century. These days popovers are also available at plenty of other restaurants, most notably the Asticou Inn (p.247) in Northeast Harbor.

Whoopie Pies

This iconic dessert was traditionally made by slathering white frosting between two chocolate cake patties. Over the past decade, however, an explosion of new whoopie flavors—pumpkin, gingerbread, blueberry, peanut butter—have flourished, significantly raising the profile of this once-humble treat. What hasn't changed is the ongoing dispute between Maine and Pennsylvania over who invented it. Pennsylvania claims whoopies were first made by Amish housewives, who packed them in their husbands' lunches. When the husbands discovered the tawdry bundle of sin, they shouted out *Whoopie!*—thus inspiring the name. Skeptical Mainers don't buy that, and in recent years they have gone to great lengths to prove their whoopie bone fides. In 2009 the town of Dover Foxcroft launched the Maine Whoopie Pie Festival, which now lures several thousands people, and in 2011 the Maine state legislature declared the whoopie pie the official "State Treat of Maine" (blueberry pie was already the official "State Dessert"). Maine also captured the record for World's Largest Whoopie Pie in 2011 with a whopping 1,062 pounder. The previous record holder, Pennsylvania, baked a paltry 200-pound whoopie. Whoopie pies are available at stores throughout Mount Desert Island, but I like the whoopies at the Pink Pastry Shop (75 Main Street, Bar Harbor).

Wild Blueberries

After lobsters, wild blueberries are Maine's most famous natural delicacy. Maine leads the nation in wild blueberry production, and over 40,000 acres of wild blueberries are harvested within 60 miles of Acadia.

Although smaller than cultivated blueberries, wild blueberries are sweeter and tastier. They also contain nearly twice the antioxidants of cultivated berries. Some studies indicate that a diet rich in wild blueberries may help improve memory.

Maine's official state berry is one of a handful of berry species native to North America (cranberries, strawberries and raspberries are the others). Blueberries were an important food for Indians, who combined dried blueberry powder with cornmeal, honey and water to make a pudding called *Sautauthig*. They also brewed a strong, aromatic tea from the root of the blueberry bush.

In 1822 Abijah Tabbutt of Sugar Hill, Maine, invented the Blueberry Rake, a hand-held harvesting tool that looks like a metal dustpan with rounded teeth. Tabbutt's invention led to wide-scale cultivation of Maine's vast blueberry fields, but it wasn't until the Civil War that the berry became famous outside New England. During the Civil War, scurvy-ravaged Union troops were in desperate need of vitamin C. Maine sardine canneries were converted to blueberry canneries, and the vitamin-rich berries were sent south. Before long the entire country had developed a taste for blueberries, and demand increased after the war.

Today Maine harvests over 80 million pounds of wild blueberries each year. Each spring over 30 million bee hives, each containing 30,000 to 100,000 bees, are brought to Maine to pollinate the blueberry fields. Harvest season starts in late July/early August and runs through the first heavy frost in September or October. These days blueberry picking machines harvest most of the crop, while migrant workers rake the areas that machines can't reach. After the berries have been picked, the bushes' green leaves turn bright red in the fall.

Wild blueberry bushes grow like weeds throughout Mount Desert Island, turning Acadia's mountains into massive, all-you-can eat buffets in late summer. During this time wild blueberries also spring up in supermarkets and roadside stands. Buy a bunch and freeze them for later. And here's an old Maine trick: spread the berries out on a cookie tray, freeze them, and then put them in a plastic bag. That way the blueberries won't clump together when you take them out of the bag.

Try the blueberry pie at Cottage Street Bakery (p.237) and the Blueberry Ale at the Atlantic Brewing Company (p.52).

Atlantic Brewing Company

The "ABC" is the oldest and most famous brewery on Mount Desert Island. Founded in 1990 in Bar Harbor's Lompoc Cafe (p.237), their first beer was Bar Harbor Real Ale, a dark, malty beer with a light, crisp finish. Real Ale was an immediate hit, and today it outsells most other beers on the island. In 1998 the brewery moved to a new location several miles west of Bar Harbor. Today they offer a wide variety of beers, including Coal Porter, Blueberry Ale made from local blueberries, and the obligatory IPA. Seasonal beers include Summer Ale, a hybrid English ale/German lager, and Leaf-Peepin Ale, an English-style red ale brewed with German noble hops. Tours of the brewery are offered three times daily at 2pm, 3pm and 4pm. As of this writing a new tasting room in downtown Bar Harbor was in the works. Call or visit their website for details. (207-288-2337, atlanticbrewing.com)

Bartlett Maine Estate Winery

For over 30 years, Bob and Kathe Bartlett have been making top-notch fruit wines from Maine blueberries, blackberries, raspberries, loganberries, apples and pears. Most of their fruit wines are dry or semi-dry, but they also produce dessert wines and honey meads. They have over 20 varieties of wine, and they produce over 7,000 cases each year. Bartlett Maine Estate Winery also distills award-winning pear eau de vie, apple brandy, and Rusticator's Rum—a gold medallist at the 2013 San Francisco World Spirits Competition. The winery/distillery is located in Gouldsboro, 23 miles east of Ellsworth near Schoodic Peninsula (p.205). Their tasting room is open Tuesday–Saturday, 10am–5pm, Memorial Day through Columbus Day. (207-546-2408, bartlettwinery.com)

Moxie

This carbonated beverage has a bittersweet flavor that divides people into one of two camps: those who like it and those who hate it. (I like it.) Created in the 1870s by Dr. Augustin Thompson, it was first marketed as "Moxie Nerve Food," a medicine that prevented "paralysis, softening of the brain, nervousness, and insomnia." Dr. Thompson claimed the drink was derived from a secret South American plant (now known to be gentian root), and he chose the name Moxie based on a supposed native word for "dark water." Following extensive advertising, the word "moxie," meaning pluck or energy, entered the popular lexicon. In 2005 Moxie was officially designated the Soft Drink of Maine.

Allen's Coffee Flavored Brandy

For better or worse, this cheap, sweet coffee-flavored liquor is the unofficial spirit of Maine. Step into any store that sells booze and notice the unusual amount of shelf space devoted to Allen's, which has been the state's bestselling liquor for over 20 years, earning it the nickname "The Champagne of Maine." The 1,750 ml bottle outsells all other liquors in the state, and the 1 liter, 750 ml and 375 ml bottles are ranked fourth, sixth and eighth respectively. In no other state does Allen's even crack the top 100—not even Massachusetts where it's made! Annual sales in Maine top one million bottles—one for nearly every man, woman and child in the state. Allen's first became popular with fishermen in the 1960s, but how it rose to its current "prominence" is a bit of a mystery. What is known is that Mainers like to mix it with milk, a concoction called simply Allen's & Milk. Not long ago many local bartenders refused to carry Allen's because of its rough and tumble reputation. As its fame/infamy has grown, however, Allen's has become available at upscale bars and restaurants—albeit ironically.

GEOLOGY

MOUNT DESERT ISLAND is one of the most fascinating geologic features on the eastern seaboard. Unlike much of the East Coast, which is sandy and flat, Mount Desert Island towers 1,500 feet above a rocky shore. No fewer than 26 mountain peaks rise above the island, some visible up to 60 miles at sea. How these mountains formed is a fascinating story that involves colliding continents, erupting volcanoes, scouring glaciers, and countless other splendid catastrophes. The end result: one of the most beautiful islands in America.

Five hundred million years ago, Maine was covered by an ancient ocean that pre-dated the modern Atlantic. Geologists call this ocean the Iapetus Ocean (Iapetus was the father of Atlas, "Atlantic"). As ancient rivers flowed into the Iapetus Ocean, vast amounts of sediment accumulated offshore. This sediment—a combination of sand, mud, and silt—piled up in thick layers, and over millions of years the bottom layers were compressed into sedimentary rock. As tectonic plates shifted, this newly formed rock was pushed deep below the surface of the Earth where extreme heat and pressure transformed the sedimentary rock into schist, a metamorphic rock similar to slate. The schist that formed is called Ellsworth schist, and it is the oldest rock found on Mount Desert Island.

After the Ellsworth schist formed, tectonic action pushed it near the surface where it became the floor of the Iapetus Ocean. As rivers from ancient continents deposited fresh sediments into the Iapetus Ocean around 420 million years ago, a new layer of sedimentary rocks formed on top of the Ellsworth schist. These new sedimentary rocks are called the Bar Harbor Formation. Roughly 20 million years later, a string of volcanic islands formed in the Iapetus Ocean, and ash from erupting volcanoes settled on top of the Bar Harbor Formation, forming a third set of rocks: the Cranberry Isles Series.

By about 400 million years ago, the three oldest rocks on Mount Desert Island—Ellsworth schist, Bar Harbor Formation, and Cranberry Isles Series—had formed. At this point all three rocks were part of an ancient continent called Avalonia, lying somewhere between North America and Europe in the Iapetus Ocean. But slowly, as tectonic plates shifted, North America and Avalonia started moving toward each other, and eventually the two continents collided.

The collision pushed up a massive mountain chain and caused huge pools of magma to rise up under the previously formed Avalonian rocks. Around 360 million years ago, some of this magma cooled into granite, creating the fourth (and most famous) rock formation on Mount Desert Island. But at this point all four rocks were still buried deep underground.

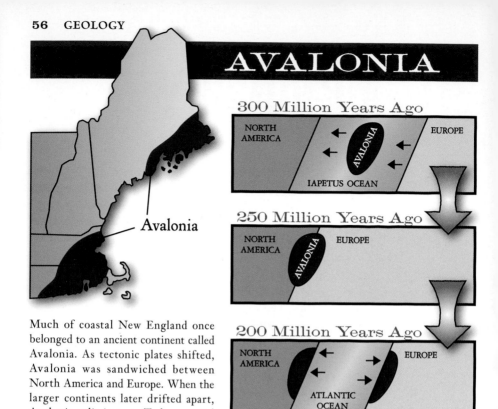

AVALONIA

300 Million Years Ago

NORTH AMERICA · AVALONIA · EUROPE · IAPETUS OCEAN

250 Million Years Ago

NORTH AMERICA · AVALONIA · EUROPE

200 Million Years Ago

NORTH AMERICA · ATLANTIC OCEAN · EUROPE

Avalonia

Much of coastal New England once belonged to an ancient continent called Avalonia. As tectonic plates shifted, Avalonia was sandwiched between North America and Europe. When the larger continents later drifted apart, Avalonia split in two. Today, coastal New England and Western Europe share many of the same Avalonian rocks.

Although geologists know a good deal about rock formation on Mount Desert Island between 500 and 350 million years ago, the last 350 million years are a bit of a mystery. Any evidence indicating what kind of landscape existed here has long since eroded away. They do know, however, that after the collision of North America and Avalonia, Africa and Eurasia smashed into North America to form a huge supercontinent called Pangea. These collisions also pushed up the Appalachian Mountains. At this point Maine was located near the geographic center of Pangea—a position close to the Equator with a warm, tropical climate.

Then, around 200 million years ago, Pangea started to break apart. Around 150 million years ago, Avalonia split in two with the western portion stuck to North America and the eastern portion stuck to Europe. (Even today, coastal Maine and Western Europe share many of the same Avalonian rocks.) As North America and Europe drifted apart, the Atlantic Ocean was born and North America moved north from the equator to its present location. During this time, erosion slowly chipped away the landscape to reveal the rocks that would ultimately form Mount Desert Island. But it would take one last dramatic act of geology before the island took on the familiar profile we know today.

THE ICE AGE

AROUND TWO MILLION years ago, Earth entered the Ice Age and thick layers of snow accumulated in the Arctic that compacted into massive sheets of ice. Soon the ice sheets were set into motion under the pressure of their own weight, at which point they became glaciers. Pushing south, the glaciers consumed everything in their path. Boulders, soil, trees—everything but the bedrock was picked up and carried along.

But even the bedrock did not escape unscathed. The glaciers, essentially dirty ice full of loose debris, acted like giant sheets of sandpaper, grinding down the bedrock and smoothing it out. The glaciers advanced over much of North America, then retreated abruptly. Then they advanced and retreated again. Then they advanced and retreated nearly a dozen more times. The most recent glacial cycle ended around 12,000 years ago.

Scientists are unsure what triggered the Ice Age (a period we are still in today) or why glacial advance has followed a somewhat predictable cycle. One culprit seems to be a small wobble in the earth's orbit that affects how much solar radiation reaches the Earth. When the wobble goes one way, solar radiation increases, temperatures rise, snowfall decreases, and the glaciers melt. When the wobble goes the other way, solar radiation decreases, temperatures drop, snowfall increases, and the glaciers advance. This cycle—earth wobbling, glaciers advancing, Earth wobbling, glaciers retreating—generally lasts about 120,000 years. Cool periods of glacial advance last about 100,000 years with warmer, interglacial periods of about 10,000 to 20,000 years in between. (We are currently about 15,000 years into the current interglacial period.)

Prior to the Ice Age, Mount Desert Island had been home to a series of jagged granite mountains separated by steep, V-shaped valleys cut by streams over millions of years. When the glaciers arrived, they flowed into the V-shaped valleys and gouged them out into graceful U-shaped valleys. Soon only jagged mountain peaks stuck out of the glacier like rocky islands in a sea of ice. But as the glacier continued to advance, even the peaks disappeared under the ice, and the jagged mountain peaks were rounded down to the graceful shapes we know today.

The most recent period of glacial advance started about 100,000 years ago. Around 25,000 years ago, massive glaciers had reached the coast of Maine, and at the glacier's maximum extent, roughly 18,000 years ago, Mount Desert Island was buried under several thousand feet of ice. The glacier covered every mountain in New England, stretched 350 miles past the present shoreline, and reached as far south as Long Island. So much of the world's water was frozen in glaciers that global ocean levels dropped roughly 300 feet. And the tremendous weight of the glacier (one cubic mile of ice weighs 4.5 billion tons) compressed the land at least 600 feet below present-day levels.

Then, around 18,000 years ago, Earth's temperatures warmed and the glacier started to melt. Within 5,000 years it had retreated as far as central Maine. Three thousand years later it disappeared from the state entirely. The melting glacier released massive amounts of water, forming huge rivers that raced to the sea and cutting deep channels into the land. Many of those Ice Age channels continue to guide the paths of major rivers flowing through present-day Maine.

As water returned to the sea, ocean levels rose roughly 300 feet, flooding the compressed land and sending saltwater up to 60 miles inland in Maine. But free of the weight of the glaciers, the compressed land slowly rebounded and rose back toward its original levels, draining the interior of the state and forming the modern shoreline. Remnants of the former shoreline can still be found on the mountains of Mount Desert Island, including cobblestone beaches stranded hundreds of feet above the present sea level.

Before the Ice Age, the coast of Maine was covered in sandy beaches—the result of waves grinding down a once rocky shore. But when glaciers descended, they pushed the sand and other sediments out to sea and permanently tilted the land near the coast, which was covered in rolling hills before the Ice Age. When ocean levels rose, those tilted hills, scraped bare by the glacier, formed the hundreds of rocky inlets and bays that now make up the present shoreline.

Today, elements such as rain, ice, and waves continue to chip away at Mount Desert Island. Some geologists estimate that erosion removes about two inches from the island every 1,000 years. A million years from now, the forces of geology will have rendered Mount Desert Island completely unrecognizable to modern eyes. In the meantime, it remains one of the most beautiful places in the world.

Georges Bank

Roughly 18,000 years ago, when a vast glacier extended nearly 350 miles past the present Maine shoreline, the front of the glacier pushed a vast accumulation of rocks and loose debris. When the glacier retreated, the debris was left behind to form what geologists call a terminal moraine. At the start of the glacier's retreat, sea levels were roughly 200 feet below present levels, and the terminal moraine formed a gravelly ridge connected to the mainland. But as the massive glacier melted, ocean levels rose and flooded the terminal moraine, creating a shallow underwater ridge that today is known as Georges Bank. (Another part of the terminal moraine, Cape Cod, still remains above sea level.) Georges Bank is one of the defining features of the Gulf of Maine, effectively separating the Gulf from the open Atlantic. From time to time fishing trawls on Georges Bank have dragged up mammoth bones and other remnants of Ice Age creatures that roamed there thousands of years ago.

ICE AGE GLACIERS

North America
18,000 years ago

At the peak of the last Ice Age, North America was covered by an enormous glacier that held 1.5 times more ice than is found on Antarctica today. At the time, Mount Desert Island was buried under several thousand feet of ice, which was so heavy that it compressed the land. At the glacier's maximum extent, the ice stretched roughly 350 miles into the Gulf of Maine.

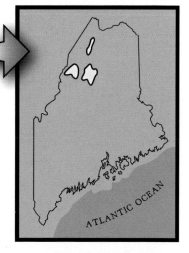

13,000 years ago

As temperatures on Earth continued to rise, the glacier continued to melt and retreat. The huge volumes of melting ice caused sea levels to rise, flooding the compressed land in Maine.

11,000 years ago

Free of the weight of the glaciers, the land in Maine began to rise. But with so much ocean water still trapped in retreating glaciers, sea levels remained below present-day levels.

ECOLOGY

From an ECOLOGICAL standpoint, Acadia is one of the most diverse national parks in America. With elevations ranging from sea-level to 1,500 feet, a location at the boundary of two of North America's major botanical zones, and a landscape filled with forests, lakes, and wetlands, Acadia is home to an astonishing number of plants and animals. All told, over 50 species of mammals, 320 species of birds, and 1,000 species of flowering plants have been identified in the park (as well as hundreds of creatures in the waters offshore). Even more amazing, Acadia's species are all found on less than 48,000 acres. Outside of a tropical rainforest, there are few places in the world with so much natural diversity packed into such a small space.

Mount Desert Island lies at the boundary of North America's northern boreal forest, found in northern Maine and much of Canada, and the eastern deciduous forest, found in southern Maine and much of the eastern U.S. The boreal forest is dominated by evergreens such as red spruce and balsam fir, hardy trees that can establish themselves in thin, poor soil. Thriving in damp, cool climates, they create a dense canopy that blocks sunlight and drops needles that create an acidic soil. As a result, spruce-fir forests tend to go unchallenged by other trees that require abundant sunlight and rich soil to grow. The nutrient-poor floor of spruce-fir forests is often covered with mosses and lichens.

In 1947 a fire burned much of the eastern half of Mount Desert Island, clearing out 17,000 acres of spruce-fir forest and allowing deciduous trees like birch, poplar, oak, and other hardwoods to grow. In contrast to trees in the boreal forest, deciduous trees drop their leaves each fall, enriching the soil and allowing other plants to grow. Today, over 30 different tree species are found on Mount Desert Island, including pitch pines growing at the northeastern limit of their range and jack pines growing at the southern limit of their range. Scattered among the trees are over 40 kinds of shrubs and hundreds of smaller plants like wildflowers, shrubs, and ferns.

Hike up the island's tallest mountains and the forests soon give way to rocky peaks. Here, small populations of alpine plants eke out a living in tiny pockets of soil. Because there is so little vegetation on the mountain peaks, there is very little soil development—a self-reinforcing process that prevents many larger plants like trees from taking root. Lying exposed at high elevations, the peaks experience cooler than average year-round temperatures. This creates an excellent habitat for several rare species of plants normally found much farther north, including Alpine clubmoss and mountain sandwort.

During the summer, the island's mountains are often bathed in thick fog, which provides moisture for the plants near the summit. Any rain that falls tends to rush off the peaks immediately because there is so little vegetation or soil to absorb the water or slow it down. As the water cascades down the rocks, it often forms dozens of temporary waterfalls. The water then gathers into numerous streams that flow into the island's lakes, ponds, and marshes.

Roughly 20 percent of Acadia is considered wetland, habitats that include saltwater marshes, freshwater marshes, bogs, and swamps. Because wetlands attract plants and animals from both land and water, they are extremely important to the park's ecology. They are among the most biodiverse of all ecosystems, and wetlands provide important stopover points for birds migrating on the Atlantic flyway. In fact, Mount Desert Island is considered one of America's premier birding locations. James Audubon, founder of the Audubon Society, did much of his research here, and birders from around the world continue to flock to Acadia. Lying on the boundary of North America's temperate and sub-arctic zone, the island attracts over 330 species of birds, many of which arrive in the spring. Among the spring arrivals are 21 species of nesting wood warblers, earning Acadia the nickname "Warbler Capital of North America." The fall migration also attracts a variety of interesting birds, but by winter Mount Desert Island's bird population is reduced to a fraction of its summertime high. Still, winter brings some fascinating migrants from the far north and arctic, including snowy owls, great gray owls, and king eiders.

Due to its coastal location, Mount Desert Island is also home to fascinating seabirds. Some, such as Leach's storm petrel, spend much of their lives on the open ocean and are rarely seen from land. Others, like common eiders and guillemots, can be spotted bobbing in the surf just off Mount Desert Island.

Mount Desert Island is also home to a wide range of mammals. Some, such as snowshoe hares and white-tailed deer, are strict vegetarians, nibbling on grasses and shrubs. Others, such as red foxes and eastern coyotes, are predators that feed on smaller animals. Acadia also contains 11 of Maine's 19 amphibian species, including 6-inch bullfrogs and the thumbnail-sized spring peeper, a tree frog that chirps up to 4,500 times per night in the spring. But because Mount Desert Island is located so far north, there are very few reptiles, which are cold-blooded and prefer a warmer climate. Only two species of turtle and five species of snake are found in the park. (None of the snake species are poisonous.)

In addition to land on Mount Desert Island, Acadia National Park also includes many smaller offshore islands. Characterized by cool climates and rocky terrain, these islands feature a habitat similar to Acadia's mountain peaks, well suited to sub-arctic plants and animals normally found much farther north. The lack of predators on many offshore islands also provides excellent breeding sites for seabirds. Great Duck Island, 6 miles south of Mount Desert Island, supports 20 percent of Maine's nesting seabirds, and Petit Manan Island, 16 miles to the east, is home to a breeding colony of puffins.

Fall Foliage

New England is famous for its fall foliage, and the changing leaves are particularly dramatic in Acadia. But what causes the leaves to change? The answer is chlorophyll—or rather, a lack of chlorophyll. In the spring new leaves contain a variety of pigments—red, yellow, orange, purple—but chlorophyll's green is the dominant color. When days grow shorter in the fall, chlorophyll production drops and the green pigment starts to fade. When it disappears entirely, the remaining colorful pigments are gloriously revealed.

Interestingly, we have Florida to thank for New England's famous foliage. Twenty thousand years ago, advancing glaciers pushed North America's ecosystems hundreds of miles south, and New England's deciduous trees migrated all the way to the tip of Florida. Had Florida not existed, it's possible that the trees might have been pushed to extinction. But when temperatures warmed and the glaciers retreated, the trees slowly migrated back to New England.

Peak foliage in Acadia usually occurs in mid-October, but the exact timing varies from year to year depending on the weather in the summer and early fall. For up-to-the-minute foliage conditions and forecasts, visit mainefoliage.com.

Barnacles & Dog Whelks

INTERTIDAL ZONE

WHEN PEOPLE THINK of marine ecology, they often picture fish, whales, and other creatures of the open sea. But between the ocean and the land lies another amazing ecosystem: the intertidal zone. This fascinating region, encompassing the shore between high and low tide, is a world unto itself. Creatures living here have adapted to a brutal environment where they must cope with life above and below water, tolerate extreme temperature fluctuations, and survive the violent pounding of the waves. During winter storms, waves in the intertidal zone can produce pressures up to 500 pounds per square inch!

Some of the most dynamic organisms on the planet are found in the intertidal zone, but much of this amazing landscape remains off limits to the public because so much of the Maine coast is privately owned. In Acadia National Park, however, over 40 miles of rocky shoreline are open to exploration, revealing the wonders of this fascinating ecosystem. And due to the Gulf of Maine's unusually large tides (8–12 feet in Acadia), the intertidal zone here is particularly dramatic.

The intertidal zone is a complex ecosystem containing a wide range of sub-ecosystems. Near the top of the intertidal zone, organisms live most of their lives above water. Only at high tide are they fully submerged, but only for a few hours. At the bottom of the intertidal zone, organisms are exposed to the air only at low tide, and they have evolved accordingly. In fact, many organisms living at the bottom of the intertidal zone will die if exposed to the air for too long. In between these two extremes lies a wide range of plants and animals adapted to specific amounts of time both above and below water.

No animal sums up the intertidal zone's evolutionary variety as perfectly as the periwinkle, a marine snail that grazes on algae. There are three types of periwinkles in Acadia, and all are adapted to different amounts of water. The smooth periwinkle spends most of its time below water and can't tolerate air. The common periwinkle can tolerate air, but not much. And the rough periwinkle prefers air, needing water only occasionally. Both smooth and common periwinkles lay their eggs in the water, but rough periwinkle babies are born live on the rocks. In fact, some scientists believe rough periwinkles are slowly evolving into land snails, and may someday disappear from the intertidal zone entirely.

Tide pools along the rocky shore are some of the best places to explore the wonders of the intertidal zone. These temporary pockets of water are filled with life-forms as small as plankton and as large as starfish and sea anemones. But even tide pools are highly varied. The location of a tide pool within the intertidal zone has a dramatic effect on the plants and animals that can survive there. Tide pools at the top of the intertidal zone experience drastic fluctuations in temperature, water level, and salinity as sunlight heats the pool and water evaporates throughout the day. By contrast, tide pools at the bottom of the intertidal zone are exposed to much less sunlight, and their fluctuations are much less severe.

INTERTIDAL ZONE

SPLASH ZONE: Although splashed by waves and spray at high tide, this zone is never fully submerged. It is sometimes called the Black Zone due to a dark algae that grows on the rocks, which is fed upon by small marine snails called rough periwinkles.

BARNACLE ZONE: This easily identified zone is home to countless tiny white barnacles, which spend their entire lives glued to a single location. When the tide is high, barnacles extend feathery legs to feed on floating food particles. When the tide is low, barnacles retract their legs and close a "trap door" at the tip of their conical shells.

ROCKWEED ZONE: Large strands of rubbery rockweeds cover this mid-intertidal zone. As the tide rises, tiny air bladders in the rockweeds lift them toward the surface where they can better photosynthesize. At low tide, rockweeds draped over the rocks provide moist protection for mussels, crabs, and dog whelks.

IRISH MOSS ZONE: This loosely defined zone often overlaps with the zones above and below it. Its namesake plant, Irish Moss, has beautiful iridescent tips and grows in small, dense clumps. Sea anemones, whose tentacles shoot microscopic spears that paralyze their victims with poison, are sometimes found in the Irish moss zone.

KELP ZONE: Thick curtains of kelp define the lowermost zone, home to such famous creatures as sea stars, sea urchins, and sea cucumbers. Kelp anchor themselves to the bottom and send up long, belt-like ribbons that can grow up to 20 feet.

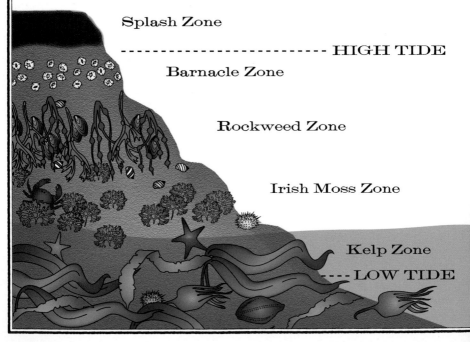

Splash Zone

------------------------- HIGH TIDE

Barnacle Zone

Rockweed Zone

Irish Moss Zone

Kelp Zone

---- LOW TIDE

Sea Stars

Sea stars (aka starfish) are found in the lower inter-tidal zones. They grow up to 10 inches across and come in a rainbow of colors. Their arms are covered with hundreds of tiny tube feet, which they use for movement and to pry open mussels. After opening a mussel, a sea star will disgorge its stomach into the open shell, digesting the victim from the inside. Sea stars can regenerate lost arms, and the tip of each arm has a tiny, primitive "eye."

Dog Whelk

This predatory sea snail (distinguished by a pointed spire) roves around the mid-intertidal zone and feasts on stationary victims. Using a tongue-like organ called a radula, dog whelks drill into the shells of barnacles and mussels. It takes roughly one hour to drill into a barnacle and 10–20 hours to drill into a mussel. Digestive enzymes are then injected into the victim's shell, creating a soup that the dog whelk sucks out. Mussels sometimes fight back by attaching threads to the dog whelk, immobilizing it until it starves to death.

Sea Cucumber

These strange, leathery creatures, found in the lower intertidal zones, grow up to 10 inches long and filter out nutrients from ingested sediments. Sea cucumbers can loosen and firm their bodies at will. If a sea cucumber wants to squeeze through a small gap, it can essentially liquefy its body to do so. When seriously threatened, it disgorges its internal organs to confuse predators (new organs will regenerate later). A sea cucumbers "breaths" by drawing water in and out of its anus.

Sea Urchin

These prickly creatures, found in the lower intertidal zones, have spiny, limestone shells that protects their soft organs from predators. They use tiny tube feet to "walk" along the rocks as they graze on algae. Seagulls pluck urchins from the intertidal zone and drop them on rocks to crack open their hard shells.

GULF OF MAINE

THE MOST fascinating aspect of Acadia's ecology is the Gulf of Maine, a shallow region (on average 500 feet deep) that covers 69,000 square miles of the Atlantic Ocean from Cape Cod to Nova Scotia. About 200 miles from the coast lies the Gulf's most prominent physical feature: Georges Bank. Only 13 feet deep in places, Georges Bank is a 10,000 square-mile shallow ridge that acts as a barrier between the Gulf of Maine and the open Atlantic, creating a semi-enclosed sea with the help of Browns Bank to the northeast. Over 60 rivers flow into the Gulf of Maine, depositing an average of 250 billion gallons of freshwater each year. Georges Bank and Browns Bank help retain this freshwater to create, in effect, a massive estuary—a place where freshwater and saltwater mix that is extremely productive biologically.

In addition to the freshwater deposited by rivers, cold arctic ocean water is cycled into the Gulf of Maine via the Labrador Current, which flows south along the eastern coast of Nova Scotia. This cold, dense, nutrient-rich water enters the Gulf of Maine via the Northeastern Channel, a deep underwater valley between Georges Bank and Browns Bank. The Northeast Channel formed at the end of the last Ice Age, when so much of the world's water was frozen in glaciers that sea levels lay hundreds of feet below present levels. As global temperatures rose and the glaciers melted, a massive river flowed across the Gulf of Maine (which was then above sea level) and helped carve the deep valley that would ultimately become the Northeast Channel.

After nutrient-rich arctic water from the Labrador Current enters the Gulf of Maine, it settles in undersea basins up to 1,500 feet deep. During the winter, when the surface water cools to the upper 30s °F, the surface water sinks to the bottom and stirs up the arctic water. By the time spring arrives, the Gulf of Maine is swirling with nutrients. As the days grow longer, abundant sunlight triggers massive phytoplankton blooms, which give the Gulf of Maine its characteristic green, murky water. (A single teaspoon of Maine seawater can hold over a million phytoplankton.) The phytoplankton are then fed upon by tiny animals called zooplankton, which form the foundation of a thriving food chain.

Zooplankton are fed upon by small fish like herring and mackerel, which often school by the thousands. Those fish, in turn, are eaten by tuna, sharks, and migrating whales, which can eat up to 5,000 herring per day. Meanwhile, the unusually craggy floor of the Gulf of Maine creates ideal habitat for lobsters, and just above the seafloor are bottom-dwelling fish such as cod, haddock, and flounder. All told, the Gulf of Maine is home to over 3,000 species, including 652 fish, 32 mammals, and over 700 species of microscopic plants.

In the summer, when surface temperatures warm to the mid-60s °F, convective mixing between the surface and the bottom slows. Nutrient-rich water settles to the bottom, and phytoplankton density drops. Closer to shore, however, dra-

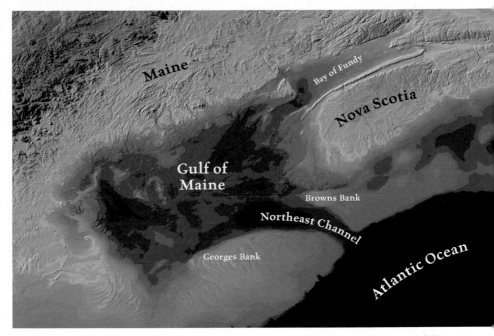

matic tides ensure continuous mixing of nutrients. Although tides rise and fall an average of three to six feet over much of the earth, in Maine tides can rise and fall up to 28 feet. Farther north in Canada's Bay of Fundy, a long channel connected to the northern tip of the Gulf of Maine, tides rise and fall an astonishing *50 feet*—the largest tidal fluctuations in the world. The Bay of Fundy's massive tides create, in effect, a giant nutrient pump. Twice a day, over 100 billion tons of water are sucked into the Bay of Fundy and then injected back into the Gulf of Maine.

The dramatic tides in the Gulf of Maine and the Bay of Fundy are due to the region's shallow underwater topography. As tides in the Atlantic rise and fall, water sloshes back and forth over the Gulf of Maine like water sloshing back and forth in a bathtub. Ultimately this sloshing water amplifies the tidal range, a phenomenon called tidal resonance. The unique shape of the Bay of Fundy has even greater tidal resonance, which accounts for its record-setting tides.

The Gulf of Maine's high tides create abundant mixing close to shore, and sinking surface water in the winter stirs up deep nutrients offshore. But another natural feature mixes the water further still: a powerful counter-clockwise current that cycles around the entire Gulf of Maine every three months. The current not only ensures further mixing of nutrients, it disperses the eggs and larvae of numerous marine animals, scattering biodiversity throughout the Gulf.

Taken together, the unique aspects of the Gulf of Maine—its shallow depth, estuary-like quality, nutrient-rich waters, and multiple circulation patterns—have created one of the most productive ecosystems in the world. According to some scientists, the Gulf of Maine is richer in nutrients than almost any other place in the earth's oceans.

HUMAN IMPACT

As EUROPEAN SETTLEMENT spread throughout coastal Maine in the late 1700s, settlers altered the environment in many significant ways. Although Indians had been altering the environment for centuries through hunting, harvesting, and intentional fires to clear brush, their activities—limited by small populations and a lack of technology—had a relatively minor impact on the land. But when European settlers arrived, their impact was swift and dramatic.

The most obvious change was to the forest. Oaks, cedars, and chestnuts were all harvested for shipbuilding and other construction, but the most important tree was the white pine, which grows up to 250 feet high and towers above all other trees in New England. Referred to as "skyscrapers" before steel buildings stole the name, white pines were perfect for ships' masts. Before long, aggressive harvesting had wiped out the white pine population along the coast. As loggers pushed farther inland, settlers along the coast cleared out large swaths of the remaining forest to farm and graze cattle. By the mid-1800s, much of the coast had been completely stripped of trees.

Human activities also took a huge toll on animal populations in coastal Maine. As trade between Indians and Europeans increased in the 1600s, Indians hunted animals in much larger numbers than their pre-contact lifestyles required. Soon, many animals, particularly beaver, had been hunted out of much of the region. Coastal residents also hunted seabirds for their meat, feathers and eggs. Because seabirds reproduce in relatively small numbers, their populations were devastated. One species, the penguin-like great auk, was hunted to extinction. Unable to fly away from humans, great auks were simply rounded up on shore and clubbed to death. Ultimately public pressure, including the founding of the National Audubon Society, encouraged protection of the remaining seabird population. The landmark Migratory Bird Treaty Act of 1918 banned seabird hunting, and many bird sanctuaries were established along the coast of Maine. Over time, many seabird populations have slowly recovered.

On Mount Desert Island, the environment has also been altered in more subtle ways. Today nearly one-quarter of the plants found in Acadia are non-native "exotics." Free from the diseases and pests that keep their populations in check back home, some exotics have thrived in Acadia. Purple loosestrife, a beautiful European plant with magenta flowers that bloom in July and August, has flourished in wetlands throughout the park and muscled out native plants. Within the boundaries of Acadia, purple loosestrife populations are kept under strict control, but outside the park the plant is thriving. About a dozen other non-native species are currently considered a disturbance to the park's native ecosystem.

The ecosystem most in peril, however, is the Gulf of Maine. For centuries the Gulf of Maine was considered one of the richest offshore fisheries in the world.

But once-abundant fish such as cod, haddock, swordfish, and bluefin tuna have seen their populations collapse over the past half century due to overfishing.

In the 1950s fears of a global food shortage were widespread, and the U.N. encouraged increases in fishing to avert the looming catastrophe. At the same time, modern fishing technology allowed catches to skyrocket—and skyrocket they did, particularly in the Gulf of Maine. In the 1960s dozens of industrial fishing vessels from the Soviet Union, Western Europe, and Japan arrived in the Gulf of Maine. At the time, the United States only had jurisdiction over waters within 12 miles of its coast. The foreign vessels, some up to 400 feet long, stayed for months at a time and hauled up astounding catches. In 1968 foreign vessels harvested 1.2 billion tons, compared to 556 million tons harvested by U.S. vessels.

Alarmed by the foreign harvests, Congress passed the Fisheries Conservation and Management Act in 1976, which extended control of U.S. waters from 12 to 200 miles offshore and prohibited foreign vessels from plundering the Gulf of Maine. The act did not, however, prohibit American vessels from plundering the Gulf of Maine, which is exactly what happened next. Government subsidies were created to expand the U.S. fishing fleet, and the massive harvests continued. Then, as powerful electronic fish-finding technology was adopted in the 1980s, harvesting ability vastly exceeded available stocks. By the end of the decade, many fish populations in the Gulf of Maine had collapsed.

In the 1990s environmental groups lobbied for, and achieved, strict fishing regulations to save the remaining fish. But the one-size-fits-all regulations were ill-suited to the complex, dynamic ecology of the Gulf of Maine and its wide variety of fishing vessels. The new regulations had the unintended consequence of actually incentivizing some unsustainable fishing practices, and they ultimately favored large fishing operations over small independent fishermen. Across Maine, small independent fisherman abandoned the fish species that had sustained their communities for generations and switched to lobster—the last commercial species in the Gulf of Maine whose population has remained healthy. But dependence on a single species is fraught with hazard. Any disturbance to Maine's lobster population could jeopardize the state's entire fishing industry and wreak havoc on small coastal communities.

Meanwhile, federal regulations have failed to adequately rebuild fishing stocks. But after decades of mutual mistrust, fisherman, lawmakers, and environmentalists could be at a turning point. They are starting to share the blame for past mistakes and work together to devise a new framework. Today some prominent thinkers have concluded that the top-down nature of federal regulations are ineffective, and a new solution based on community-centered management practices and local stewardship could be more preferable. This radical idea, it turns out, is not so radical after all, for it has worked exceptionally well over the past several decades for Maine's signature marine species: lobster.

LOBSTERS

THE LOBSTER IS the quintessential symbol of Maine. Although billboards are proudly banned throughout the state, it's impossible to drive through a coastal town without being bombarded by dozens of lobster images. And rightly so. Although there are roughly 30 species of clawed lobsters in the world, no seafloor on the planet is as densely populated with lobsters as the Gulf of Maine. And the specific species found here, Homarus americanus, is one of the ocean's most unusual and fascinating creatures.

The American lobster is found on the ocean floor from North Carolina to Newfoundland, but they thrive in the Gulf of Maine due to its cold, shallow waters and rocky, craggy seafloor. Lobsters seek out shelter among the rocks. Large lobsters snag the best hiding spots and vigorously defend them, while smaller lobsters are often forced to burrow into the sand like rodents. In some parts of the Gulf of Maine, the density of lobsters is roughly one per square meter.

Because lobsters are almost neutrally buoyant, they tiptoe across the sea floor with ease. In the spring, millions of lobsters migrate towards the warmer waters closer to shore. In the fall, when water temperatures near the shore drop due to cold winds, lobsters crawl back to the warmer water offshore where they spend the winter. Lobsters can travel up to four miles per day, and if threatened they can propel themselves backward more than 25 feet per second by flapping their powerful tail.

Young lobsters start out with two claws of equal size, but as they mature they develop a preference for one or the other, much as people become right- or left-handed. The preferred claw becomes the powerful "crusher" claw, which is used to crush the shells of prey. The smaller, "shredder" claw is used to tear and shred flesh. As food is brought close to the face, a vast array of tiny appendages near the mouth are employed as forks, clamps, brushes and shredders. After the food is ingested, it is chewed in the stomach by teeth-like grinders. Lobsters feed on just about anything, including mussels, crabs and starfish. Lobsters, in turn, are preyed upon by skates, sharks and groundfish that swallow them whole.

Because lobsters grow throughout their lives, they must periodically shed their shells to accommodate larger bodies. This process, called molting, is similar to how a snake sheds its skin. In a lobster's first five years, it will molt roughly 25 times, gaining 15 percent body length and 50 percent volume each time. As adults get larger, they molt fewer and fewer times. A three- to four-pound lobster may only molt every three to five years.

Prior to a molt, a new shell forms just under the lobster's old shell. The lobster then drains the remaining calcium out of its old shell and stores it in a reservoir to be recycled into the new shell. When the lobster is finally ready to molt, it secretes enzymes that soften the old shell. It then swells its body with saltwater, and splits the old shell open. As it backs out of the old shell, the lobster attempts

to pull its large claw muscles through the shell's narrow claw joints. Occasionally a claw muscle won't fit through the old shell, and it tears off in the process. But claws, like all other lobster appendages, have the ability to regenerate over time. The entire molting process can take anywhere from five minutes to half an hour.

After a molt, the lobster's Jell-O-like muscles are almost completely exposed. At this point it is almost totally defenseless. This is one of the most dangerous periods in a lobster's life. The lobster eats its old shell to absorb additional calcium and minerals stored in the old shell, then seeks out shelter while it waits several days for the new shell to harden.

A lobster's shell offers good defense, but it also poses some unique challenges. Because the shell reduces access to a female's anatomy, lobsters have sex only after the female has molted. During courtship, an alpha male will wander around the ocean floor and evict several females from their shelters before returning to his own shelter. Interested females, who only mate with the dominant alpha male, then wander over to the alpha male's shelter and pee inside. The alpha male, in turn, happily swirls the urine around himself. (If this wasn't strange enough, lobsters pee through an opening in their face.) Eventually the female moves in, sheds her shell, and the lobsters copulate. For the next week or so, as the female waits for her new shell to harden, she will stay in the male's shelter under his protection. When she leaves, a new female immediately takes her place.

Females can carry the male's sperm for several month before putting it to use. They can even store some sperm for a second batch of eggs. Eggs develop inside the female before attaching themselves to the underside of her tail. Depending on the size of the female, her tail can carry anywhere between 5,000 and 100,000 eggs.

When the eggs hatch, tiny lobster larvae are dispersed into the ocean and float aimlessly wherever the currents take them. Only a few will survive this dangerous period—most will be eaten by predators. After molting four times in three weeks, the tiny, half-inch long lobsters settle to the ocean floor where they will spend the rest of their lives. Baby lobsters that settle on sandy bottoms are often eaten immediately by predators. Baby lobsters that settle on cobble-covered bottoms—of which there are plenty in the Gulf of Maine—often grow to adulthood.

Some scientists believe that lobsters are one of a handful of species that do not die of old age. If they can survive predation, disease, and entrapment, they can grow to monstrous proportions. The largest known lobster, caught in Nova Scotia in 1977, weighed 44 pounds and was estimated to be over 100 years old. In the early 1800s, before lobsters were commercially harvested, reports of four-foot lobsters weighing up to 50 pounds were not uncommon.

A lobster's shell has multiple dark pigments, although a bright red pigment is all that remains after a lobster is cooked. In rare cases, lobsters are born with a genetic mutation that gives them just one pigment. Every few years a blue or yellow lobster is caught, and in extremely rare cases a lobster's coloration is split down the middle—half yellow, half blue.

ANATOMY OF A LOBSTER

Shredder Claw

This sharp, slender claw shreds the flesh of victims. It is composed of fast muscle fibers, which contract rapidly but tire easily.

Crusher Claw

This large, powerful claw is used to crush the shells of prey such as clams and mussels. It is composed of slow muscle fibers, which produce strong contractions of long duration.

Antennules

A lobster's antennules contain hundreds of chemical receptors that give lobsters an extraordinary sense of smell. Lobsters "sniff" by flicking the antennules up and down.

Carapace

This large backplate stretches from the eye socket to the top of the tail. Lobstermen measure the carapace to determine legal size.

Legs & Feet

Lobster have 10 legs, including the claws, which are covered with thousands of tiny hairs that sense touch and function as taste buds.

Antennae

These whip-like antennae are highly mobile, moving swiftly from side to side to detect motion. The two antennae can also sense bidirectional movement to determine water current direction.

Tail

A lobster's powerful tail can propel it backwards at speeds up to 25 miles per hour. Female lobsters carry eggs on the underside of their tails, and they have wider tails to accommodate more eggs. Large females can carry up to 100,000 eggs.

MAINE LOBSTERMEN

It's impossible to talk about coastal Maine without talking about lobstermen. Proud, tough, and independent minded, they are the economic heart of small coastal communities and a vital cultural symbol of Maine. But it wasn't always this way.

Until the 1800s, lobster was largely considered a "garbage fish" barely worthy of harvesting. Lobster was collected close to shore by old men and young boys who lacked the strength to fish at sea. Then New Yorkers discovered the taste of fresh lobster, and demand increased. The 1840s saw the invention of the "lobster smack," a sailboat that could transport live lobsters over long distances, and canned lobster became big business in the 1870s. In the 1840s, there were only a few dozen lobstermen in Maine. By 1880, there were over 1,800.

When settlers first arrived in Maine, it was possible to gather large lobsters among the rocks at low tide. When harvesting reduced lobster populations along the shore, wooden traps were invented and launched from rowboats. As the lobster industry grew, rowboats were abandoned for sailboats—most notably Friendship Sloops built in Friendship, Maine—and in the 1930s and 1940s sailboats were abandoned for diesel-powered motorboats.

The next major change came in the 1970s, when wooden traps were abandoned for more durable metal traps. Today lobster traps measure roughly four feet long and are divided into two chambers. The first chamber, the "kitchen," has twin, funnel-shaped openings where lobsters can enter the trap. From the kitchen a third funnel-shaped opening leads to the "parlor," where a bag of smelly bait has been placed. Once a lobster wanders into the parlor, it is effectively trapped.

Each trap is connected by rope to a floating buoy, which is painted with a color pattern unique to each lobsterman. After snagging a buoy, the lobsterman hauls the trap onboard with the aid of an electric motor. He then removes any lobsters, puts a fresh bag of bait in the trap, and throws the trap overboard. In Maine, lobstermen are allowed a maximum of 800 traps.

According to the Gulf of Maine Research Institute, the average lobsterman is 50 years old and has been lobstering for 30 years. His boat is 32 feet long, 17 years old, and has a 260 horsepower engine. If he works with

a sternman (assistant), he lands roughly 24,000 pounds of lobster and earns an average of $25,000 after expenses. Lobstermen can earn significantly more, however, depending on their work ethic, the wholesale price of lobster, and the price of gas.

Today nearly every fisherman in Maine is a lobsterman. After other fish stocks collapsed in the early 1990s, lobstering took up the slack. Today there are roughly 7,000 lobstermen in Maine—up from 2,500 lobstermen in the 1970s. From an annual harvest of 20 million pounds in the 1980s, annual catches have skyrocketed to well over 100 million pounds today. Amazingly, lobster populations in Maine appear to be stable. This is due, in large part, to the lobstermen themselves, who adhere to strict conservation measures that have allowed lobsters to flourish

Lobster conservation laws were first enacted in the late 1800s, but back then they were largely ignored. When lobster catches collapsed in the 1920s, averaging five to seven million pounds, lobstermen finally embraced the conservation laws. Today all lobsters are measured, and lobstermen only keep lobsters with a carapace between 3.25 and 5 inches. All other lobsters are returned to the sea. This allows small lobsters to reach sexual maturity, and big lobsters (which produce exponentially more eggs) to reproduce. In addition, when lobstermen catch an egg-bearing female they cut a permanent V-notch on the tip of her tail. Once a female lobster acquires a V-notch, she can never be harvested.

Perhaps most fascinating, these conservation measures are almost entirely self-regulated. Lobstermen belong to unofficial "gangs" which work a specific harbor or territory. If anyone is caught breaking the rules, they face the wrath of the entire gang. Likewise, if a lobsterman encroaches on another gang's territory, subtle warning signals are sent. At first, knots are tied on the offending lobsterman's buoy. If the violations continue, trap ropes are cut. And in severe cases, lobsterboats are vandalized. This social pressure, it turns out, is far more effective than government intervention, especially when there are only 32 wardens to patrol 2,500 miles of Maine coast. It also helps that lobstermen have good working relationships with government officials and a strong personal sense that the system works for them.

In recent years, the Maine lobster industry's unusual success has drawn the attention of prominent researchers. In 2009 the Nobel Prize in Economics was awarded to Elinor Ostrom (the first woman ever to win the prize) for her work on the management of common property by common ownership, which examined Maine lobstermen. Someday, the unorthodox solutions developed on the coast of Maine may help conserve other natural resources around the world.

WHALES

THE GULF OF MAINE'S cold, nutrient-rich water and shallow depth make it one of the most biologically productive marine habitats in the world. In the summer, when the nutrients are at their peak, hundreds of migrating whales arrive here to feast on the natural bounty. From 85-foot finback whales to 5-foot harbor porpoises, the variety of whales found in the Gulf of Maine is extraordinary.

Whales are warm-blooded mammals that breath air, have hair, and give birth to live young. Although mammals evolved roughly 200 million years ago, whales did not appear until roughly 50 million years ago. Around that time, some land mammals began spending more and more time in the ocean, and after several million years they had evolved into purely marine animals—the ancestors of modern whales. Even today, whale fetuses develop a pair of rear legs that are genetic remnants of their land-dwelling ancestors. Although these tiny legs fail to fully develop, tiny "leg bones" are visible in the skeletons of many whales.

Whales are divided into two major categories: toothed whales and baleen whales. Toothed whales, such as sperm whales, have teeth in their mouths which they use to grind up fish and other prey. Baleen whales, such as humpbacks, have mouths filled with hundreds of fibrous, closely-spaced baleen plates. These plates are made of keratin—the same substance found in human fingernails—and they allow whales to filter out plankton and fish from swallowed seawater. Although there are over 70 species of toothed whale and only 12 species of baleen whales, baleen whales are the most commonly spotted large whales in the Gulf of Maine.

Because whales are warm-blooded, they must maintain a constant body temperature of 98.6 °F, which can be difficult in frigid waters like the Gulf of Maine. To help retain warmth, whales have a thick layer of blubber (fat) located under their rubbery skin. In large baleen whales the blubber layer can be up to two feet thick. Although blubber helps whales survive in cold water, it nearly resulted in their extinction in modern times.

Three hundred years ago, people relied on oil rendered from whale blubber to fuel lamps and lubricate machines. In the 1700s whales were aggressively hunted in New England, and by the early 1800s global whale populations were in steep decline. It wasn't until petroleum was developed as a cheap alternative to whale oil in the late 1800s that the whale oil industry collapsed.

Several decades later, however, motorized boats and exploding harpoons allowed whalers to hunt species that had previously been too fast to catch. At the same time, new chemical processes allowed whale oil to be rendered into a variety of products, including margarine and soap. Blue whales and finback whales suffered massive population declines before a moratorium on commercial whaling was established in 1986. Although some whale populations are recovering, many remain threatened due to deaths by fishing nets and accidental boat strikes.

Allied Whale

For nearly 40 years, researchers at Allied Whale have been studying migrating whales and other marine mammals off Mount Desert Island. Founded in 1972 as a non-profit research arm of Bar Harbor's College of the Atlantic, Allied Whale pioneered identifying humpback whales by studying their unique tail markings. Today they keep a database of over 25,000 whale photos to help track population and migration patterns. In 2010 Allied Whale researchers used photos to identify a humpback whale that had traveled over 6,000 miles between Brazil and Madagascar—the largest mammal migration ever documented. Allied Whale also operates the most remote field research station on the eastern seaboard: Mount Desert Rock (p.113), a tiny island 20 miles south of Mount Desert Island. To find out more, visit the George B. Dorr Natural History Museum (p.229).

Humpback Whale
Megaptera novaeangliae

Famous for their acrobatic displays and crooning songs, humpbacks grow up to 60 feet long and weigh up to 45 tons. Over 10,000 humpbacks spend their summers feeding in the western North Atlantic, eating up to 3,000 pounds of fish and krill per day, and often doubling their weight by fall. After storing up enough fat to carry them through the winter, the whales migrate to the warm Caribbean to breed and raise calves. During this time adults do not feed at all, but calves consume up to 100 gallons of mother's milk each day. A pronounced back arch gives the whale its common name, while long flippers—the longest of any whale—give humpbacks their scientific name: *Megaptera novaeangliae*, "Big Wing of New England." (Humpbacks were first studied in New England.) Humpbacks are found throughout the world's oceans, and they have the longest migration of any animal—5,000 miles.

Northern Right Whale
Eubalanea glacialis

The northern right whale is one of the rarest animals in the world—less than 350 remain in the North Atlantic. Among the bulkiest of whales, they are slow moving giants that can weigh up to 100 tons, which made them the main target of whalers in the 1800s. Right whales—so named because they were the "right" whales to hunt—were nearly extinct by the 1900s. Although an international hunting ban was enacted in 1931, their populations have barely recovered since then. In the winter, mothers and calves swim in the waters off northern Florida and Georgia. Right whales grow up to 60 feet long, and their heads are often covered in large skin growths called callosities, which are home to several species of whale lice.

Finback Whale
Balaenoptera physalus

Finbacks, the most commonly spotted whales off Mount Desert Island, are the second largest whales in the world after blue whales. Finbacks can grow up to 85 feet long and weigh up to 70 tons. They are named for a prominent dorsal fin located two-thirds of the way down the back. After coming to the surface for air, a finback will breath 5 to 15 times in a row, diving a short distance between breaths. Each breath raises their back and dorsal fin higher and higher out of the water. The final breath leads to a "terminal dive," where the finback arches its back five to six feet above water, then dives underwater for up to 15 minutes. During this time, the finback can reach depths up to 750 feet. Finbacks return to the same feeding areas in the North Atlantic year after year, but where they mate and give birth remains a mystery. There are an estimated 16,000 finback whales in the North Atlantic.

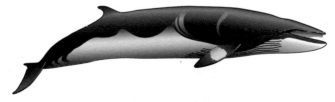

Minke Whale
Balaenoptera acutorostrata

Minke whales are relatively small whales, growing up to 30 feet long and weighing up to 11 tons. Because of their size, they avoided the attention of whalers. Today they are the world's most common baleen whale with an estimated population of one million. Minke whales are found in all oceans of the world, but they prefer cold environments like the North Atlantic. Larger minke whales tend to migrate farther north in the summer than smaller minke whales, and adult females migrate farther north than males. In the Gulf of Maine, the majority of minke whales are smaller juveniles. Because they venture closer to shore than larger whales, minke whales are sometimes seen in harbors and bays.

Harbor Seals & Gray Seals

Harbor seals (*Phoca vitulina*) are often seen swimming in the waters off Mount Desert Island and basking on offshore ledges. They are five to six feet long, weigh up to 290 pounds, and come in a wide range of colors including black, gray, tan, and white. Harbor seals have large, round eyes that give them superior vision in dark, murky water. But because they lack ducts to drain eye fluids, tears flow continuously down their eyes. They can swim up to 12 mph, dive down 300 feet, and stay submerged for up to 28 minutes. While diving their heart rate slows from 120 beats per minute to six beats per minute to conserve oxygen.

Gray seals, which are much larger than harbor seals, can grow up to eight feet long and weigh up to 800 pounds. They are identified by their distinctive, horse-like faces and prominent curved noses. (The gray seal's scientific name, *Halichoerus gryphus*, means "hook-nosed sea pig.")

In the late 1800s, fishermen put a bounty of $1 per head on seals to reduce competition for fish. By the time the bounty was repealed in 1905, seals were nearly exterminated along much of the Maine coast. In 1972 the Marine Mammal Protection Act banned hunting of all marine mammals, and seal populations have slowly rebounded since then.

BIRDS

Acadia National Park is a birdwatcher's paradise. Over 335 bird species have been identified in the park—roughly one-third of all bird species found in the United States—including 36 species of warbler. Acadia's impressive bird diversity is due to the park's diverse habitat. Onshore there are lakes, ponds and marshes surrounded by extensive conifer and hardwood forests. Offshore there are dozens of pristine islands surrounded by the biologically rich Gulf of Maine, which attracts seabirds from both north and south. Over two dozen seabird species have been identified near Acadia, including rarely seen pelagic (open ocean) species that venture onshore only to nest.

If you're a serious birder looking for an great guide, contact Rich MacDonald (207-266-9461, thenaturalhistorycenter.com) or Michael Good (207-288-8128, downeastnaturetours.com). Seasonal events include the Acadia Birding Festival (acadiabirdingfestival.com) in late spring, Peregrine Watch at the Precipice in spring and early summer, and Hawk Watch on Cadillac Mountain in the fall. Cadillac Mountain offers some of the best views on the East Coast, making it a great place for Hawk Watch volunteers to study annual raptor migrations.

Peregrine Falcon
Falco peregrinus

Peregrine falcons are among the world's most formidable birds of prey. Their diet consists mainly of medium-sized birds such as pigeons, ducks and shorebirds. They can spot victims from thousands of feet above, then dive bomb them at speeds topping 200 mph—the fastest speed of any animal. The collision creates an explosion of feathers. Victims that don't die upon impact have their necks broken by the peregrine's powerful beak. Peregrine falcons are such successful strikers that they were used to kill Nazi carrier pigeons in World War II. By the early 1970s, however, U.S. populations had plummeted due to the toxic effects of the pesticide DDT. To save the remaining birds, young peregrines were captured, bred in captivity, then reintroduced into the wild. Today peregrine falcons nest on several cliffs in Acadia, most notably the Precipice (p.146). Adult peregrines weigh up to 3.3 pounds with a 3.9-foot wingspan.

Atlantic Puffin
Fratercula arctica

Beloved for their colorful beaks, these adorable seabirds spend most of their lives on the open ocean, returning to land only to raise chicks in the spring and summer. Amazing swimmers, puffins use their wings to "fly" underwater. They hunt small fish and can carry up to 60 fish in their beaks at one time. In the air they flap their wings up to 400 times per minute. Puffins were hunted by early settlers, and by 1900 only one colony remained in Maine. In the 1970s puffin chicks from Newfoundland were reintroduced to a handful of Maine islands, and today there are several breeding colonies in Maine—including Petit Manan Island near Schoodic Peninsula. (Bar Harbor Whale Watch offers puffin tours, p.230.) Atlantic puffins grow up to one foot long. Their scientific name, *Fratercula arctica*, means "little friar of the north," a reference to their robe-like coloration.

Common Loon
Gavia immer

Famous for their haunting call, which echoes across lakes in the summer, loons are one of Acadia's most recognizable birds. Their summer range includes most of Canada and the northern boundary of the U.S. Winters are spent in coastal areas as far south as Mexico. Summer plumage is striking: jet black covered with bright white points. Winter plumage is drab brown. Unlike most flying birds loons have relatively solid bones that help them dive deep underwater. They can hold their breath up to 90 seconds and reach depths of 150 feet. Bright red eyes give them superior vision underwater. Loons pursue fish with dagger-like bills, which they use to stab and grasp prey. Loons also use their bills against other loons, engaging in underwater fights to defend territory. Although loons are powerful swimmers, they are famously clumsy on land. The word "loon" is supposedly derived from the Scandinavian word *lom* ("clumsy person"). Chicks often take to the water within hours of hatching.

Osprey
Pandion haliaetus

Osprey fly high above water in search of fish, which are the vast majority of their diet. When a fish is spotted—sometimes from as far as 130 feet in the air—the osprey swoops down and snatches it out of the water with powerful talons. Up to 80% of strikes are successful, and osprey occasionally catch two fish at once with each talon. Backwards-facing scales on the talons act as barbs that help grasp slippery fish. Osprey wingspans measure up to six feet across, and their nests can exceed 12 feet in height. Their call is a sharp, high-pitched *cheep cheep*. Osprey are found along the entire East Coast in the summer, but those north of South Carolina migrate to the tropics for the winter. Osprey from Mount Desert Island have been recorded as far south as Haiti and Honduras. The osprey's only natural predators are great horned owls, golden eagles and bald eagles.

Bald Eagle
Haliaeetus leucocephalus

One of the largest birds in North America, bald eagles weigh up to 14 pounds with 7.5-foot wingspans. Their tree nests—the largest of any animal—measure up to eight feet across, 13 feet high and weigh up to 2,000 pounds. The bald eagle's call is a high-pitched *kleek kik ik ik ik*. Fish make up the majority of their diet, but bald eagles also prey on birds and small mammals. When attacking they can achieve dive speeds of nearly 100 mph. In 1782 bald eagles were declared the national bird of the U.S. (Ben Franklin didn't like the choice because of the bird's "bad moral character.") By the 1960s, however, there were fewer than 900 bald eagles in the lower 48 states. Populations had plummeted due to hunting, habitat loss and the toxic effects of the pesticide DDT. Today, following effective conservation programs, there are over 30,000 bald eagles in the lower 48 states.

Blackburnian Warbler
Setophaga fusca

With its vibrant orange and black plumage, the Blackburnian warbler is one of the most striking warblers in North America. Their summer breeding range extends from southeastern Canada down the Appalachian Mountains as far south as North Carolina. In the winter they migrate to Central America and northern South America, where they are found in tropical montane forests between 2,000 and 8,000 feet. Their winter range extends down the Andes Mountains as far south as Peru. Blackburnian warblers measure up to five inches long with an 8.5-inch wingspan. Their song is a series of high simple notes, often ascending in pitch, sometimes described as *zip zip zip zip zip zip zip zip*. They spend much of their time high in the treetops, and their diet is almost entirely insects, with a particular fondness for caterpillars. Not surprisingly, their migration corresponds with the vast number of insects that thrive in North America in the summer.

Herring Gull
Larus argentatus

The most commonly spotted bird in Acadia is, without question, the herring gull. From the park's rocky shoreline to its highest peaks, these medium-sized birds are ubiquitous. Adult birds, which grow up to two feet in length, have white bodies, gray wings and black wing tips. Juveniles are mottled brown. Herring gulls eat just about anything, including fish, shellfish, garbage and baby seabirds. To crack open the shells of clams and mussels, herring gulls drop them onto hard surfaces. Like all gulls, herring gulls have unhinged jaws, which allows them to swallow large prey. The red spot on a gull's yellow bill is a target for chicks, who peck at it to indicate hunger. When pecked, adults regurgitate food into a chick's mouth. Although common today, herring gull populations collapsed in the 1800s due to egg poaching, habitat loss and hunters seeking feathers for hats. Following the passage of conservation laws, populations have rebounded. Today there are over 200,000 herring gulls in Maine.

Great Shearwater
Puffinus gravis

These seabirds, which spend most of their lives on the open ocean, circumnavigate the Atlantic every year. From September to May they breed on a handful of small islands (Gough, Nightingale, Tristan da Cunha) in the middle of the South Atlantic, then migrate up the coast of South America. By June they are extremely common in North American waters. In late summer they migrate to Europe, then head down the African coast en route to their breeding grounds. This migration pattern—breeding in the southern hemisphere, then flying to the northern hemisphere—is the reverse of most long-distance migrants. Great shearwaters measure up to 1.7 feet long with four-foot wingspans. Like all shearwaters they have stiff wings that enable them to "shear" across wave fronts, reducing physical exertion with a minimum of active flight.

Common Eider
Somateria mollissima

The common eider is the largest duck in the northern hemisphere, growing up to 28-inches long and weighing up to five pounds. Adult eiders feed primarily on shellfish, swallowing mussels and crabs whole. Their stomachs are specially designed to crush shellfish, digesting both the shell and its contents. During breeding season in the spring, adult males sport dramatic black and white plumage with white cheeks and yellow/greenish coloration on the back of the neck. Females eiders, which are completely brown year-round, are solely responsible for incubation of the egg. Males leave immediately after breeding, and females work cooperatively raising "crèches" of 60 or more chicks. Although common today, Maine eider populations plummeted in the late 1800s. They were aggressively hunted for their soft down, which was used in pillows and quilts. By the early 1900s just one breeding population remained in Maine. Following a hunting ban, eider populations slowly recovered. Today they can be seen gathering in large "rafts" of several thousand birds on the open water.

Arctic Tern
Sterna paradisaea

This remarkable bird is famous for its annual migration—the longest of any animal. Arctic terns spend June, July and August in the arctic and subarctic regions of North America, Europe and Asia. When temperatures drop, they migrate to Antarctica—a minimum distance of 12,000 miles. Some arctic terns travel up to 56,000 miles *each year*. Those that live 30 years or more can travel over 1.5 million miles during their lifetimes. This "Endless Summer" migration—enjoying both northern summer and southern summer—means arctic terns see more daylight than any other creature on the planet. Those that summer in Maine follow a migration route along the west coast of Europe and North Africa, crossing the North Atlantic to reach North America. Arctic terns breed and raise chicks in their northern range. They are fierce defenders of their nests, attacking any animals—including humans—that wander too close. From beak to tail arctic terns measure up to 14 inches with a 2.5-foot wingspan.

Black Guillemot
Cepphus grylle

The black guillemot is one of Acadia's most easily identifiable seabirds. In summer look for a medium-sized black body with bright red feet, striking white patches on the top and underside of the wings, and a rapid flapping motion in flight. Winter plumage is whitish/gray. Black guillemots grow up to 15 inches long with a 23-inch wingspan. They are found on both sides of the North Atlantic, but Maine marks the southern limit of their North American range. Black guillemots are members of the alcid family, which includes puffins. Unlike puffins, however, they prefer foraging for fish and crustaceans in relatively shallow waters near shore. Black guillemots are non-migratory birds, spending their winters near the rocky cliffs and islands where they breed.

White-Tailed Deer

Odocoileus virginianus

White-tailed deer are the most abundant large mammal in North America. Their range extends from Canada to Peru, with the largest whitetails found in the U.S. and Canada. The flash of their tail, which sports a bright white underside, serves as a warning to other deer when danger is present.

Bucks (males) are distinguished by their antlers, which grow up to two feet across. Antlers are used as sparring weapons during the fall rut, and the most dominant bucks breed with the most does (females). During this time bucks are so focused on finding does that they rarely eat or rest. Bucks shed their antlers each winter, then regrow them the following spring.

In the spring does give birth to one to three fawns, which are virtually defenseless when born. During their first month fawns lie hidden in vegetation while their mothers forage. To avoid detection by predators, fawns have white spots on their backs that help them blend in with the sun-dappled forest floor. After the first month fawns follow their mothers on foraging trips, and by summer their spots have disappeared. Bucks leave their mother after one year, while does leave after two. When fully grown, does can weigh up to 200 pounds and bucks can weigh up to 350 pounds.

Deer are ruminants with four-chambered stomachs. This allows them to digest rough vegetation such as shoots and leaves. They can also eat mushrooms and plants that are toxic to other animals. Although classified as herbivores, white-tailed deer opportunistically feed on small animals.

Highly adaptable, white-tailed deer are found in forests, swamps, deserts, plains, mountains—even in densely populated cities. Prior to European colonization, North America's white-tailed deer population may have numbered as high as 40 million. But by the mid-1800s, hunting had reduced that number to roughly 1 million. Hunters, alarmed at the decline, pushed for wildlife management practices that allowed populations to bounce back. But the near extermination of natural predators such as mountain lions and wolves means that white-tailed deer are now entirely dependent on humans to keep their population in check. Without adequate hunting, deer populations would explode to unsustainable levels.

White-Tailed
Deer Range

Moose
Alces alces

Weighing up to 1,800 pounds, moose are the largest members of the deer family. They stand up to 7.5 feet tall at the shoulder, and the tips of their antlers can tower 10 feet above the ground. Despite their massive size, moose are surprisingly nimble animals. They can swim up to six miles per hour and run at speeds up to 35 miles per hour—nearly as fast as a white-tailed deer. Their long, gangly legs are well-adapted to walking through deep snow.

Moose are solitary animals that do not form herds. Males (bulls) are distinguished by massive antlers, which can stretch six feet across and weigh up to 50 pounds. Antlers start growing in the spring and are shed by December. They grow progressively larger each year until a bull reaches about five years in age. Antlers are used to mark territory, dig up plants from the bottom of ponds, and fight with other males. During the fall rut, when bulls are stoked by testosterone, spectacular fights erupt among bulls competing for females (cows). About eight months after mating cows give birth to one or two offspring, which weigh up to 35 pounds. Adult moose can live up to 20 years in the wild.

Moose require 50 to 60 pounds of vegetation daily. They feed by wrapping their thick, rubbery lips around a twig and, in a single motion, stripping away the leaves, bark and buds. The name "moose" comes from the Algonquian *moosu*, which has been translated as "twig eater" or "he who strips off." Moose meat was a staple of Native American diets, and moose hides were used to make leather moccasins.

Moose are relatively recent arrivals in North America. They are believed to have crossed the Bering land bridge from Siberia during the last Ice Age. Although once common throughout New England, by the late 1800s populations had plummeted due to hunting and habitat loss. Populations have since rebounded, and today Maine has an estimated 75,000 moose—the largest population south of Canada, where 80% of North America's moose population lives. Although moose are rarely seen on Mount Desert Island, they are occasionally spotted on Schoodic Peninsula or swimming among the islands of Blue Hill Bay.

Moose Range

Black Bear

Ursus americanus

Black bears are the most common bear in North America with roughly 800,000 black bears in the U.S. and Canada. Of the three bear species in North America—black, grizzly and polar— black bears are the smallest and most common. They grow up to three feet high at the shoulder and weigh up to 550 pounds. Despite their roly poly appearance, black bears can reach top speeds of 30 mph over short distances. They are also excellent tree climbers. A few years back, a black bear wandered into downtown Bar Harbor and spent an afternoon in a tree in front of city hall. Although a handful of black bears live and breed on Mount Desert Island, they are rarely seen.

Black bears are highly intelligent, and their sense of smell is roughly 100 times more powerful than a dog's. Black bears are omnivores that eat just about anything—grasses in the spring, berries in the summer, acorns in the fall, and ants, termites, and insect larvae whenever they can. Roughly 80% of their diet consists of vegetation. In autumn black bears consume up to 20,000 calories per day to prepare for hibernation, often doubling their weight by winter. But black bears are not true hibernators. Entering their dens in October or November, they enter a "light" hibernation referred to as Seasonal Lethargy. During this time their heartbeat drops from 60–80 beats per minute to as low as eight beats per minute. Compared to true hibernators, however, a black bear's body temperature drops relatively little. Winter dormancy lasts three to five months, during which time the bear will consume 25–30% of its body weight.

Black bears live about 18 years in the wild. Between the ages of three and five, females produce their first offspring, and they breed about every two years after that. Mating occurs in the summer, but embryos do not develop until the mother has put on adequate weight to survive the winter. Cubs are born in late January/early February while the mother is in her den. Most litters consist of one to three cubs, which generally weigh less than a pound at birth. Youngsters stay with their mother throughout their first year while they learn how to fend for themselves.

Black Bear Range

Coyote
Canis latrans

Nocturnal by nature, coyotes are seldom seen in Acadia during the day, but their haunting howls can echo through the park at night. One long, high-pitched howl calls a pack of coyotes together, and when the pack has gathered a cacophony of yips and yelps are often added to the mix.

Today coyotes range from Canada to Panama, but historically they were confined to the open spaces of the Western U.S. and Mexico. Following the extermination of wolves in the 1800s, coyotes spread rapidly throughout North America. Coyotes first appeared in New England in the 1930s and 40s. Eastern coyotes mixed with the remaining wolf population, and today they are considered a genetically distinct subspecies

Intelligent, adaptable animals with a knack for scavenging, coyote populations have held steady and even increased in some places despite years of being hunted, poisoned and trapped. This is partly due to an amazing reproductive adaptation: when coyote populations decline, the remaining animals produce larger litters. Coyotes often travel in packs of six or so closely related family members. Their diet, which is 90% animal-based, consists mostly of rodents and small mammals. But coyotes are highly opportunistic, and they will eat just about anything, including birds, snakes, insects and trash. Working in teams, coyotes sometimes hunt larger animals such as deer. While pursuing prey, they can reach top speeds of over 40 mph and jump up to 13 feet in length.

Coyotes mate in the winter, and they are strictly monogamous. Mothers give birth to an average of six pups in the spring. Young coyotes are extremely vulnerable, however, and up to two-thirds of pups do not survive to adulthood. Those that do survive their first year often live over 10 years in the wild. Adult coyotes grow up to four feet in length and can weigh up to 40 pounds.

In the legends and myths of native tribes, coyotes often played a central role. Among a small cast of human and animal characters, Coyote was portrayed as a scheming, meddling trickster that scraped by on his cunning and charm. The word "coyote" is derived from the Aztec word *cóyotl*. Coyote's Latin name, *Canis latrans*, means "barking dog," a reference to its famous vocalizations.

Coyote Range

Beaver
Castor canadensis

Beavers are the largest rodents in North America, weighing up to 80 pounds. They use their large incisors to gnaw on tree trunks, toppling trees and dragging them to streams to build dams. The resulting pond creates prime wetland habitat for beavers and other animals. Beaver dams are made of logs, sticks and rocks cemented together with mud. A separate living space, called a lodge, is built by heaping together a separate pile of debris, then gnawing out a roomy chamber from the bottom up. Excellent swimmers, beavers can remain submerged for up to 15 minutes. They have large, webbed hind feet that aid in swimming. They use their long, flat tails as rudders while towing trees and branches in water. On land, beavers use their tails to prop themselves up while gnawing on trees. The beaver's thick fur coat was so prized by early European trappers that beavers were hunted out of much of their natural range. In the early 1900s protective laws were enacted to increase beaver populations, and beavers were reintroduced to Acadia in 1920. Since then the North American beaver population has recovered to roughly 10–15 million—a fraction of the 100–200 million present before Columbus.

Raccoon
Procyon lotor

Famous for the black "mask" that covers their faces, raccoons are intelligent, crafty creatures. Their eyes are incredibly well adapted to darkness, allowing them to carry out mischievous deeds at night, such as removing trash lids and prying open coolers to steal food. Raccoons eat just about anything they can get their hands on, including frogs, birds, fruits, nuts, worms, slugs and garbage. They are especially ravenous in the fall, increasing their body fat up to 50 percent to prepare for the lean winter months. Although raccoons prefer wooded areas near streams, they have adapted remarkably well to urban environments, traveling along sewage pipes and living in attics and chimneys. Despite their cute and cuddly appearance, raccoons have a nasty disposition and a tendency to carry rabies. As a result, they should never be approached. The name raccoon is supposedly derived from the Algonquian *arakunem*, which means "one that scratches with its hands."

Red Fox
Vulpes fulva

Sleek and swift, crafty and cunning, red foxes are highly adaptable animals. Their range includes North America, Europe, Asia, North Africa, Iceland and Japan. Although members of the dog family, foxes display many feline characteristics such as stalking, pouncing and toying with wounded prey. Their elliptical cat-like pupils can shrink to a narrow slit, giving them exceptional vision in bright light. A reflective membrane at the back of the eye causes light to pass over the retina twice, giving them excellent vision at night. Their superior vision, combined with exceptional hearing and a sense of smell 100 times greater than that of humans, makes foxes highly skilled hunters. Foxes eat virtually anything they can catch, including grasshoppers, crickets, small birds, squirrels, rabbits and lizards. Mothers bring partially dead animals back to the den so pups can sharpen their survival skills. While still less than a month old, pups fight among themselves to establish dominance, and parents feed the most dominant pups first.

Snowshoe Hare
Lepus americanus

Snowshoe hares are masters of disguise. In the summer they sport a grayish brown coat that helps them blend in with grasses and shrubs. As winter approaches, shorter days trigger a biological response that turns their coats almost entirely white, providing excellent camouflage in the snow. Snowshoe hares are preyed upon by foxes, coyotes, owls and hawks. When the hare senses a predator, it freezes to avoid detection. If necessary, it can flee at speeds up to 30 mph, hopping 12 feet in a single bound and making sharp zigzags. Snowshoe hares often spend their days sleeping in hidden locations, becoming active only at night or in the low light of dawn or dusk. They mate and give birth year-round, with females producing up to eight young per litter, up to four times per year. Young hares run within hours of birth. The populations of snowshoe hares are highly cyclical, becoming extremely plentiful every 10 years or so, then plummeting dramatically. During population booms some areas contain up to 10,000 snowshoe hares per square mile.

Passamaquoddy Man

HISTORY

NOT LONG AFTER Ice Age glaciers retreated from New England, people settled the land. Around 11,000 years ago, paleo-Indian hunters arrived in Maine and scraped out a living on the tundra left in the glacier's wake. At the time, Ice Age creatures such as mammoths, mastodons and six-foot beavers roamed the inland regions. The hunters chased game throughout the interior of the state, and they likely hunted seals and walrus on the coast.

As temperatures warmed, trees such as spruce and fir took root, followed by birch, alder and other hardwoods. By around 5,000 years ago the modern ecology of Maine had started to take shape. By that point many large Ice Age mammals had become extinct, and many arctic and sub-arctic species had migrated north. Taking their place in the forest were deer, moose and a variety of small mammals.

By the time of European contact, French explorers called the tribes living in Downeast Maine "Etchemins." The name may have been derived from the native word *skicin*, which translates as "the real people." Following the upheaval that came with European contact, the Etchemins merged with other tribes, and collectively they became known as the Wabanaki—an Algonquian-speaking group that includes the Penobscot, Passamaquoddy, Mi'kmaq and Maliseet. *Wabanaki*, loosely translated, means "People of the Dawnland," a reference to Maine's eastern location. The Wabanaki were highly mobile, with a seasonal cycle adapted to take advantage of various plants and animals. They paddled birch-bark canoes and established villages on the banks of lakes, rivers and along the coast.

Of the four Wabanaki tribes, the Penobscot and the Passamaquoddy are the two most closely associated with Mount Desert Island. They called the island *Pesamkuk,* and they lived in seasonal villages in present-day Northeast Harbor and Bar Harbor.

The Wabanaki diet was rich in seafood. They used nets, bone hooks and harpoons to catch cod, swordfish, flounder and salmon. At night they hunted sturgeon from canoes, using birch bark torches to attract the fish. The Wabanaki collected clams, mussels and shellfish near the shore. (They refer to Bar Harbor as *moneskatik*, "The Clam-Gathering Place.") Extra seafood was smoked and stored for winter use.

Native Objects

Spear Points

The first people to arrive in Maine 11,000 years ago hunted with spears and spear-throwers. Most spear points were made from stone that, when struck with another stone, flaked off to form sharp edges. Some points were carved from animal bones, such as the whale bone point pictured here. Native tribes hunted large Ice Age animals like mastodons with large spear points. When those animals disappeared (possibly due to overhunting), tribes hunted smaller animals with smaller spear points.

Arrowheads

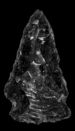

Sometime between 2,000 and 1,000 years ago, bows and arrows replaced spears and spear-throwers as the primary hunting weapons. Arrows travel up to 300 feet—much farther than the 90-foot range of spear throwers. Bows were made from beechwood or rock maple, then strung with animal sinew. Arrows were fashioned from ash, fletched with crow or hawk feathers, then tipped with flaked stone points.

Birch Bark Canoes

These elegant boats were so vital to local tribes that early European settlers often referred to the Wabanaki as "Canoe Indians." Maine is crisscrossed with lakes, rivers and streams, making water transport superior to overland travel. The earliest people made dugout canoes, but these were ultimately replaced by birch-bark canoes, which are lighter and easier to portage. Large canoes reached up to 20 feet in length, weighed just 85 pounds, and could hold up to 12 people. Birch-bark—which is waterproof, rot-resistant and flexible—was harvested in the winter when thickest. It was then sewn over a beechwood frame using split spruce root. Leaks were fixed with a mixture of spruce gum and animal fat.

Penobscot N.M. Francis and his wife

Pottery

The use of clay pottery began around 3,000 years ago. Prior to that time, native tribes used bark, wood and animal skin containers for cooking and storage. To boil liquids, they heated rocks in a fire, then dropped the hot rocks in a liquid-filled container. Pottery, by contrast, could be placed directly in a fire to boil liquids and cook soups and stews. Pottery is fragile, however, and it tends to fragment over time. Today pottery shards are the only archaeological evidence of this ancient craft.

Baskets

The Wabanaki wove beautiful baskets from sweetgrass and thin strips of the ash tree, which they called the "basket tree." Basketmaking was one of the most important aspects of Wabanaki culture. One myth tells how Gluskabe, the creator, split an ash tree with an arrow, and from that tree emerged the ancestors of the Wabanaki. Baskets and birch bark containers were sometimes decorated with dyed porcupine quills.

Wigwams

The Wabanaki lived in portable wigwams that could be easily assembled in a few hours. Wooden poles formed a basic conical framework to which birch bark panels were lashed. The structures measured 8–12 feet across, and moose or deer hide was hung as a door. Inside there was a central fire pit and sleeping areas carpeted with fragrant balsam tips and soft animal hides. An overhead platform provided extra storage space for utensils, dried food and extra furs. A hole in the roof allowed smoke to escape. During bad weather the hole was covered with a birch bark flap. When it was time to move on, wigwams were disassembled and birch bark panels were rolled up for easy transport.

On land the Wabanaki supplemented their diet with nuts, berries and maple sap. They hunted moose and deer with arrows and spears, and they trapped smaller animals such as beaver and otter. In the winter the Wabanaki chased game on snowshoes, which allowed them to move quickly across deep snow. Unlike tribes to the west, the Wabanaki in Downeast Maine did not practice agriculture. Wild food was abundant, and they were happy to trade surplus meat and animal hides for beans, corn and squash grown by neighboring tribes.

When European explorers first arrived in Maine in the early 1600s, there were an estimated 32,000 Wabanaki living in Maine and Canada (about 41 people per 100 square miles). As one European explorer noted, "I should consider these Indians incomparably more fortunate than ourselves ... their lives are not vexed by a thousand annoyances ... They mutually aid one another in their needs with much charity and without selfseeking. There is a continual joy in their wigwams." Another observer claimed the Wabanaki "start off to their different places with as much pleasure as if they were going on a stroll ... for their days are all nothing but pastime."

Physical differences were also noted. One early European explorer observed that the Wabanaki "have no beards, the men no more than the women ... They have often told me that at first we seemed to them very ugly with hair both upon our mouths and heads; but gradually they have become accustomed to it, and now we are beginning to look less deformed."

Although Europeans did not settle coastal Maine until the mid-1700s, European contact had an immediate impact on Wabanaki life. In the early 1600s, a European fad for beaver-pelt hats decimated beaver populations in Europe, and trappers soon set their eyes on North America. The Wabanaki were happy to trade beaver pelts for guns and metal weapons, which gave them a strategic advantage over rival tribes. As trade with Europeans increased, the Wabanaki began to abandon their traditional self-sufficient lifestyle.

At the same time, European diseases such as smallpox, cholera and influenza ravaged Wabanaki communities. These diseases had ravaged Europe centuries earlier, and the survivors had developed a crude immunity. North American tribes had no immunity, and in 1618 alone a massive plague killed nearly three-quarters of coastal Maine's native population. Within a few decades, up to 90 percent of the Wabanaki population perished. With their communities decimated, many remaining Wabanaki abandoned their traditional religious beliefs for the Christianity introduced by missionaries.

By the late-1700s, the Wabanaki population in Maine had fallen to roughly 1,200 individuals. The white population in Maine, meanwhile, had jumped from 54,000 to 300,000 in a matter of decades. As a result, the remaining Wabanaki lost access to much of their traditional territory, including parts of Mount Desert Island. Much of Maine's coast remained unoccupied, however, and for several decades the Wabanaki continued to spend part of the year near the ocean to fish, hunt and gather food along the shore.

EUROPEAN DISCOVERY

SOME HISTORIANS BELIEVE Vikings were the first Europeans to visit Maine. Others have speculated that European fisherman secretly fished Maine's waters long before Columbus set sail. (Some believe that Columbus overheard fisherman discussing North America, thus inspiring his historic voyage.) But the first recorded voyage to Maine comes from Giovanni De Verrazano, an Italian navigator who led a French expedition to the New World in 1524.

By the time Verrazano set sail, Spain and Portugal had explored the New World from Florida to the tip of South America, and John Cabot had led an English expedition to Newfoundland. Most of North America, however, remained a mystery. Searching for a northern passage to Asia, Verrazano landed at present-day North Carolina and named it "Archadia" based on a mythical landscape described by the Greek poet Virgil. He then sailed north to explore the unknown coast.

When Verrazano reached Maine, he encountered the Wabanaki, whom he described as "of such crudity and evil manners, so barbarous, that despite all the signs we could make, we could never converse with them." As Verrazano's boat approached the shore, the Wabanaki yelled and shot arrows at them. They then indicated their desire to trade with the Europeans for metal tools—albeit with the aide of a basket on a line shuttled safely between the ship and the shore. When Verrazano's ship departed, the Wabanaki sent them off by "exhibiting their bare behinds." Verrazano returned the favor by naming the Maine coast *Terra Onde di Mala Gente*, "Land of Bad People."

The Wabanaki's less than hospitable *bon voyage* to Verrazano, and their desire to trade for metal tools, indicate that they had encountered Europeans before. But Verrazano was the first to officially map the region. Included on his map was a spot near Mount Desert Island mysteriously labeled "Oranbega."

Despite Verrazano's successful exploration, no permanent settlement was attempted in New England for almost a century. Europe, preoccupied with wars at home and the plunder of Central and South America to the south, paid little attention to chilly, remote New England. Although the rich waters off the coast of Maine were filled with fishermen by the late 1500s, they did little more than set up seasonal camps on offshore islands.

Before long, however, rumors of a fantastic city of gold located somewhere in Maine began to spread through Europe. The rumor is believed to have originated from a group of English sailors who were stranded in Mexico in 1567 and spent the next three years traveling on foot to New Brunswick, Canada. From there they hopped a fishing boat back to England and immediately hit the pubs, telling drunken stories of a fabulous city of gold located somewhere in Maine. They called the city "Norumbega"—a name strikingly similar to the "Oranbega" found on Verrazano's map.

Mount Desert Island lay at the center of a native community that stretched from Blue Hill Bay to Frenchman Bay, including the surrounding watershed. Samuel Champlain's 1607 map of the region shows a large village along the Union River in present-day Ellsworth. This was likely the community's main village, which may have been home to about 150 people.

Champlain's 1607 map of Mid-Coast Maine

In the mid-1500s, the idea of a golden city in Maine would not have seemed that far-fetched. Spain had hauled away enormous quantities of gold from the Aztecs and Incas, and it seemed only logical that more riches lay awaiting discovery in the New World. In 1579 and 1580, England sent two expeditions to mid-coast Maine to search for Norumbega. Although the expeditions failed to find the golden city, the British officially named the entire region "Norumbega." (In 1606 the name Norumbega was changed to "Virginia," and fourteen years later Virginia was changed to "New England.")

But England was not the only country with an eye on the region—and dreams of easy riches were not so quickly forgotten. In 1603, seventeen years before the Pilgrims landed at Plymouth Rock, France sent an expedition to North America led by Samuel Champlain. After landing at the mouth of the St. Croix River in Canada, Champlain sailed south to explore the coast of Maine. When he spotted the bald peaks of Mount Desert Island, he noted in his log:

"The island is very high and notched in places, so that there is the appearance to one at sea, as of seven or eight mountains extending along near each other. The summit of most of them is destitute of trees, as there are only rocks on them. The slopes are covered with pines, firs, and birches. I named it *L'isle des Monts-déserts* [Island of Barren Mountains]."

Although earlier explorers had noticed the island before, Champlain was the first to give it a name. He was also the first to note that Mount Desert is, in fact, an island—previous maps had shown it connected to the mainland.

Continuing on, Champlain sailed up the Penobscot River, which empties into the Atlantic southwest of Mount Desert Island. If Norumbega existed, he hoped to find it there. Champlain made his way as far as present day Bangor, where he found, to his dismay, nothing more than a regular Indian village. Frustrated, he concluded that the city of Norumbega was a myth. He did point out, however, that the region as a whole was "marvelous to behold."

By the time of Champlain's voyage, Verrazano's name for North Carolina, Archadia, had slowly migrated north on French maps. As Verrazano's map was drawn and re-drawn by countless map makers, Archadia became "L'Acadie" and began to refer to the region between Philadelphia and Montreal—a region that would soon become a major point of contention between the English and the French.

SAMUEL CHAMPLAIN

THE FRENCH JESUITS

ALTHOUGH THERE WAS no gold in Maine, the region was overflowing with natural resources. "The aboundance of Sea-Fish," wrote one early fisherman, "are almost beyond beleeving." Cod grew up to six feet in length and could be gathered by simply dropping a bucket into the water. Sturgeons were so numerous near the shore that they were considered a navigational hazard. The natural bounty was all the more dramatic compared with Europe's own depleted resources. And the items that Europe needed most—timber, cod, beaver, and sassafras (mistakenly thought to cure syphilis)—were among the most abundant in New England. For over a century, Europe had virtually ignored the region. But once New England's natural resources were recognized, it began to look a lot more promising.

By the time of Champlain's voyage, both England and France claimed that they were the rightful owner of North America. But with no English settlements in the New World, and only a handful of French settlements in Canada, there were no actual conflicts over the land. Then, in 1607, England established a permanent settlement at Jamestown, Virginia. In response, France's Louis XIII granted North America to French noblewoman Antoinette de Pons, Marquise de Guercheville, who proposed a Jesuit mission on the coast of Maine.

In May of 1613, two Jesuits and 48 settlers set sail from France, hoping to establish a mission along the Penobscot River. As they neared the coast of Maine, they became surrounded by a thick fog. Unable to see more than a few feet ahead, the Jesuits grew terrified. If their ship ran aground it could easily sink, and they would be stranded with no supplies. Poor winds prevented the boat from retreating to deeper water, and the helpless French settlers simply huddled together and prayed. For two days, their ship drifted aimlessly through the fog. When the fog finally lifted, they found themselves staring at Mount Desert Island.

Overjoyed, the settlers rowed to shore and raised a cross. Not long after they landed, they were approached by a group of Wabanaki Indians who introduced themselves and encouraged the Frenchmen to stay on the island—presumably to benefit from the lucrative fur trade. But the Jesuits insisted that they would continue to the Penobscot River. The Wabanaki then informed them that their leader, Sagamore Asticou, was mortally ill and wished to be baptized before he died. Eager to save a soul, the Jesuits climbed into the Indians' canoes and were paddled to the southern end of the island.

When the Jesuits met Asticou, they found him suffering from nothing more than a common cold. Some historians have speculated that Asticou faked sickness to draw the Jesuits near and convince them to stay. If that was the case, it worked. Asticou was baptized and the Jesuits established a small settlement named Saint Sauveur just north of present-day Southwest Harbor.

Unfortunately for the French, English settlers in Jamestown, Virginia caught wind of their settlement plans, and a 14-gun warship was dispatched to deal with the problem. When the warship's captain, Samuel Argall, reached Penobscot Bay, he encountered a group of Wabanaki fishing among the offshore islands. The Indians, assuming the white men were friends of the French, tipped them off to the Jesuit's settlement. By the time they realized their mistake, it was too late. Argall's ship sailed toward Mount Desert Island ready to attack.

The French, caught entirely by surprise, fired off a single shot before their settlement was laid to waste. Argall allowed 14 Frenchmen to flee to Nova Scotia in an open boat, but the rest were taken to Jamestown as prisoners. Upon arriving in Jamestown, the Governor threatened to hang the prisoners, but they were ultimately sent back to France.

The battle on Mount Desert Island was one of the first skirmishes between the English and the French in North America. It would hardly be the last. For the next 150 years, the two countries battled over the region, and during that time Mount Desert Island became a virtual no man's land.

The Original Cadillac

In 1688 a young French lawyer named Antoine Laumet was granted 100,000 acres along the coast of Maine by the King of France. Undaunted by the violent land disputes in the region, the ambitious Laumet sailed to Mount Desert Island to oversee his new domain. Upon arriving in the New World, he changed his name to the noble sounding, yet completely fabricated, "Antoine de La Mothe, Sieur de Cadillac" and created a noble-looking coat of arms to complement his new name. But desolate Mount Desert Island offered little in the way of social mobility, and Cadillac headed west after only one summer. He later founded Detroit, Michigan, and today a modernized version of his fake coat of arms still graces the hood ornaments of Cadillac automobiles.

In 1786 Cadillac's granddaughter, Maria Teresa de Gregoire, contacted American authorities and claimed that she was the rightful owner of Mount Desert Island. Although her claim was legally dubious, the newly independent American government granted her the eastern half of the island as a show of goodwill toward the French. De Gregoire and her husband then moved to the island and started a real-estate company, selling land at $5.00 per 100 acres. Today, there are only two places in the United States where real estate titles can be traced back to the King of France: Louisiana and Mount Desert Island.

SETTLEMENT BEGINS

ONGOING BATTLES BETWEEN England and France kept many would-be settlers out of Maine until the late 1700s. During this time, Mount Desert Island was used primarily as a navigational tool (on clear days its mountains can be seen up to 60 miles at sea). As one Englishman put it, the region north of the Penobscot River was "a Countrey rather to affright then delight one, and how to describe a more plaine spectacle of desolation, or more barren, I know not." But shortly before the 1763 Treaty of Paris, which granted England control of New England, Mount Desert Island received its first permanent settlers.

In 1761, 22-year-old Abraham Somes sailed north from Gloucester, Massachusetts to Mount Desert Island and settled the town of "Betwixt the Hills" (later named Somesville). At the time, Mount Desert Island was owned by Francis Bernard, the royal governor of the Province of Massachusetts. Following the Revolutionary War, however, Bernard fled to England and the Americans confiscated his land. Bernard's son, who had sided with the Americans, ultimately petitioned the new government for his father's land, and being a good patriot he was granted it. But shortly after the transaction he sold the land and hightailed it back to England to join his father.

By the late 1700s, fertile land near the coast was in short supply in southern New England, and ambitious settlers began heading north to the undeveloped harbors in Maine. Before long, Mount Desert Island was growing at a healthy clip. Initial development took place in Somesville, but settlement soon spread throughout the island. In 1796 the town of Eden (later named Bar Harbor) was incorporated. Fishing, shipbuilding and lumbering were the primary occupations of the island's residents, who soon numbered several thousand, and for the most part they led peaceful, industrious lives. As one observer noted, "The women do the most of what there is in the way of farming, while the men, from early boyhood, are upon or in the water, chiefly as fishermen, but always as sailors, and unquestionably the best sailors in the world."

The island's economy revolved around the sea, and each day hundreds of sailboats could be seen in the waters offshore. Local sailors shipped goods around the world, and many knew the coastlines of Europe and South America as well as the coast of Maine. But sailing and fishing were rugged occupations. Men spent up to eight months of the year at sea, leaving their wives and children to fend for themselves at home.

Although Mount Desert Island continued to grow throughout the mid-1800s, access to the island remained challenging. The journey was a multi-day affair that required a train ride to Portland, a steamboat cruise to Castine, and a schooner trip to Mount Desert Island. As a result, few outsiders knew much about this remote, beautiful island. But following the arrival of a handful of landscape painters from New York, all that was about to change.

Lobstermen, 1800s

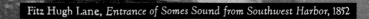
Fitz Hugh Lane, *Entrance of Somes Sound from Southwest Harbor*, 1852

BOOM to BUST
Coastal Maine in the 1800s

As the Industrial Revolution swept across North America in the 1800s, demand for natural resources boomed. And everything that America needed—fish for food, lumber for ships, granite for construction—Maine had in abundance. In an era when virtually everything was transported by ship, Maine also boasted a coastline filled with sheltered, deep-water harbors and thousands of offshore islands. After plodding along for centuries as an economic backwater, Maine had finally hit the jackpot.

The fishing industry in Maine, which had always been big business, revolved around cod, which were easily caught, cured and transported. As American and European populations grew, demand for dried cod skyrocketed. Fishing villages flourished, and the new settlers cut down trees at a furious rate for fuel, building material and to clear farmland. After the coastal forests had been plundered, lumber barrens turned their eyes to the state's vast interior. By 1880, nearly half of Maine's forests had been chopped down.

Granite also became big business, and many entrepreneurs (including my own great-grandfather) set up quarries on offshore islands. Because the islands were located along popular shipping routes, transportation was easy. On Mount Desert Island, Hall Quarry churned out enough granite to fill 10 to 15 schooners *each day*. Hall Quarry granite was used, among other things, to construct the Library of Congress.

Even the ice was valuable. In winter, huge blocks of ice were carved from rivers and ponds, covered in sawdust, and shipped around the world. From Bourbon Street to Bombay, Maine ice was considered a delicacy.

For a while, it seemed like everything in Maine turned to gold. But a few decades after the Industrial Revolution showered Maine with easy riches, it took them away just as quickly.

It started with the railroads, which opened up the vast virgin forests west of the Appalachian Mountains. This new form of transportation also permanently reduced America's reliance on coastal shipping routes. Maine's offshore islands, previously the best places to live and work, suddenly became the worst places to live and work. Coastal commerce collapsed, and hundreds of islands were abandoned.

At the same time, many independent fisherman found they couldn't afford the new, modern technologies being used by larger fishing operations. Maine's fishing fleet, once the nation's largest, shrank by over 70%. When reinforced concrete was introduced, the granite industry collapsed. Then mechanical refrigeration destroyed demand for Maine ice. As the decades wore on, coastal Maine watched its once vibrant economy collapse. It wasn't long before people turned to the only lucrative industry that was left: tourism.

LIGHTHOUSES

Back before trains and planes, the world relied on boats to transport nearly all commercial goods. And in the days before radar and GPS, boats depended upon lighthouses for navigational guidance. Due to the craggy, treacherous nature of Maine's shoreline, 68 lighthouses were constructed along the coast. By the late 1800s, it was possible to sail from one end of the state to the other and always be within sight of a lighthouse. The earliest beacons were lit with whale oil and attended by a keeper who lived at the lighthouse full-time. Lighthouse keepers and their families lived on remote islands for months or even years at a time. Infrequent supply ships provided their only link to the mainland. By the late 1970s, however, all lighthouses had been automated, and lighthouse keepers were no longer necessary.

Bass Harbor Light (p.266) is the only lighthouse on Mount Desert Island. Nearby lighthouses include Bear Island (p.248), Egg Rock (p.143), Baker Island (p.273), Winter Harbor (p.207), Burnt Coat Harbor (p.281), Isle au Haut (p.213), and Petit Manan (right), at 96 feet the second tallest lighthouse in Maine.

Mount Desert Rock Lighthouse

Mount Desert Rock is one of Maine's most famous lighthouses due to its remote location (20 miles south of Mount Desert Island) and the island's exceptionally small size (1.5 acres, with a maximum height 15 feet above sea level). Originally built in 1830, the lighthouse was later fortified with granite walls four feet thick to withstand pounding waves. During particularly fierce storms, keepers took shelter in the tower. In the 1880s, three keepers lived here with their families, and a school teacher visited in the summer to teach the children. One keeper's family lived on the island for eight straight years without visiting the mainland. The last keepers left in 1977. Today the lighthouse is used as a whale research station by Allied Whale.

THE HUDSON SCHOOL PAINTERS

IN THE MID-1800S, American cities faced immense growing pains. Overpopulation and the effects of the Industrial Revolution transformed previously habitable cities such as Boston, New York, and Philadelphia into filthy, wretched urban nightmares. Indoor plumbing had not yet been invented, and trash and human waste were left in the street to rot.

Not surprisingly, the art world experienced an overwhelming demand for landscape paintings during this time. City dwellers, disgusted with the stink and grime of city life, were desperate for wholesome scenes of unspoiled nature—hung conveniently on their townhouse walls. At the same time, railroads were creating an entirely new middle-class industry: tourism, which further fueled the demand for paintings of scenic destinations.

One of the first artists to visit Mount Desert Island was Thomas Doughty, who worked his way up the Maine coast in the early 1830s, booking passages on small sailing vessels. Doughty's paintings were later exhibited in New York, where they received moderate acclaim. They also caught the eye of his student, Thomas Cole, who was maturing into one of America's leading landscape artists.

In 1844 Cole traveled to Mount Desert Island with fellow artist Henry Cheever Pratt. The pair stayed at a farm near Schooner Head and painted dramatic scenes of Sand Beach, Otter Cliffs, and Frenchman Bay. Cole was in awe of the rugged, coastal scenery. His diary from the trip includes passages describing "threatening crags, and dark caverns in which the sea thunders" and "a range of mountains of beautiful aerial hues."

When Cole's work was exhibited in New York the following summer, it opened to mixed, but predominantly negative, reviews. One critic chided Cole for painting red rocks, noting "the rocks are of a kind that no geologist would find a name for; the whole coast of Maine is lined with rocks nearly black in color." (In fact, the rocks on Mount Desert Island do have a reddish hue.) Another critic complained that "the ocean appears like a vast cabbage garden."

Despite the poor reviews, Cole's paintings were a hit with the public. Several years later, Cole's aspiring young student, Frederic Church, set off to create his own paintings of Mount Desert Island. Only 24 years old, Church was considered something of a prodigy. He spent his days exploring the island's rugged terrain and produced a series of dramatic paintings that were received the following year with enormous success.

In the days before television or photography, landscape paintings offered a rare glimpse of exotic destinations, and landscape painters were treated like A-list celebrities. Church's stunning depictions of Mount Desert Island created a public frenzy. Thousands of people lined up outside galleries in New York to view his work, and other painters rushed to follow in his footsteps. Suddenly, Mount Desert Island found itself thrust into the national spotlight.

the Hudson River School

FREDERIC CHURCH

The painters of the Hudson River School not only introduced Mount Desert Island to the masses in the 1800s, they also helped launch the American conservation movement. Two hundred years earlier, when the Puritans first arrived in New England, wilderness was viewed as a sinister, dangerous place— and back then it often was. The Puritans believed it was their moral duty to tame the wilderness so religious communities could flourish. But even after the landscape had been tamed, their harsh view of nature persisted, and generations of Americans grew up viewing the frontier as an obstacle to be conquered. But as more and more pristine wilderness disappeared, a backlash began to develop.

Leading the charge were landscape painters such as Frederic Church and Thomas Cole, members of the Hudson River School of Art (which was not an actual school but an artistic movement). Cole rallied against the "apathy with which the beauties of external nature are regarded by the great mass, even of our refined community." Another artist declared, "Yankee enterprise has little sympathy with the picturesque, and it behooves our artists to rescue from its grasp the little that is left before it is for ever too late."

Artists of the Hudson School painted breathtaking scenes of the American wilderness that ignited the passions of the American public. They also used subtle visual techniques to convey their belief that wilderness was an extension of God, not an obstacle to His progress. One of their favorite tricks was to hide human features in the contours of rocks. This not only turned picture viewing into a kind of game, but also established a direct link between man and nature—and by extension God.

By portraying the American wilderness as a spiritual destination, the Hudson School hoped to dispel the notion that nature was an obstacle to be conquered. They also wanted to prove that American landscapes were just as beautiful as European landscapes, creating a much needed sense of national pride for the young democracy. On both counts, they succeeded. Hudson School exhibitions drew huge crowds and lured thousands of tourists to beautiful American destinations such as Mount Desert Island.

"The ladies wear wide-brimmed hats and picturesque costumes ... cut short above the feet and ankles, which, in turn, are incased in stout walking shoes. The gentlemen appear in warm, rough clothing, which will stand the wear and tear of a tramp over the rocks."

—*Harper's Magazine*, 1872

THE RUSTICATORS

CHURCH'S PAINTINGS GENERATED a flurry of interest in Mount Desert Island, and before long both artists and tourists were making the multi-day journey to see the island firsthand. In the summer of 1855, Church returned to Mount Desert Island with 26 friends, a group that included artists, writers, businessmen, and their families. The group stayed at a Somesville tavern and spent their days hiking, fishing, sailing, picnicking, and otherwise thoroughly enjoying themselves.

Although artists like Church were present, the excursion was first and foremost a social expedition. What little drawing was done generally consisted of humorous sketches mocking members of the party. At the end of their month-long stay, the group threw a large party. They invited dozens of locals and imported a piano, the island's first, specifically for the event. Church held forth at the piano, indulging in his "perfectly inexhaustible" capacity for entertainment late into the night.

What seemed like nothing more than a deliriously satisfying summer actually set the tone for the first wave of visitors to Mount Desert Island. Later named "Rusticators," these early tourists—for the most part artists, professors, and other intellectuals with leisure time on their hands—came to experience the simple outdoor pleasures of rugged coastal life.

Rusticators required no fancy accommodations. They often rented out attic space from locals and paid for an extra spot at the family's dinner table. Locals, eager for some extra cash, were more than happy to accommodate the easy-to-please visitors, creating a wonderfully symbiotic relationship. An 1872 travel article in *Harper's Magazine* summed up the rusticator's lifestyle: "Now, most of the visitors to Mount Desert, even the prosaic folk, go prepared to enjoy the picturesque, the beautiful, the sublime."

Another article that year stated that "During the day parties of several persons, ladies and gentlemen, start off on a walking expedition of five, ten, and fifteen miles to one or another of the many objects of interest on the sea-shore or up the mountains. There is a vigorous, sensible, healthy feeling in all they do, and not a bit of that overdressed, pretentious, nonsensical, unhealthy sentimentality which may be found at other places."

But changes to the rusticator lifestyle were already under way. Several years earlier, a New York journalist named Robert Carter had chartered a fishing sloop in Boston and taken a pleasure cruise to Mount Desert Island. At the time, there were no summer homes on the island and only two small inns. Carter reported that "of late years [Mount Desert Island] has become attractive to artists and summer loungers, but it needs the hand of cultivated taste." Although he could hardly have imagined it at the time, the arrival of a "cultivated hand" was not far away, and it would forever change the character of the island.

THE COTTAGERS

As STORIES, ARTWORK, and magazine articles about Mount Desert Island continued to spread, interest in the island soared. But tourism was limited by the physical challenge of actually getting there. Few would-be tourists had the time, money, or patience required for the multi-day journey. Then, in 1868, direct steamboat service was started between Boston and Mount Desert Island. A steamboat route drastically reduced the time it took to get to the island. It also dramatically increased the reliability of the voyage because travelers were no longer at the mercy of the wind. Within a few years, Mount Desert Island had become a major tourist destination.

Between 1868 and 1882, at least one hotel was built or thoroughly expanded on the island each year. The largest, Rodick House in Bar Harbor, contained over 400 rooms and was the largest hotel in Maine. Locals welcomed the flood of cash, but some were left feeling a bit perplexed. When one visitor told a local innkeeper that "It's the scenery we wish to see," the innkeeper replied, "Yes, I know, it's what them artist men come here for. But what it amounts to, after all their squattin' and fussin', I don't know."

In 1882 luxuries such as electricity and telephones arrived on Mount Desert Island, followed two years later by train service from Boston to Hancock Point, which was a short ferry ride away from Bar Harbor. The new train service cut travel time to Mount Desert Island down to a single day. The result was predictable: the number of summer visitors quadrupled.

The tourist explosion quickly changed the face of Bar Harbor. As more and more wealthy visitors arrived, upscale development proceeded at a breakneck pace. Luxury hotels sprouted up on Bar Harbor farmland, and quaint general stores were replaced with boutiques showcasing the latest Parisian fashions.

An 1886 article in *Harper's* neatly summed up the situation: "For many years [Bar Harbor] had been frequented by people who have more fondness for nature than they have money, and who were willing to put up with wretched accommodations, and enjoyed a wild sort of 'roughing it.' But some society people in New York, who have the reputation of setting the mode, chanced to go there; they declared in favor of it; and instantly, by an occult law which governs fashionable life, Bar Harbor became the fashion."

The writer went on to describe a typical day at Rodick House: "The first confused impression was of a bewildering number of slim, pretty girls, nonchalant young fellows in lawn-tennis suits, and indefinite opportunities in the halls and parlors and wide piazzas for promenades and flirtations ... The big office is a sort of assembly room, where new arrivals are scanned and discovered, and it is unblushingly called the 'fish-pond' by the young ladies who daily angle there."

Hoping to distance themselves from hotel life, which was becoming increasingly less exclusive, the wealthiest visitors built giant mansions along the shore. So as not to appear pretentious, they referred to their mansions as "cottages." The name fooled no one, however, and before long the social epicenter had shifted from hotel lounges to private dinner parties. The wealthiest families in America all added Bar Harbor "cottages" to their portfolio of homes, and the arrival of these families firmly cemented Bar Harbor's reputation as one of the most exclusive summer destinations in America.

By 1896 there were nearly 200 mansions in Bar Harbor, and the tone of the town had completely changed. As longtime summer resident Edward Godkin put it, "The Cottager has become to the boarder what the red [squirrel] is to the gray, a ruthless invader and exterminator ... caste has been established ... the community is now divided into two classes, one of which looks down on the other."

Bar Harbor, late 1800s

Lost "Cottages" of
BAR HARBOR

WINGWOOD

Wingwood was the most extraordinary summer cottage in Bar Harbor. It belonged to Edward T. Stotesbury, who grew up poor in Philadelphia, started working at age 12, and eventually became a senior partner at J.P. Morgan & Company. In 1925, flush with cash, Stotesbury purchased a large mansion in Bar Harbor. His wife Eva took one look at the new property, hired an architect, and ultimately spent over one million dollars remodeling the house. When the remodeling was complete, Wingwood boasted 80 rooms, 26 hand-carved marble fireplaces, 52 telephone lines, and a 30-room servants' wing. Some of Wingwood's bathrooms (28 total) featured gold fixtures, which Eva claimed were "economical" because "they saved polishing." For Edward, his wife's excesses were a bit much. He once remarked to his gardener that he would have been content with a small cottage and a supper of beans. Instead, his meals were served on one of two 1,200 piece dining sets. Eva's spending habits were legendary. She hired gardeners to move plants around Wingwood's grounds on a weekly basis, and she employed a full-time fashion designer and "costume secretary." At one point, Eva organized a $500,000 alligator safari to gather leather for a set of matching luggage. Following her death in 1946, Eva was remembered fondly as an exemplary hostess, one who "made every guest feel as if he or she were the only one invited." After the death of the Stotesburys, Wingwood fell into disrepair, and it was ultimately demolished in 1953.

CHATWOLD

Chatwold was the summer home of famed millionaire Joseph Pulitzer, by far the strangest cottager in Bar Harbor. After earning a fortune in the newspaper business—where he introduced such revolutionary concepts as the daily sports page and the color comic strip—Pulitzer added Chatwold to his collection of mansions in New York, Georgia, and the French Riviera. His idiosyncrasies were legendary. Pathologically sensitive to noise, the sound of a nut cracking is said to have made him wince. When Pulitzer stayed in hotels he required the rooms above, below, and on either side of him to be kept vacant. To combat the irritating sounds of everyday life, Pulitzer spent $100,000 constructing the "Tower of Silence"—a massive granite structure on the right side of Chatwold that was designed to be 100 percent soundproof. The mansion also boasted the first heated swimming pool in Bar Harbor and a master bedroom that rotated on ball bearings.

Despite Pulitzer's legendary aversion to noise, he required a servant to read him to sleep each night—and continue reading, in monotone, for at least two hours after he had fallen asleep. Legend has it he would awaken at the slightest change in pitch. Pulitzer also spent at least 12 hours a day in bed, dictating letters to his secretaries in a self-devised code that contained over 20,000 names and terms (Pulitzer was "Andes," Theodore Roosevelt was "Glutinous"). Chatwold was ultimately demolished in 1945, several decades after Pulitzer's death.

JOSEPH PULITZER

ACADIA NATIONAL PARK

BY THE TURN of the century, train service to Mount Desert Island had improved to the point that New Yorkers could hop a train in the morning and arrive in Bar Harbor by evening. As more and more tourists flooded the island, some citizens grew alarmed at the speed of development taking place. Speculators were snatching up real estate, and the lumber industry, equipped with modern machinery, was eyeing the island's vast untouched forests.

Among the citizens most alarmed was former Harvard president and longtime summer visitor Charles Eliot. With the help of his friend, wealthy island resident George Dorr, Eliot organized a group of private citizens dedicated to preserving Mount Desert Island for future generations. As savvy as they were civic minded, the Hancock County Trustees of Public Reservations (as they later came to be called) obtained a tax-exempt charter and quickly set to work purchasing land. Dorr enthusiastically took charge and acquired Eagle Lake, Cadillac Mountain, Otter Cliffs, and Sieur de Monts Spring—all told over 6,000 acres.

Things were going well until 1913, when the Maine Legislature, under pressure from a variety of sources, attempted to revoke the Trustee's tax-exempt charter. Worried that the charter might ultimately be dissolved, Dorr suggested that the Trustees donate their land to the federal government. This was easier said than done. More government land meant more government spending, and Dorr was dispatched to Washington to convince lawmakers that land preservation on Mount Desert Island was worth the extra money.

Using his considerable wealth and influence, Dorr pulled strings and cashed in on personal favors to arrange a meeting with President Woodrow Wilson. He also convinced the editors at *National Geographic* to publish an article about Mount Desert Island that generated tremendous public support for the cause. Two years later, a National Monument was created by Presidential Proclamation. Dorr's next move was to elevate the monument to national park status, which required an act of Congress. Despite the government's preoccupation with World War I, Dorr was able to gather the Congressional support he needed, and on February 26, 1919 Lafayette National Park was created. (The name Lafayette was chosen to reflect America's pro-French sentiment in the wake of the war.) Lafayette was the first national park established east of the Mississippi, and the first national park donated entirely from privately owned land.

Dorr became the park's first superintendent—at a salary of one dollar per year—and he worked hard to expand Lafayette's holdings. In the late 1920s, a family of Anglophiles donated Schoodic Peninsula with the stipulation that the name of the park be changed to something less French. And so, in 1929, Lafayette National Park became Acadia National Park. (Ironically, Acadia was based on an early French name for the region.) A decade later, the park acquired the southern half of Isle au Haut, a small island 15 miles south of Mount Desert Island.

the Father of Acadia
GEORGE DORR

Without George Dorr, Acadia National Park would not exist as we know it today. His tireless lobbying in Washington, D.C. was responsible for the creation of the park in 1919, and he devoted the rest of his life to preserving and expanding Acadia's holdings.

Dorr first visited Mount Desert Island in 1868 when his wealthy family purchased a summer home in Bar Harbor. As a young man, Dorr attended Oxford University and traveled extensively throughout Europe, exploring the Scottish highlands and hiking the Swiss Alps. When Dorr inherited his family's vast textile fortune at the turn of the century, he could have lived anywhere in the world. His choice: Mount Desert Island, where he could spend his days immersed in outdoor activities. When he wasn't hiking or biking across the island, he was hard at work building new trails and paths for such pursuits. Locals never ceased to marvel at his boundless energy, which included a frigid morning swim in the Atlantic each morning until Christmas. As his good friend Charles Eliot once put it, "George Dorr is an impulsive, enthusiastic, eager person who works at high tension, neglects his meals, sits up too late at night, and rushes about from one pressing thing to another. But he is very diligent, as well as highly inventive."

In 1944, at the age of 94, George Dorr died an impoverished man. He had spent his entire fortune purchasing additional land for Acadia National Park. Toward the end of his life, shabby clothes replaced once expensive suits, and he could not even afford to buy new books. His estate, once valued at over $10 million, had $2,000 for his funeral only because its trustees had secretly set the money aside, preventing Dorr from giving it all away.

Reflecting on the creation of Acadia National Park, Dorr once noted, "It never will be given up to private ownership again. The men in control will change. The government itself will change. But its possession, by the people, will remain."

Millionaire's Row, after the fire

THE GREAT FIRE OF 1947

By THE TIME Acadia National Park was established, Bar Harbor was a town in decline. The Cottage Era had started to fade following the introduction of the personal income tax in 1913, and its fate was sealed by the Great Depression. By the late 1940s, many of Bar Harbor's once grand mansions had fallen into disrepair.

The next tumultuous chapter in the island's history began on a dry October day in 1947, a year in which a record drought had engulfed the state. That summer and fall, Maine received just 50 percent of its normal rainfall. By mid-October, Mount Desert Island was experiencing the driest conditions ever recorded. On October 17, at the height of the drought, a small fire broke out in the town dump north of Bar Harbor. Firefighters managed to control the blaze, but they were unable to completely put it out. When the fire started to grow, firefighters from across the state were dispatched to prevent a possible catastrophe.

For six days firefighters battled the stubborn blaze. Then, just when the fire was about to be declared out of control, gale force winds descended on the island, whipping up even more flames with 60 mph gusts. It was a nightmare scenario. At 4 P.M. the fire covered 2,000 acres. Eight hours later, over 16,000 acres had burned. "It looked like two gigantic doors had opened and towering columns of roaring flames shot down," recalled one firefighter. Many trees in the fire's path simply exploded as extreme heat pressurized their moist interiors.

Fueled by the howling winds, the fire raced along the northeastern shore of Mount Desert Island and approached Bar Harbor. A lucky shift in wind pushed the fire south, sparing the downtown section, but the fire's destruction blocked all roads leading out of town. To evacuate the trapped citizens, fishermen from nearby towns were dispatched to the Bar Harbor town pier. Over 400 people escaped by boat before bulldozers cleared a path through the rubble north of town. Shortly thereafter, a caravan of 700 cars fled to safety along Route 3 as sparks from the lingering fire shot past their vehicles.

South of Bar Harbor the fire continued to rage, roaring around the eastern edge of the island with no signs of slowing down. As it approached Sand Beach, another shift in wind pushed the fire to the tip of Great Head Peninsula. With winds pounding the inferno, flames leapt nearly a mile over the ocean, forcing nearby sailors to turn away to avoid igniting their sails. But confined to the peninsula, the fire's progress was finally contained.

On October 27, the fire was officially declared under control. But two weeks later, even after rain and snow had fallen, scattered fires continued to smolder below ground. On November 14, the fire was finally declared out. When all was said and done, it had burned over 17,000 acres (10,000 in Acadia) and caused five deaths. It had also destroyed nearly $20 million worth of property, including five hotels, 127 homes, and 67 mansions along once-fabled "Millionaires Row."

PRESENT DAY

As THE SCARS of the fire started to heal, the island took on a new character that defined it for several decades. Although the fire destroyed much of Bar Harbor's gilded era, the island was no longer confronted with its reputation as a faded bastion of wealth. With Acadia National Park acting as its main draw, Mount Desert Island began to attract a new type of visitor: vacationing middle-class families.

To accommodate the new arrivals, dozens of budget hotels and campgrounds sprang up around the park. Bar Harbor reinvented itself as a sleepy tourist town full of fried seafood shacks and nautical trinket shops. But as visitation increased year after year, the town grew increasingly less sleepy and increasingly more upscale. By the end of the century, it had become one of the most popular summer destinations in New England.

Today the economy of Mount Desert Island revolves around tourism. Acadia National Park is tied with L.L. Bean's flagship store in Freeport, Maine, as the state's most visited destination (roughly 3 million visitors annually), and each year over 100 cruise ships drop anchor in Bar Harbor. Although summer is by far the busiest season on the island, more visitors are arriving in the fall, when the crowds are light and the weather is crisp. Not long ago, Labor Day was considered the end of the tourist season. Today many hotels, shops and restaurants stay open through October to accommodate the leaf-peeping crowd. But by November most business are closed and the island is back in the hands of the locals.

Today year-round residents have a surprisingly wide variety of career options. In addition to fishing and boat building, occupations that have flourished here for hundreds of years, Mount Desert Island has become a hotbed of scientific research. The Jackson Lab, the largest employer in Hancock County, is a world-renowned mammalian research facility with over 1,400 employees. Since it was founded in 1929, over 20 Nobel Prizes have been linked to the lab, which breeds hundreds of strains of genetically pure research mice. (Locals have affectionately nicknamed the lab "the Mouse House.") In addition, the Mount Desert Island Biological Laboratory is at the forefront of genetic research in marine biology.

Bar Harbor's College of the Atlantic (COA) has also had a profound impact on the culture of the island. Founded in 1969, COA offers a single major: human ecology, which explores how humans interact with the environment. Not surprisingly, COA students are a rather crunchy bunch. But their boundless enthusiasm for the natural world finds plenty of productive outlets on Mount Desert Island—from volunteering for Acadia National Park to assisting whale watch researchers at Allied Whale (p.86). In addition to COA's 300 active students, dozens of alumni choose to stay on Mount Desert Island after graduation because they simply can't imagine living anywhere else.

College of the Atlantic

For many year-round locals, the problem these days isn't finding a job, it's finding a house. As wealthy individuals have snatched up summer homes, real-estate prices have skyrocketed. The total value of all private property on Mount Desert Island is now over five billion dollars. These days many locals struggle to afford a house and pay property taxes. As a result, many people and businesses have moved off the island. Lobstermen may launch their boats from island harbors, but many of them live on the mainland and commute.

These days Mount Desert Island appears to be in the grip of a Second Cottage Era. On summer weekends, the Bar Harbor Airport is crowded with dozens of private jets, and megayachts often drop anchor offshore. But this new Cottage Era seems distinctly different. These days there's considerable social pressure from Old Money families to downplay wealth (after they climb out of their Gulfstreams, of course). And the shameless social climbing that defined Bar Harbor in the late 1800s has migrated to other, trendier locales. On Mount Desert Island, ostentatious displays are frowned upon, fleece is considered haute couture, and hiking remains the distinguished activity of choice.

For the moment, Mount Desert Island continues to fly somewhat under the national radar, commanding nowhere near the same name recognition as Martha's Vineyard or Nantucket, two islands of comparable size yet wide reaching fame. Only time will tell if Mount Desert Island will continue to remain one of America's best kept secrets.

ACADIA NATIONAL PARK

As NATIONAL PARKS go, Acadia is posh. Real posh. The wealthy families that flooded the island in the late 1800s may have brought some blue-blooded attitude, but they also brought plenty of cash. And when they decided to create Acadia National Park, no expense was spared. Hiking trails were built with hand-cut stones. The Park Loop Road was designed by America's leading landscape architect. And John D. Rockefeller, Jr. personally commissioned a network of gravel roads through the forest exclusively for horse-drawn carriages—*horse-drawn carriages!*

Acadia's scenery is scattered in non-contiguous chunks along the coast of Downeast Maine. The largest and most famous part of the park covers 30,000 acres on Mount Desert Island (about 40% of the island). Acadia also includes 2,400 acres on Schoodic Peninsula (5 miles east of MDI on the mainland), 2,700 acres on Isle au Haut (a large island 15 miles to the southwest of MDI), and about half a dozen tiny offshore islands.

If you're only visiting for a weekend, focus on Mount Desert Island, which is home to the park's most spectacular sights. The Park Loop Road (p.133) is Acadia's most famous attraction, but there are also 125 miles of hiking trails (p.17) and 47 miles of Rockefeller carriage roads (p.195). Instead of driving and fighting for parking spaces, consider riding the free Island Explorer Shuttle (p.30), which offers rides around the island.

If you're here for a week—or you've already explored Mount Desert Island—Schoodic Peninsula (p.205) and Isle au Haut (p.213) are worth a visit, especially if you're looking to get away from the crowds. Even in July and August, Isle au Haut is delightfully uncrowded.

To enter Acadia you'll need a park pass. You can purchase a seven-day pass ($25 per vehicle), annual pass ($50) or the America The Beautiful Pass ($80), which grants you access to all U.S. national parks and federal lands for one year. Passes are available at Hulls Cove Visitor Center (p.134), Thompson Island Visitor Center (p.30), the Bar Harbor Village Green (p.228), Blackwoods or Seawall campgrounds (p.31), and the Park Loop Road entrance station near Schooner Head. Also pick up a copy of the *Beaver Log*, Acadia's free publication that lists ranger programs, tide schedules, sunrise/sunset times, and a wealth of other useful information.

PARK LOOP ROAD

THE PARK LOOP ROAD is Acadia's star attraction. Twisting 27 miles through the spectacular eastern half of Mount Desert Island, it shows off bold mountains, rocky shorelines, dense forests and pristine lakes. Then, saving the best for last, the road twists and turns to the top of Cadillac Mountain—the highest point on the eastern seaboard—where stunning 360-degree views roll down from the peak.

The Park Loop Road is the main artery of the park, pumping millions of visitors through Acadia each year. But no matter how crowded it gets—and during peak season it can get very crowded—the Park Loop Road is always worth it. If you only have one afternoon to spend in the park, spend it on the Park Loop Road.

There are three popular ways to explore the Park Loop Road: drive your own car, pay for a guided bus tour, or take the free Island Explorer shuttle. Taking your own car offers the most flexibility, but traffic and parking can be a hassle during in July and August. Guided bus tours (p.231) offer narrated commentary and remove the hassle of driving and parking, but they whisk you through the park on a set schedule with little time to explore the many interesting sights on your own. The Island Explorer Shuttle (p.30) offers flexibility (it stops at popular destinations about every 30 minutes) and relaxation (no driving, no parking), but it doesn't follow the Park Loop Road in a continuous loop (it's broken up into two separate routes) and it doesn't go to the top of Cadillac Mountain.

Whatever method you choose, plan on at least three hours to explore the Park Loop Road. If you want to drive your own car, the best place to start is the Hulls Cove Visitor Center (p.134), north of Bar Harbor off Route 3.

The Park Loop Road was the brainchild of John D. Rockefeller, Jr., who championed the idea of a new motor road over the opposition of some who felt it would ruin the park. The way Rockefeller saw it, automobiles were inevitable. The park could either thoughtfully plan for their arrival or ignore the issue until it was too late. Not surprisingly, the deep-pocketed Rockefeller, who had donated much of the land that became Acadia, won the battle. To ensure that the new road blended in with the scenery, he commissioned renowned landscape architect Frederick Law Olmsted, Jr. (whose father had designed New York's Central Park) to oversee the project. Construction began in 1922 and finished in 1953. Today, the results speak for themselves. The Park Loop Road is, without question, one of the most beautiful drives in America.

1 Hulls Cove Visitor Center

Acadia National Park's main visitor center is located at the start of the Park Loop Road. There's a large parking area here, and from late-June to mid-October the visitor center is serviced by the Island Explorer shuttle. A 52-step staircase ascends from the parking area to the visitor center. (People with disabilities can use an alternate parking area reached via a short road at the south end of the main parking area.) Inside you'll find a help desk, free park publications like the Beaver Log, a giant relief map of the island, restrooms, and a store overflowing with books, calendars, and assorted goodies. A small auditorium also shows a free 15-minute movie about the park. The visitor center is open mid-April through October, 8am-4:30pm (8am to 6pm in July and August). During peak summer months, up to 9,000 people pass through the visitor center each day. It's busiest between 10am and 2pm, so try to arrive earlier or later if you can.

Rules of the Park Loop Road

- The speed limit never exceeds 35 mph, and it is strictly enforced

- Parking is allowed on the right-hand side of the road between mile 3 and mile 19 (the one-way section of the loop)

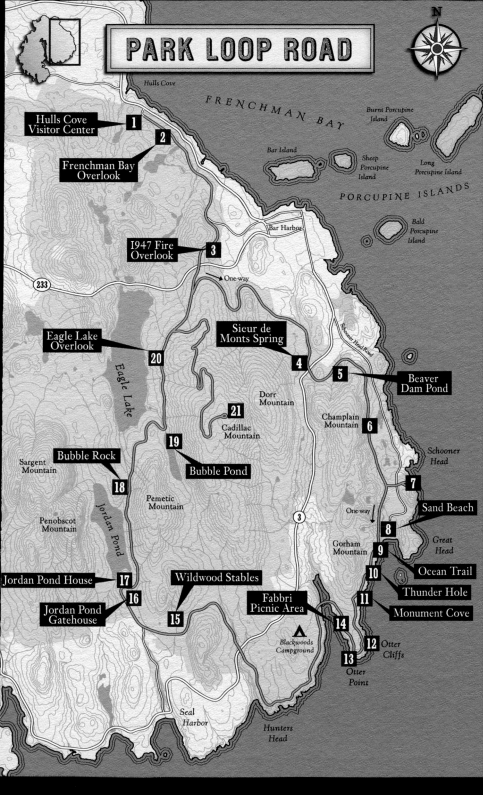

2 Frenchman Bay Overlook

The first viewpoint you'll come to on the Park Loop Road overlooks Frenchman Bay, which lies between Mount Desert Island and Schoodic Peninsula to the east. From the overlook you can see several of the Porcupine Islands (p.174), which lie just off Bar Harbor. The closest island to the overlook is Bar Island, which is connected to Bar Harbor twice a day at low tide by a shallow sandbar (p.226). Although the Frenchman Bay Overlook is nice, you'll be treated to much better views of the Porcupine Islands farther down the Park Loop Road.

Frenchman Bay

Grammar nerds take note! The name of the beautiful bay just east of Mount Desert Island is Frenchman Bay, not Frenchman's Bay (with a possessive "s"). Acadia National Park, being a good grammatical citizen, always spells it right. But as you wander outside the park on Mount Desert Island, you'll undoubtedly encounter maps, signs, and menus that refer to "Frenchman's Bay."

③ 1947 Fire Overlook

In 1947 Maine suffered its worst drought in decades. After a summer and fall with very little rain, Mount Desert Island experienced the driest conditions ever recorded. Then, in mid-October, a massive fire broke out that burned over 17,000 acres—nearly half the eastern side of Mount Desert Island (p.127).

Before the fire, the island had been dominated by evergreen forests of spruce and fir. These dark, shady forests deterred the growth of sun-loving deciduous tree species, but the 1947 fire dramatically shook up the landscape. At first only blueberry bushes, wildflowers and small ground plants grew in the fire's charred wake. But later a wide range of sun-loving broad-leafed deciduous trees such as birch and poplar took root in the sunny, open spaces created by the fire. This new mixed deciduous forest diversified the landscape, created new habitat for wildlife such as deer and songbirds, and resulted in brilliant fall foliage displays. But as the deciduous trees have flourished, they have created a nursery for shade-loving spruce and fir, which may one day muscle out the colorful deciduous trees and reclaim their lost territory.

From the 1947 Fire Overlook you can still trace the path of the fire, marked by the light green patches of deciduous leaves against the dark green evergreens in the summer. This contrast becomes surreal in the fall, when the deciduous trees' brilliant yellow, orange and red leaves seem to reenact the historic blaze.

4 Sieur de Monts Spring

This peaceful, wooded setting is home to a natural spring that was once used by Indians and early settlers. In many ways, it is the spiritual home of the park. The area around the spring was one of the first pieces of property acquired by George Dorr (p.125), who was one of the driving forces behind the creation of Acadia National Park. Dorr purchased the property in a last-minute deal, snatching it away from real-estate speculators who, aware of Dorr's interest in acquiring land for a park, hoped to buy it first and drive up the price. Dorr later described Sieur de Monts Spring as "one of the foundations on which the future park was built."

Today the spring is covered by an arched dome built by Dorr, who also had "Sweet Waters of Acadia" inscribed on a nearby rock. The inscription was inspired by Dorr's travels in Turkey, where he had seen springs labeled "Sweet Waters of Europe" and "Sweet Waters of Asia." Sieur de Monts Spring was one of Dorr's favorite places, and Dorr Mountain, which rises above the spring to the southwest was named in his honor. Due to its wet, wooded location, the area around Sieur de Monts Spring is excellent for bird watching.

Next to the parking area is the **Acadia Nature Center**, which offers exhibits about Acadia's native species, and information about efforts to preserve and protect the park's natural resources. There's also a desk where friendly park rangers answer any questions you might have, and ranger talks are sometimes given outside. Just up the hill from the nature center is the small **Abbe Museum** ($3.00 admission), which displays artifacts from local Indian tribes. Among the objects on display are stone tools, weapons, pottery, and small flutes carved from animal bones. The museum, open since 1928, displays native artifacts collected by summer resident Robert Abbe. Today this museum is overshadowed by the Abbe's much larger sister museum in downtown Bar Harbor (p.223), but the impressive collection of artifacts here still makes a visit worthwhile. A small gift shop inside also sells baskets and jewelry made by native artists.

Finally, the **Wild Gardens of Acadia**, located adjacent to the parking area, are filled with over 400 species of native flowers, trees, shrubs, and other plants. If you're interested in the local flora, it's definitely worth a stroll along the gardens' rambling paths. The Wild Gardens of Acadia are open from dawn to dusk.

5 Beaver Dam Pond

This small pond is home to several beavers, whose dam is visible at the far side of the pond. Beavers are most active at dawn and at dusk, so keep your eyes out for ripples in the water if you visit the pond during these times. By 1900 trappers had exterminated beavers from Mount Desert Island, but in 1920 two beaver pairs were successfully reintroduced to the park by George Dorr. The large buildings across the Park Loop Road from the pond belong to the Jackson Lab (p.128).

Sieur de Monts Springs

Beaver Pond

Egg Rock Overlook

Marked by an obvious pull-off on the left side of the road, this overlook provides sweeping views of Frenchman Bay, Egg Rock Lighthouse, and Schoodic Peninsula beyond. Egg Rock was named by early coastal settlers who gathered seabird eggs on its rocky ledges. Egg gathering was later banned when several seabird species, such as eider ducks and herring gulls, nearly went extinct.

In 1875 Egg Rock Lighthouse was built to help ships navigate the rocky entrance to Frenchman Bay. Because Egg Rock is so small, the lighthouse beacon was built on top of the keeper's residence to conserve space. (Most lighthouses place their beacon in a separate tower). For over a century, Egg Rock was manned by lighthouse keepers, who lived year-round on the island and rowed four miles to shore for supplies. The beacon was originally lit by whale oil, which was stored in barrels in the adjacent shack. Whale oil was later replaced by kerosene, which was then replaced by electricity from gas-powered generators. Today the lighthouse is fully automated. Electricity is delivered from Bar Harbor via an underwater cable, and solar panels provide backup energy.

As guardian of Frenchman Bay, Egg Rock has seen some remarkable comings and goings over the years. During World War II, a 250-foot German submarine snuck past Egg Rock and deposited two spies at Hancock Point, just north of Mount Desert Island. The spies, carrying $60,000 cash and a bag of diamonds, made their way to New York City before they were captured.

Highseas

This spectacular brick mansion, perched above the ocean just south of Egg Rock Overlook, was built in 1912 by Princeton professor Rudolf Brunnow. The 32-room mansion was intended as a wedding gift for Brunnow's fiancée, who was then living in Europe. Tragically, his fiancée booked her passage to America on the Titanic, and she perished in the North Atlantic.

In 1924 Highseas was purchased by wealthy New York City divorcée Mrs. Eva Van Cortland Hawkes. The sum: $25,000. Mrs. Hawkes kept a large staff at Highseas that included a butler, two footmen, a downstairs maid, upstairs maid, kitchen maid, personal maid, cook, laundress, cleaning woman, chauffeur, and gardener. During World War II, Mrs. Hawkes threw lavish parties at Highseas for the American and British navies that called to port in Bar Harbor. Champagne flowed freely and lobster Newburg was cooked in 30-gallon drums.

When the great fire of 1947 swept through this part of the island, Highseas was spared destruction by a faithful gardener who kept the mansion doused with water. Following Mrs. Hawkes' death, the estate was donated to the Jackson Lab. Today the building is used as a dormitory for high school and college students participating in the Jackson Lab's exclusive Summer Student Program—which counts *three* Nobel Prize winners among its alumni.

6 Champlain Mountain

Past Egg Rock Overlook, the Park Loop Road descends alongside the sheer eastern flank of Champlain Mountain, which rises nearly 1,000 vertical feet above the road. These cliffs—the steepest on the island—are home to the Precipice hiking trail (p.180), which starts from a small parking area on the right side of the road. In the spring and early summer, the Precipice Trail is often closed to protect nesting peregrine falcons. During this time the park sets up viewing scopes in the parking area from 9am to noon.

Peregrine falcons (p.86) are one of Acadia's most fascinating birds. Tragically, their populations plummeted in the eastern U.S. in the 20th century due to hunting and the toxic effects of pesticides. The last known nesting pair on Mount Desert Island was seen in 1956. By 1969 peregrines had completely disappeared from the island. Following the passage of the Endangered Species Act, conservationists set out to restore peregrine populations. In 1984 peregrine chicks were reintroduced to Acadia National Park as part of a captive breeding program. The chicks were hatched in captivity, then transferred to nesting sites in Acadia when they were 3 to 4 weeks old. Over the next several weeks, trained specialists monitored the chicks and made "food drops" through long tubes, which were designed to prevent the chicks from associating food with humans. Eventually, when their wings were strong enough to fly, the chicks fledged and hunted on their own.

Between 1984 and 1986, over 20 chicks were raised in Acadia. In 1987 captive bred chicks returned to Acadia as adults, but none produced any young. Then, in 1991, a successful peregrine nesting occurred in Acadia for the first time in 35 years. Over the past two decades, nesting peregrines in Acadia have produced nearly 100 chicks, 60 of which have fledged from the Precipice. Peregrine recovery efforts like those in Acadia have been so successful that peregrines were removed from the federal endangered species list in 1999.

7 Schooner Head

Just before the park entrance station, a short spur road heads left to an overlook with dramatic views of Schooner Head and Egg Rock Lighthouse. Schooner Head is named for several white markings on the rocks that resemble the sails of a ship when viewed from sea. During the American Revolutionary War, a British warship supposedly fired upon Schooner Head during a snow squall, mistaking the white markings for an American ship. A short path descends from the Schooner Head parking area to some rocky cliffs below.

The giant, modern house perched on top of Schooner Head is owned by Dan Burt, a wealthy attorney-turned-poet. Burt once told a local newspaper that he had traveled all over the world, but "I've never seen a piece of land or area more beautiful than Mount Desert."

Peregrine Falcon Chicks

8 Sand Beach

Lying at the far end of Newport Cove, Sand Beach is one of the highlights of Mount Desert Island. On clear summer days, hundreds of visitors flock here to soak in the sunshine and scenery. If the water wasn't so bone-chillingly, teeth-chatteringly cold, Sand Beach would be perfect. But this is Maine, and even in the summer ocean temperatures rarely crack 60 degrees. Whether you find a swim here refreshing or masochistic, you can rest assured that the beach will be packed on sunny days in July and August. During this time, finding a parking spot in one of the two adjacent lots feels like winning the lottery (yet another reason to ride the Island Explorer shuttle).

A staircase descends to the beach from the lower parking area. The fragile sand dunes behind the beach are protected by a long wooden fence. On the far, eastern side of the beach, a moderate, 1.8-mile trail rises above the beach and loops around the rocky promontory called Great Head. Another popular hike, the Beehive (p.178), starts across the road from Sand Beach.

Why, on the famously rocky coast of Maine, did a sandy beach form here? The answer is secluded Newport Cove, which shelters Sand Beach from powerful waves and currents, allowing small particles to accumulate over time. The "sand" you see is actually a combination of sand and crushed seashells. A close examination of the particles reveals colors such as blue, green, purple and cream from the shells of mussels, urchins and barnacles.

Although Sand Beach is generally protected from powerful waves and currents in the summer, seasonal storms do pull away sand in the winter. At times enough sand is removed to reveal the hull of the schooner *Tey*, which crashed on Old Soaker (the rock ledge at the head of Newport Cove) and washed up on Sand Beach in 1911. Back then, the beach was privately owned by financier J.P. Morgan. In 1949 Morgan's granddaughter donated Sand Beach to the park.

9 The Ocean Trail

This easy, 2-mile path parallels the Park Loop Road and offers fantastic views of the rocky shoreline between Sand Beach and Otter Cliffs. In my opinion, a stroll on the Ocean Trail is the best way to enjoy this magnificent stretch of the Park Loop Road, which is known as Ocean Drive. Walking allows you to get out of your car, breath the pine-scented air, and enjoy the scenery at nature's pace. On days when the tide is low and the ocean is calm, you can wander out on the rocks and explore the tide pools. You might even catch a glimpse of local lobstermen hauling up their traps offshore.

The Ocean Trail starts from the far end of the upper parking area at Sand Beach. If you're riding the Island Explorer, you can follow the Ocean Trail to Thunder Hole, which is the next shuttle stop.

10 Thunder Hole

Thunder Hole is a narrow rock crevice that booms like thunder when waves hit it just right. The trick is to visit at just the right time (about two hours before high tide) in just the right seas (about three to six feet). With luck and timing, you might hear the famous boom.

What causes the sound? At the end of the crevice lies a small cave, and when waves rush in they compress the air inside. If enough pressure builds, air explodes outward in a burst of spray, producing a deep, thundering boom.

But don't get your hopes up. Although Thunder Hole is one of Acadia's most famous sights, many visitors walk away disappointed. Expecting dramatic booms, they encounter pathetic gurgles and sloshes. But "Sloshing Hole" or "Hole That Thunders Only Occasionally" is no name for a star attraction.

When seas are stormy, however, Thunder Hole is one of the most spectacular—and terrifying—sights on the island. Unlike much of Mount Desert Island, which is sheltered by offshore islands, this stretch of coast is almost fully exposed to the open ocean. In high seas, waves crash into Thunder Hole with a particular fury. If you happen to visit during a storm, use extreme caution and *do not wander out on the rocks.* I took these photos on August 23, 2009, when the remnants of Hurricane Bill kicked up 15-20 foot seas in the Gulf of Maine. Against the warnings of park rangers, dozens of people wandered out onto the rocks. Suddenly, a large wave swept a father and his 7-year-old daughter into the 55-degree water. Although the Coast Guard rescued the father, the little girl drowned.

Monument Cove

11 Monument Cove

Most people drive past Monument Cove without even realizing it's there. But this tiny cove, sheltered by tall pine trees on either side, is a testament to the power of erosion. The "monument" of the cove is an obelisk-like spire at its north end. Over thousands of years, erosion widened natural cracks in the rocks surrounding the cove. As rock chunks fell away, the monument was left behind. The fallen chunks were then tumbled by the waves, eroding to form rounded, pumpkin-sized boulders. Like Sand Beach, Monument Cove is partially sheltered from waves and currents. But because Monument Cove is more exposed to the ocean than Sand Beach, waves and currents are powerful enough here to wash away any sand or small cobblestones that might form, leaving only large, heavy boulders behind.

12 Otter Cliffs

These vertical cliffs rise 110 feet above the ocean, making them irresistible to rock climbers who scamper up the sheer walls nearly every day in the summer and fall. In fact, Otter Cliffs is one of the only places on the eastern seaboard where you can rock climb directly above the ocean. (If you're interested in rock climbing lessons, there are two good rock climbing outfitters in Bar Harbor, p.17.) Despite Otter Cliff's name, there are no sea otters here. In fact, there are no sea otters on the entire East Coast. Otter Cliffs and Otter Point—as well as Otter Cove and Otter Creek—were probably named after *river* otters (which are found in Acadia) or the now-extinct sea mink, which was sometimes mistaken for an otter.

13 Otter Point

About half a mile past Otter Cliffs lies the Otter Point parking area on your right. From the parking area, a short path crosses the road and heads down to Otter Point, which at low tide is one of the best places in the park to explore tide pools. Head towards the southwestern tip of Otter Point to find the largest and most impressive tide pools. Look closely and you can probably find barnacles, dog whelks, sea stars, and other creatures of the intertidal zone (p.68).

14 Fabbri Picnic Area

This small picnic area is a good place to stop if you brought a picnic lunch. Across from the picnic area is a memorial that commemorates a strategically important naval radio station that operated here during World War I. The station received important information from the European front, but in 1932 it was relocated to Schoodic Peninsula to make way for the Park Loop Road.

Otter Cliffs

Otter Cliffs

Little Hunters Beach

This small cobblestone beach is a geological delight. The cobblestones come from rocks in Acadia's "Shatter Zone," which formed roughly 370 million years ago when a large plume of magma rose under the previously formed bedrock. When the scorching hot magma came into contact with the cool bedrock, the bedrock shattered into pieces. Some of those pieces then fell into the magma. When the magma cooled into granite, the shattered pieces were suspended in the granite like plums in plum pudding. These "plum pudding" rocks make up the Shatter Zone. At Little Hunters Beach you can see chunks of the older, mostly darker bedrock (the "plums") embedded in the granite cobblestones. The rusty coloration found on some rocks is due to iron oxide. To reach Little Hunters Beach, drive roughly two miles past Otter Point. Look for a small wooden staircase on the left side of the road, then follow the stairs down to the beach.

15 Wildwood Stables

Wildwood Stables offers horse-drawn buckboard rides ranging from one to two hours on the famous Carriage Roads (p.195). Two rides are available: Day Mountain, which offers sweeping views of the coast, and the Rockefeller Bridge Tour, which passes through the forest en route to several beautiful stone bridges. Private carriage rides are also available. (Open mid-June to mid-Oct, 877-276-3622, carriagesofacadia.com)

16 Jordan Pond Gate Lodge

In 1932 John D. Rockefeller, Jr. financed this gate lodge as a checkpoint to keep automobiles off the Carriage Roads. (Today it serves as a residence for lucky park personnel.) Rockefeller believed the architecture in many national parks was random and haphazard, and he was determined to make the buildings in Acadia better. In 1929 he sent architect Grosvenor Atterbury on a tour of national parks to study their architectural successes and faults. Atterbury returned with several important guidelines, most notably: (1) buildings should not compete with the local scenery, and (2) if no local style of architecture exists for reference, a suitable foreign style should be chosen. No local style existed in Acadia, so Atterbury designed the Jordan Pond Gate Lodge based on French Romanesque design. Look closely and you'll notice several whimsical details, including birdhouses in the garage gables and shutters with the letter "A" for Atterbury.

Wildwood Stables

17 Jordan Pond House

This restaurant, which has been serving guests for over a century, is one of the highlights of Acadia. Located on the southern shore of Jordan Pond, it offers spectacular views of the glacially sculpted scenery. Lunch and dinner are served, but many people come just for the house specialty: oven-fresh popovers (p.50) and tea. The menu also includes stews, chowders, salads, sandwiches and plenty of lobster. Open mid-May to mid-October. Local tip: During the busy summer months make a reservation (you'll avoid a long wait) and arrive via the Island Explorer shuttle (nearby parking is extremely limited). For reservations call 207-276-3316. The last Island Explorer shuttle (p.30) leaves Jordan Pond at 8:45pm.

The original Jordan Pond House opened its doors in the late 1800s. Back then, it was little more than a rambling, birchbark farmhouse. Visitors arrived on foot from Seal Harbor. Later John D. Rockefeller, Jr. bought the property and donated it to the park, but a fire destroyed the original building in 1979. The modern restaurant was built in 1982.

At 150 feet, Jordan Pond is the deepest freshwater body on the island. Towering over its north shore are the Bubbles, two glacially sculpted mountains that appear symmetrical. The symmetry is an optical illusion. North Bubble, on the left, is actually 100 feet taller than South Bubble, but it's situated 2,000 feet north. You can walk to the base of the Bubbles along the Jordan Pond Trail, a moderate 3.2-mile hike that loops around the pond. Hiking nearby Penobscot Mountain (p.186) is another great way to work up an appetite.

Jordan Pond House, early 1900s

Jordan Pond from South Bubble

18 Bubble Rock

As the Park Loop Road rises above the eastern shore of Jordan Pond, it heads between Pemetic Mountain (on your right) and the Bubbles (on your left). Keep your eyes out for rock climbers on the cliffs of South Bubble, then shift your gaze upward for a glimpse of Bubble Rock. Perched precariously on a high ledge, this 14-ton boulder was deposited by a melting glacier roughly 15,000 years ago. Geologists refer to such rocks as *glacial erratics*, and Bubble Rock is one of the most famous glacial erratics in the world.

As massive glaciers advanced over Maine during the last glaciation, loose rocks and boulders were picked up and carried along by the moving ice. Geologists believe Bubble Rock was picked up somewhere near Lucerne Lake, roughly 20 miles to the northwest. By the time it had been carried over the top of South Bubble, global temperatures started to warm and the glacier stopped advancing. As the glacier slowly melted, Bubble Rock settled on top of South Bubble in the unlikely position you see today.

Although Bubble Rock looks like it could topple over at any moment, it's actually quite secure. You can see for yourself via the short Bubble Rock Trail, a moderate, 0.7-mile round-trip trail that starts from the Bubble Rock parking area. A close examination of Bubble Rock reveals black and white crystals that are distinct from the pinkish crystals found in South Bubble's bedrock. Even if you're not interested in geology, a walk to the top of South Bubble is worth it for the stunning views of Jordan Pond just past Bubble Rock.

19 Bubble Pond

Nestled between Cadillac Mountain and Pemetic Mountain, Bubble Pond rests in a graceful, U-shaped valley that's a tell-tale sign of a glacially carved landscape. A carriage road curves around the western shore (great for a quick stroll), but swimming is prohibited because Bubble Pond is a public water supply. The stone bridge next to the pond is the only bridge in the carriage road system made entirely of stone. Most carriage road bridges are made of reinforced concrete, which was then covered with an outer layer of cut stone.

20 Eagle Lake Overlook

This small overlook offers sweeping views of Eagle Lake, the second largest lake on Mount Desert Island after Long Pond. In the late 1800s, before the Park Loop Road existed, the steamship *Wauwinnet* ferried tourists across Eagle Lake to the base of Cadillac Mountain. From there a small cog railroad hauled tourists to the top of the mountain. The venture was not profitable, however, and the *Wauwinnet* was sunk in Eagle Lake, where it still rests today.

Porcupine Islands

As you drive along the Park Loop Road up Cadillac Mountain, you'll be treated to sweeping northeastern views of Bar Harbor, Frenchman Bay, and the Porcupine Islands. During the French and Indian War (1754–1763), French gunboats hid behind the Porcupine Islands to ambush British vessels, which is probably how Frenchman Bay got its name. Even after the war, the islands continued to make fabulous hiding places. One of the islands, Rum Key, got its name during Prohibition when rum runners smuggled liquor into Frenchman Bay from Canada. Today four of the Porcupine Islands are owned by Acadia National Park. Burnt Island, which is privately owned, belongs to the town of Gouldsboro across Frenchman Bay.

Blue Hill Overlook

The best place to watch sunset on Cadillac Mountain is the Blue Hill Overlook. From the parking area, almost everyone follows the crowds to the open area to the right, but the best views are actually to the left! Follow the sidewalk to some small steps, then continue over the granite. You'll soon come to an even higher area with stunning views of Eagle Lake and Blue Hill, plus dramatic views of the Cranberry Isles to the south.

21 Cadillac Mountain

Saving the best for last, the Park Loop Road heads up a 3.5-mile spur road to the top of Cadillac Mountain. At 1,530 feet, Cadillac is the highest mountain on the island and the highest point on the Atlantic north of Rio de Janeiro. From roughly October 7 to March 7, Cadillac Mountain is the first place in the United States to see the sunrise.

The road to Cadillac's summit is filled with hairpin turns and spectacular views of the island. A pullout on the right offers western views of Eagle Lake, Sargent Mountain, and the back side of the Bubbles. Continuing on you'll twist around to eastern views of Bar Harbor, the Porcupine Islands, and Frenchman Bay. Then, after a long, straight ascent along the western side of Cadillac, the road wraps around a hairpin turn with a small pullout, which offers great views of the island's southern shore and the smaller islands beyond. Just past the turn is the Blue Hill Overlook, the most popular sunset spot on Mount Desert Island. (Arrive well before sunset during peak season to snag a space in the parking area.)

At Cadillac's summit you'll find a large parking area, restrooms, and a small store selling gifts and snacks. The 0.3-mile Summit Trail loops around the eastern edge of Cadillac, offering sweeping views of the coast. As you walk around Cadillac, take a moment to imagine the landscape 20,000 years ago at the peak of the last Ice Age. Back then, a massive glacier buried Cadillac Mountain under several thousand feet of ice. The glacier covered much of North America and stretched over 200 miles into the Gulf of Maine.

If the crowds on the Summit Trail are crazy (as they often are in the summer) you can probably find solace at Cadillac's *true* peak, reached via a short trail/access road adjacent to the gift shop. Keep your eyes out for the metal USGS marker embedded in the rock and the tremendous views of the southern shores of Mount Desert Island and the Cranberry Isles beyond.

Contrary to popular belief, Cadillac's summit does not lie above treeline. But conditions here are so harrowing that, on much of Cadillac's peak, only small, rugged plants can survive. Plants living here must cope with strong winds, freezing temperatures, and rapid erosion from run-off. The constant erosion and sparse vegetation lead to poor soil development, which often prevents larger plants like trees from taking root. The landscape here is fragile, so watch where you step. Each year millions of visitors explore Cadillac's summit, and all those footsteps add up. The park recommends sticking to Cadillac's half-mile loop trail to preserve the sparse vegetation.

In the late 1800s, a small cog railroad chugged up the side of Cadillac (then called Green Mountain). The half-hour ride cost $2.50 and brought visitors to the summit where they could spend the night in the 50-room Summit Hotel. The railroad was short-lived, however, going bankrupt after only a decade, and the Summit Hotel was torn down in 1896.

Sunrise, Cadillac Mountain

‒ᅯ **BEEHIVE TRAIL** ᅩ‒

SUMMARY: Short, steep, and sweet, the Beehive Trail is one of the most popular trails in Acadia. Rising to the top of a beehive-shaped dome that towers above the Park Loop Road, the trail provides unbeatable views of Sand Beach and Great Head Peninsula. Although the Beehive Trail is one of the shorter trails in Acadia, it's not for the faint of heart. A few steep sections require climbing iron rungs, and several precipitous drop-offs won't sit well with anyone with a fear of heights. If you are afraid of heights, the route up the steep southern face of the Beehive Trail is probably not for you, but you can still enjoy the views from the top via the Bowl Trail, which wraps around the backside of the Beehive. No matter which route you choose, be sure to check out the Bowl, a small mountain pond nestled in the granite behind the Beehive. The Bowl is a perfect place to soak your feet or jump in for a refreshing swim.

TRAILHEAD: The Bowl Trail starts across the Park Loop Road from the Sand Beach parking area. Follow the Bowl Trail 0.2 miles to its intersection with the Beehive Trail, which veers off to the right.

▶ TRAIL INFO ◀

RATING: Strenuous, Ladder

DISTANCE: 1.6 miles, round-trip

HIKING TIME: 1–2 hours

ELEVATION CHANGE: 520 feet

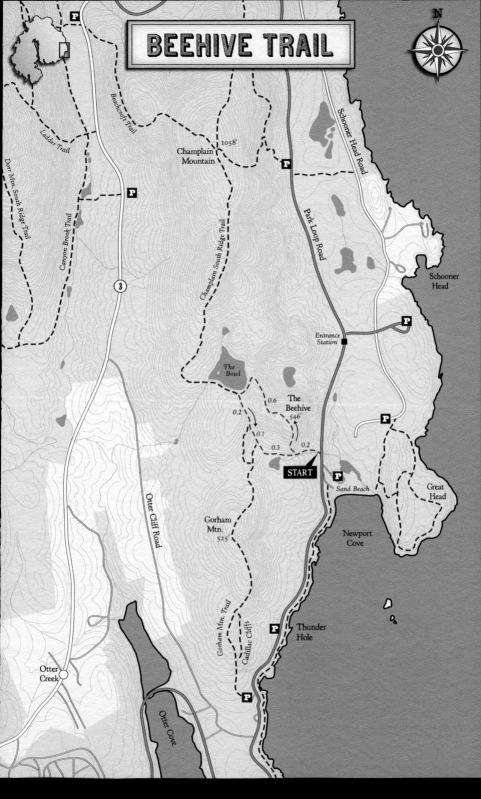

BEEHIVE TRAIL

N

P

Ladder Trail

Beachcroft Trail

Canyon Brook Trail

Dorr Mtn. South Ridge Trail

P

3

Champlain Mountain
1058'

Champlain South Ridge Trail

P

Schooner Head Road

Park Loop Road

Schooner Head

P

Entrance Station

P

The Bowl

0.6

The Beehive
546'

0.2

0.1

0.3   0.2

START

P

Sand Beach

Great Head

Otter Cliff Road

Gorham Mtn.
525'

Newport Cove

Gorham Mtn. Trail

Cadillac Cliffs

P

Thunder Hole

P

Otter Creek

Otter Cove

~d THE PRECIPICE ɔ~

SUMMARY: Rising nearly 1,000 feet up the sheer east face of Champlain Mountain, the Precipice might be the most challenging trail in the park. It's certainly the most famous. A jungle gym of iron rungs guides hikers up this sheer cliff, which offers thrilling ascents and tremendous views of Frenchman Bay. Despite the hype, it takes more mental strength than physical strength to conquer the Precipice. Other than some exposed, 100-foot plus drop-offs and a few steep sections that require ladder-style climbing, the Precipice is no worse than many other challenging yet less-heralded hikes in Acadia. But if you do have a fear of heights—or if the Precipice is closed due to nesting peregrine falcons—you can still reach the top of Champlain via the 1.2-mile Beachcroft Path, which starts off Route 3. From the summit of Champlain, follow the North Ridge Trail and Orange and Black Path back to return to the Precipice parking area.

TRAILHEAD: The Precipice Trail starts from the Precipice parking area off the Park Loop Road, two miles south of Sieur de Monts entrance off Route 3.

TRAIL INFO

RATING: Strenuous, Ladder   **HIKING TIME:** 2–3 hours

DISTANCE: 2.5 miles, round-trip   **ELEVATION CHANGE:** 978 feet

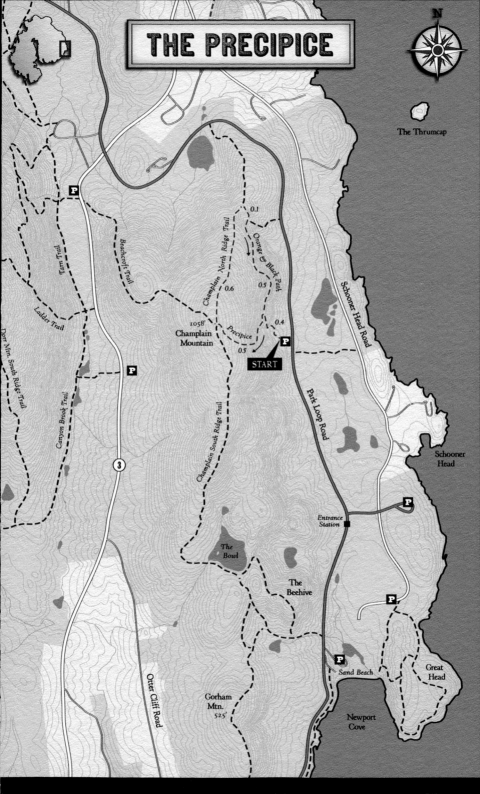

THE PRECIPICE

N

The Thrumcap

Tarn Trail

Beachcroft Trail

Champlain North Ridge Trail

0.1

Orange & Black Path

0.6

0.5

Ladder Trail

0.4

1058'
Champlain
Mountain

Precipice

0.5

Schooner Head Road

START

Dorr Mtn. South Ridge Trail

Canyon Brook Trail

Park Loop Road

Schooner
Head

3

Entrance
Station

The Bowl

The
Beehive

Otter Cliff Road

Gorham
Mtn.
525'

Sand Beach

Great
Head

Newport
Cove

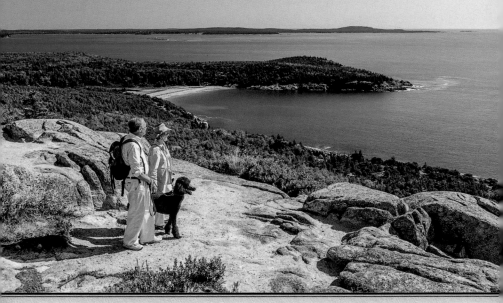

❧ GORHAM MOUNTAIN ❧

SUMMARY: Gorham Mountain offers the best views of any moderate hike in the park. Great for families with young children, the trail rises to the summit of Gorham Mountain, providing dramatic views of Otter Cliffs, Sand Beach, and the gorgeous stretch of shoreline along Ocean Drive. Cadillac Cliffs, a short spur trail that branches off from the main trail, passes by an ancient sea cave that sat at sea level several thousand years ago (at the time, in the wake of the glaciers, the land was compressed and sea levels were relatively higher). As you climb towards the summit, be sure to turn around and enjoy the dramatic views to the south (they're better than the views from the summit). After reaching the summit, follow the trail north to the Sand Beach parking area. From the parking area, stroll back to the Gorham Mountain trailhead along the easy Ocean Path.

TRAILHEAD: The Gorham Mountain Trail starts from the Gorham Mountain parking area, located on the right side of the Park Loop Road about half a mile past Thunder Hole.

TRAIL INFO

RATING: Moderate   **HIKING TIME:** 1–2 hours

DISTANCE: 3.2 miles, round-trip   **ELEVATION CHANGE:** 525 feet

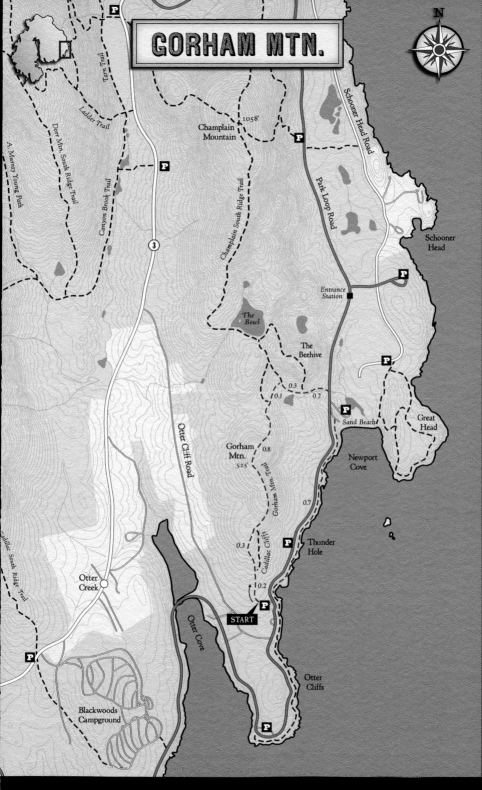

❧ CADILLAC MOUNTAIN ☙

SUMMARY: At 1,530 feet Cadillac Mountain is the island's highest peak, offering stunning 360-degree views of coastal Maine. Although you'll be sharing those views with everyone who arrived by car, your endorphin-soaked brain will be enjoying them more! There are four possible routes up Cadillac, but I like heading up the North Ridge Trail, which offers terrific views of Bar Harbor and the Porcupine Islands. After reaching the summit, follow the dirt path next to the gift shop to the island's true peak (look for the USGS marker embedded in the bedrock) and continue down Cadillac's South Ridge Trail. On clear days you'll be treated to spectacular views of the dozens of small islands lying off MDI's southern shore. The South Ridge Trail ends at Blackwoods Campground, where you can catch the Island Explorer Shuttle (p.30) back to downtown Bar Harbor.

TRAILHEAD: The Cadillac North Ridge trailhead is located along the Park Loop Road, 1/3 of a mile past the Y-intersection where the Park Loop Road becomes one-way. There's a small pull-out across from the trailhead. The Island Explorer "Loop Road" route stops at the Cadillac North Ridge trailhead.

◀ TRAIL INFO ▶

RATING: Strenuous **HIKING TIME:** 3–4 hours

DISTANCE: 5.7 miles, round-trip **ELEVATION CHANGE:** 1,463 feet

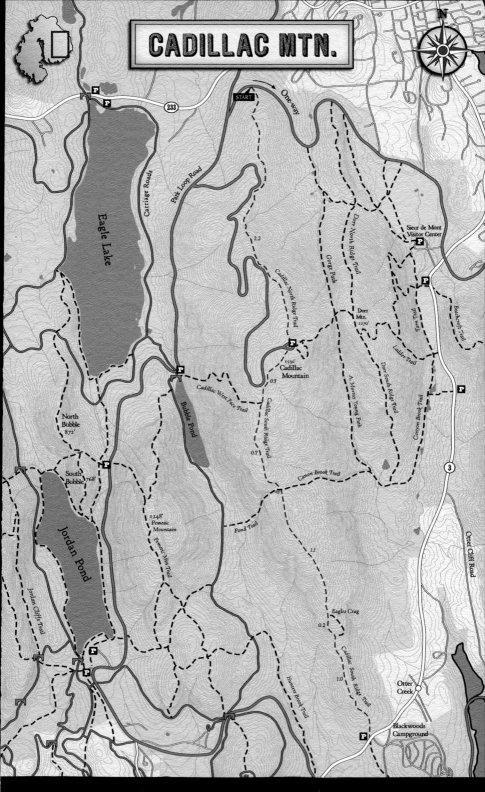

◦◦ PENOBSCOT MOUNTAIN ◦◦

SUMMARY: Penobscot Mountain is my favorite hike in the Jordan Pond area. The trail to the summit is classic Acadia—a dramatic hike up a bare granite ridge with spectacular views of the Gulf of Maine. The trail starts near the Jordan Pond House and rises quickly through dense forest. After scrambling over a few iron rungs, you'll reach Penobscot Mountain's dramatic granite ridge. Hiking above treeline, you can see the Cranberry Isles to the south and, if it's a clear day, Great Duck Island and Little Duck Island beyond. After passing over the summit, the trail dips back into the forest and descends rapidly to Jordan Pond along the Deer Brook Trail, which passes under a magnificent carriage road bridge. From the northern tip of Jordan Pond you can follow the Jordan Pond Shore Trail back to the Jordan Pond House. Local tip: Fresh popovers at the Jordan Pond House are even more delicious after a hunger-inducing hike up Penobscot Mountain.

TRAILHEAD: The Penobscot Mountain Trailhead is located behind the Jordan Pond House. Follow the trail into the woods and look for a carved signpost.

TRAIL INFO

RATING: Strenuous   **HIKING TIME:** 2–3 hours

DISTANCE: 3.7 miles, round-trip   **ELEVATION CHANGE:** 973 feet

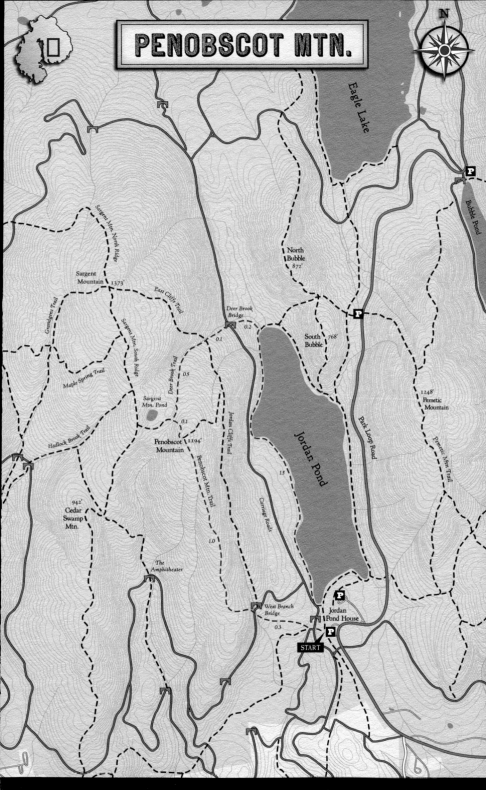

⊰ SARGENT MOUNTAIN ⊱

SUMMARY: At 1,373 feet Sargent Mountain is Acadia's second highest peak, just 157 feet shy of Cadillac Mountain. Like Cadillac, Sargent has sweeping 360-degree views rolling down from a bare granite summit. Unlike Cadillac, it's not swarming with tourists who arrived by car. In fact, because Sargent Mountain is one of Acadia's most remote and challenging hikes, you might have the views all to yourself. There are several possible approaches, but my favorite heads up and over Parkman Mountain. From there head up the western face of Sargent Mountain along the Grandgent Trail. As you climb the steep Grandgent Trail, be sure to rest and take in the terrific views of Somesville and Somes Sound to the west. After reaching the summit, head down Sargent's gorgeous southern ridge to the Hadlock Brook Trail, which passes gurgling streams, shimmering cascades, and one of the Carriage Roads' most spectacular stone bridges.

TRAILHEAD: Head to the small parking area just north of Upper Hadlock Pond, next to the Norumbega Mountain trailhead. The Hadlock Brook Trail starts across the street from the parking area.

TRAIL INFO

RATING: Strenuous   **HIKING TIME:** 4–5 Hours

DISTANCE: 4.6 miles, round-trip   **ELEVATION CHANGE:** 1,152 feet

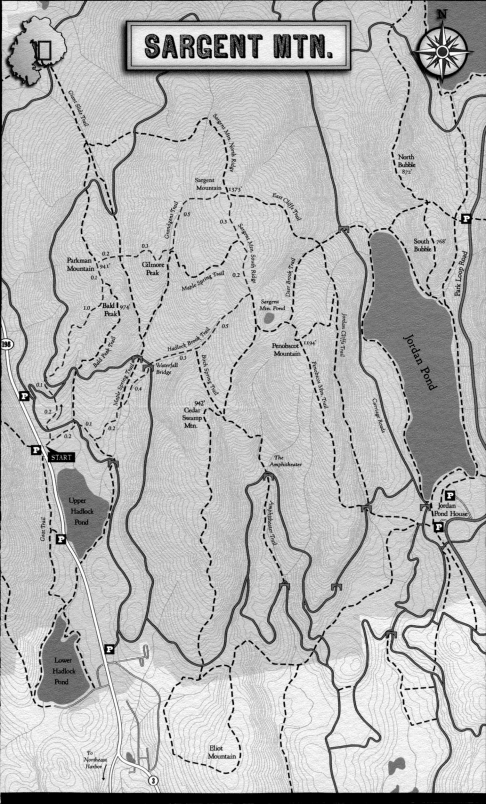

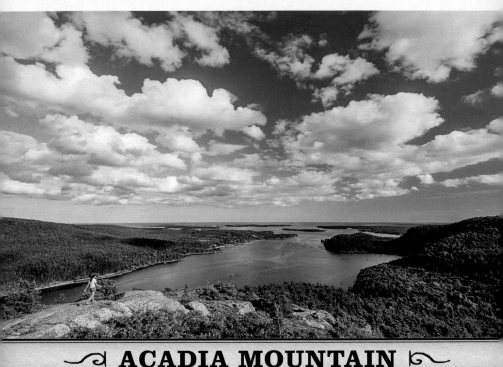

~&〉 ACADIA MOUNTAIN 〈&~

SUMMARY: Acadia Mountain is my favorite hike on the western side of Mount Desert Island. Perched high above Somes Sound, it offers spectacular views of the East Coast's loveliest fjard and the beautiful islands lying south. The trail starts in a shady spruce-fir forest, then scrambles over a large granite ledge en route to the top of Acadia Mountain. The view from the peak is nice, but there's an even better viewpoint a short distance farther. Just past the viewpoint the trail drops roughly 600 feet in half a mile. Near the base of the mountain a small trail leads to Man 'o War Brook Waterfall, a small cascade where 18th century ships would replenish their water barrels. Somes Sound is so deep near the waterfall that ships would simply pull up alongside the cascade. From Man 'o War Brook, follow the dirt access road back to the trailhead. Local tip: After hiking Acadia Mountain, head to Echo Lake Ledges for a refreshing swim!

TRAILHEAD: The trail starts across the street from the Acadia Mountain parking area on Route 102, about two miles north of Southwest Harbor.

TRAIL INFO

RATING: Strenuous

DISTANCE: 2.6-miles, round-trip

HIKING TIME: 2 hours

ELEVATION CHANGE: 581 feet

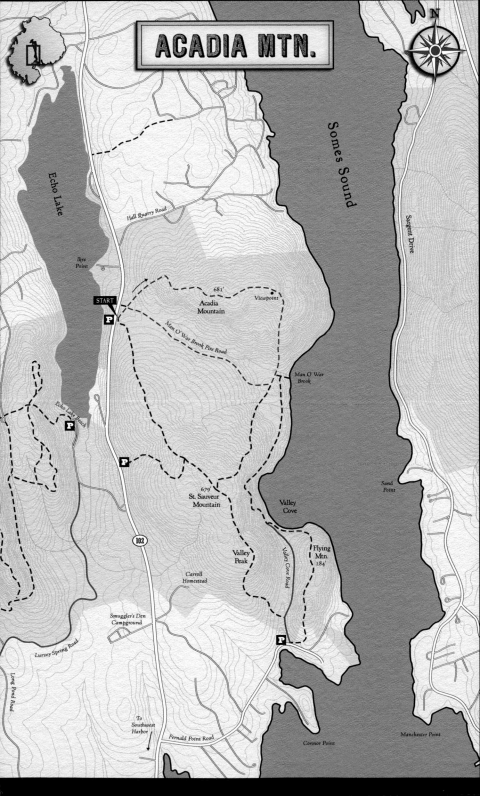

⊰ BEECH MOUNTAIN ⊱

SUMMARY: This peaceful hike, far removed from the crowds on the eastern side of the island, reveals some of the island's most overlooked and underrated scenery. From the Beech Mountain parking area, follow the Valley Trail through a lush spruce-fir forest, then climb a series of exquisite granite steps up the Beech Mountain South Ridge Trail. After a long ascent you'll reach Beech Mountain's peak. From the top you'll enjoy terrific views of the southern shore of western Mount Desert Island. The fire tower on top of Beech Mountain was last used in 1976 (today most fire patrols are done by small planes). The tower is closed to the public except on special weekends in the fall; check local papers for details. From the summit, follow the western branch of the Beech Mountain Trail back to the parking area. Along the way you'll be treated to gorgeous views of Long Pond.

TRAILHEAD: Follow Route 102 south of Somesville, then turn right onto Pretty Marsh Road. After 0.3 miles turn left onto Beech Hill Road, which heads south for three miles before dead ending at the Beech Mountain parking area. The Valley Trail starts at the southern end of the parking area.

TRAIL INFO

RATING: Moderate

HIKING TIME: 2 hours

DISTANCE: 2.9 miles, round-trip

ELEVATION CHANGE: 589 feet

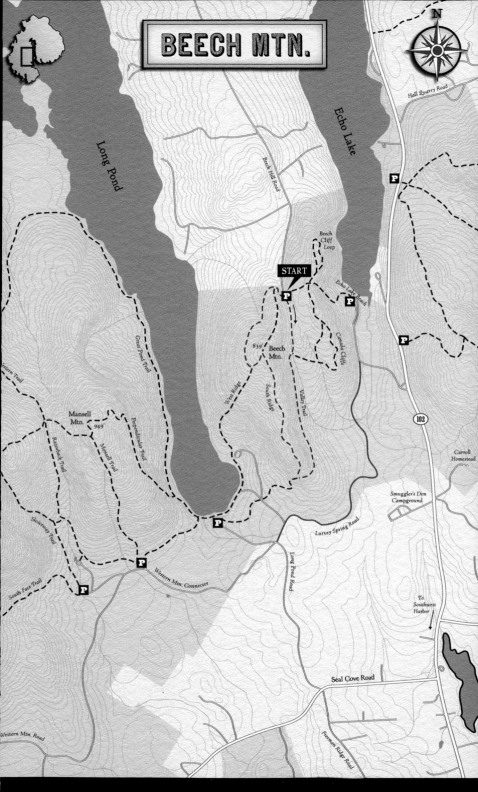

BEECH MTN.

N

Hall Quarry Road

Echo Lake

Long Pond

Beech Hill Road

Beech Cliff Loop

START

Echo Lake Beach

Canada Cliffs

839'
Beech Mtn.

West Ridge

South Ridge

Valley Trail

Great Pond Trail

Western Trail

Perpendicular Trail

Mansell Mtn.
949'

Mansell Trail

Razorback Trail

102

Carroll Homestead

Smuggler's Den Campground

Lurvey Spring Road

Sluiceway Trail

Western Mtn. Connector

Long Pond Road

South Face Trail

To Southwest Harbor

Western Mtn. Road

Seal Cove Road

Freeman Ridge Road

Duck Brook Bridge

CARRIAGE ROADS

Acadia's carriage roads are like a fairy tale come to life. Originally constructed on the private estate of John D. Rockefeller, Jr., they were later donated to the park for the enjoyment of the public. Today over 57 miles of gravel roads twist through Acadia, revealing the island's lush interior—a land of leafy forests, sparkling streams, and stunning lakes. Sprinkled along the carriage roads are 17 exquisite stone bridges, hand-crafted by stonemasons out of native rock. When the bridges first opened, they regularly saw the comings and goings of horse-drawn carriages. Today, bicycles are the most popular form of transportation along the carriage roads, and many people consider a pedal-powered romp on the carriage roads to be one of the highlights of Acadia National Park.

The carriage roads form a network of car-free roads on the eastern half of Mount Desert Island, extending from Paradise Hill (near downtown Bar Harbor) south to the Rockefeller family estate in Seal Harbor. There is no official start or end to the carriage roads. There are, however, six popular parking areas next to the carriage roads where most people begin their journey, and from there you can choose your own adventure. Although the intricate network of roads can be confusing at first, numbered signposts at every intersection make it hard to get lost when you have a good map (included at the end of this chapter). Bicycles can be rented in Bar Harbor (p.223), or you can head to Wildwood Stables near Seal Harbor for a genuine horse-drawn carriage ride (p.160). Of course, walking the carriage roads is also an option. (Note: Twelve miles of carriage roads in Seal Harbor are open only to hikers and horseback riders—no bicycles are allowed. Keep your eyes out for the "No Bicycle" signs posted at intersections.)

The fascinating history of the carriage roads traces its roots to the year 1837, when a wooden bridge first connected Mount Desert Island to the mainland. Before the bridge, Mount Desert Island was only accessible by sea. After the bridge, visitors could arrive by land. For decades this minor improvement produced relatively little change in island life because ships remained the primary mode of transportation. But with the dawn of the automobile age in the late 1800s, the tiny bridge became a vital link between Mount Desert Island and the modern world—a fact that did not sit well with the summer residents who came to Mount Desert Island to *escape* the modern world.

By the time Henry Ford introduced his Model T to the masses in 1908, cars were already banned on Mount Desert Island. The ban served two purposes: it allowed rich summer visitors to take refuge from the sputtering, soot-spewing automobiles that were flourishing in big cities, and it allowed year-round residents to limit the pretentious lifestyles of the rich. All that changed with the introduction of the Model T. As moderately priced cars flooded the nation, local islanders were determined not to be left out of the fun. On a more practical level, cars also offered a cheap, efficient method of transport for local businesses. In 1909 a group of locals attempted to repeal the ban on cars, but their efforts were blocked by a group of wealthy summer residents who lobbied hard to keep the ban in place. The locals, vowing revenge, promised to revisit the matter as soon as possible.

Two years later, a temporary compromise was reached limiting cars to the town of Bar Harbor. But when a local man died because a horse-drawn carriage could not reach the hospital in time, the automobile ban was widely denounced. By 1915 cars were allowed in every town on Mount Desert Island.

Among the summer residents most alarmed at this turn of events was John D. Rockefeller, Jr. A recent arrival to Mount Desert Island, Rockefeller had purchased a home in Seal Harbor as a summer refuge from New York City. At a time when most wealthy Manhattan businessmen commuted to work in shiny new cars, Rockefeller drove himself to work in a horse-drawn carriage—a habit that spoke volumes about his poor fit among the office buildings of New York City. Since birth Rockefeller had been groomed to take over his family's vast oil business, but Rockefeller and Standard Oil were hardly a match made in heaven. Happiest outdoors, Rockefeller coped with the stress of Manhattan office life by chopping wood after work. After a few years at the helm at Standard Oil, he quit the family business, devoted himself to a life of philanthropy, and purchased his 150-acre Seal Harbor estate.

When Rockefeller arrived in Seal Harbor in 1910, the Great Automobile War (as it was later called) was just beginning. Perhaps sensing the inevitable, Rockefeller began building a series of gravel roads on his sprawling Seal Harbor property where he could enjoy the simple pleasures of a horse-drawn carriage ride. As his network of roads grew, he decided to connect them in a continuous loop. To do so, however, required passing through land owned by the Hancock County Trustees of Public Reservations (the predecessor of Acadia National Park). Rockefeller tried to buy the land in question, but his offer was refused. He was allowed, however, to build roads through the land with the knowledge that they might one day be shut down.

Rockefeller accepted this risk, and over the next decade he continued to expand his network of roads through the park. Things went well until one planned road in Northeast Harbor drew heat from local conservationists who felt it would be a blight on the natural landscape. Northeast Harbor summer resident George Wharton Pepper fired off a letter to Rockefeller. "In my judgement," he wrote, "it

JOHN D. ROCKEFELLER, JR.

Without John D. Rockefeller, Jr.'s deep pockets and even deeper sense of philanthropy, Acadia National Park would not exist as we know it today. He is the park's most famous benefactor, embodying both the generosity and public-minded spirit that defines Acadia.

Rockefeller was born in 1874, the sole male heir to John D. Rockefeller's vast Standard Oil fortune. Influenced by his family's pious values, he did not drink alcohol and was a deeply religious man. He was also a lover of nature, spending as much time as possible outdoors. After graduating from Brown University he went to work for Standard Oil in New York City. But Rockefeller ultimately decided the family business was not for him, and in 1910, at age 36, he retired from the working world and devoted himself to a life of philanthropy.

Rockefeller first visited Mount Desert Island when he was in college, but it wasn't until he returned in 1908 with his wife, Abbey, that he fell in love with the island. Two years later, Rockefeller bought a spectacular hilltop estate in Seal Harbor. Shortly after his arrival, Rockefeller was approached by local philanthropist George Dorr, who was soliciting funds to protect land on the island from private development. Rockefeller listened to Dorr's vision of a national park, then opened his enormous wallet.

Over the following decades, John D. Rockefeller Jr. became Acadia's greatest benefactor. When Rockefeller met Dorr the future park consisted mostly of mountaintops. Rockefeller spent millions of dollars buying the land between the mountains, unifying and protecting Mount Desert Island's most spectacular scenery. All told Rockefeller donated roughly one-third of Acadia National Park.

Rockefeller also spearheaded and financed both the Park Loop Road and the Carriage Roads, both of which drew strong opposition at the time. Some conservationists felt the roads would ruin the wild nature of the park. Rockefeller disagreed. A firm believer that nature could make people "happier, richer, better," Rockefeller argued that roads and paths were necessary to make nature more accessible to the public.

Rockefeller's work in Acadia set the stage for decades of involvement with the National Park Service. In 1927 he donated five million dollars to help establish Great Smoky Mountain National Park in Tennessee. In 1943 he donated 35,000 acres of land in Wyoming to help create Grand Teton National Park.

John D. Rockefeller Jr. died in 1960, but his family's philanthropic legacy lives on. In 2015 his son, David, celebrated his 100th birthday by donating 1,000 acres of family property in Seal Harbor to the local Land and Garden Preserve.

would be a serious mistake to extend your well conceived system of roads into this area." Rockefeller reluctantly agreed, and he halted construction of the road in question. But by this point many people were using and enjoying the roads that were already built. In fact, many locals openly supported Rockefeller's plans. A group of locals circulated a petition urging Rockefeller to continue construction, and the *Bar Harbor Times* published an op-ed in full support of the carriage roads. But despite the outpouring of support, the ever-cautious Rockefeller stayed out of the fray and did not resume construction of the road in question.

The sudden controversy was particularly worrisome to George Dorr, the savvy superintendant of the park. Dorr knew that Rockefeller's deep pockets were essential to acquire additional land for the park, and he did not want to alienate the park's wealthiest benefactor. Recognizing Rockefeller's obvious enthusiasm for road building, Dorr suggested that Rockefeller help build an "access" road next to Jordan Pond. Rockefeller jumped at the idea, and by 1921 the "access" road had expanded to include a series of roads connected to Rockefeller's previously built roads. Although the new roads were officially ordered by Dorr, it was Rockefeller who studied and planned them, simply making "suggestions" as to where they might be placed.

Rockefeller financed these new roads with one condition: that a new motor road would also be constructed through the park. Although Rockefeller was hardly thrilled with the steady stream of automobiles pouring onto the island, he realized that they were inevitable, and he wanted to plan for them wisely.

Rockefeller's proposed motor road immediately drew heat from the same small group of wealthy summer residents who opposed his carriage roads. Again it was George Pepper, by this time a Senator from Pennsylvania, who led the charge. Pepper contacted Secretary of the Interior Hubert Work and used his influence to halt construction of both the motor road and the new carriage roads. Pepper and others felt the new park was already drawing too many people to Mount Desert Island. A motor road, they argued, would only encourage more to come. Such feelings were summed up in a 1924 article in the *Boston Evening Transcript*: "Protests were especially emphatic from the view-point of many of the summer residents, who had long enjoyed the blissful quiet and primitive beauty of the island. They freely stated their fear that the proposed development would

> "When I thought a thing was worth doing, I made up my mind that the annoyances, the obstacles, the embarrassments had to be borne because the ultimate goal was worthwhile."
> —John D. Rockefeller, Jr.

bring in a 'peanut crowd' of the Coney Island type, and that the park would speedily be littered with egg shells, banana peels, old tin cans."

Rockefeller saw things differently. As he had pointed out during a similar road building incident at another national park, "What are these parks for ...? The average American can't afford to go into the secluded areas or to have private trips into the parks. He must travel on such a highway. That's the whole point of the national park system." Rockefeller, ever the populist, believed in making the parks accessible for the common man, as well as for the elderly and handicapped.

Rockefeller had the full support of year-round residents, who welcomed the flood of money that road construction and increased tourism would bring. With the backing of local residents and Maine politicians, Rockefeller and Dorr pushed hard to continue construction of both the motor road and the carriage roads. In the face of such strong opposition, Senator Pepper backed down. Shortly thereafter, the Secretary of the Interior came to the island to examine the situation firsthand. After viewing the roads, he concluded that they were indeed a worthy improvement. He gave his full blessing to the roads already under construction—with the stipulation that any future roads be approved by his office.

Emboldened by the overwhelming public support for his cause, Rockefeller charged ahead with plans for an even larger network of carriage roads and an expanded motor road. To bypass the approval demanded by Secretary Work, Rockefeller built new roads on land earmarked for (but not yet donated to) the park. Only when the roads were finished would the land be transferred to the park. Another round of protests erupted, but this time there was nothing that could be legally done to halt the construction.

By 1940 Rockefeller's grand vision was complete. A 57-mile network of carriage roads stretched from Bar Harbor to Seal Harbor, passing mountains, lakes and ponds. Curving gracefully through the woods, the roads revealed some of the park's most beautiful, hidden scenery. Every twist and turn was personally selected by Rockefeller, whose knowledge of road building and hands-on involvement in the undertaking were legendary. Rockefeller also commissioned 17 exquisite stone bridges along the carriage roads. Each bridge, unique in design, was handcrafted by stonemasons and financed by Rockefeller at extraordinary cost.

When all was said and done, Rockefeller had spent nearly 30 years and several million dollars building the carriage roads. When construction first began in 1913, horse-drawn carriage rides were still a popular aspect of island life. By 1940, however, they had turned into a quaint pastime for the rich. At the same time, bicycle use had taken off in America. Rockefeller was aware of this fact, and he was one of the first to encourage opening the carriage roads to bicycles. Today, bicycles are the most popular way to explore the carriage roads.

Following Rockefeller's death in 1960, the carriage roads fell into disrepair. To remedy the situation, the non-profit Friends of Acadia established a multimillion dollar endowment for the ongoing upkeep of the carriage roads. After several years of rehabilitation, Mr. Rockefeller's roads were restored to their full glory, and today they are as magnificent as ever.

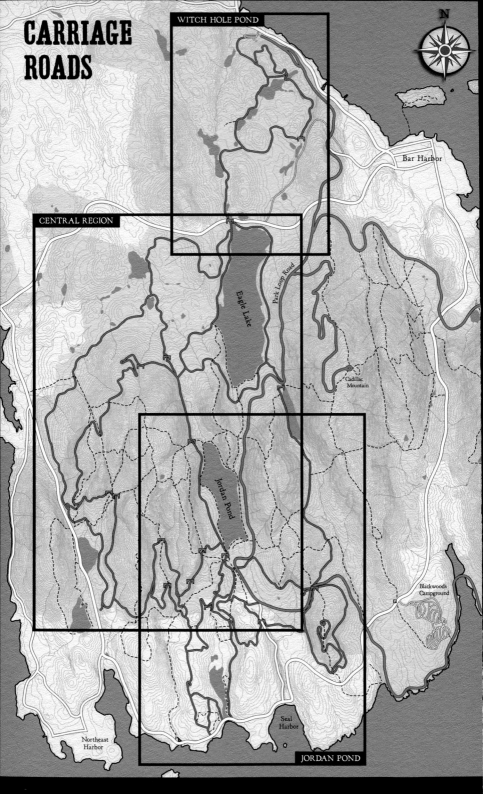

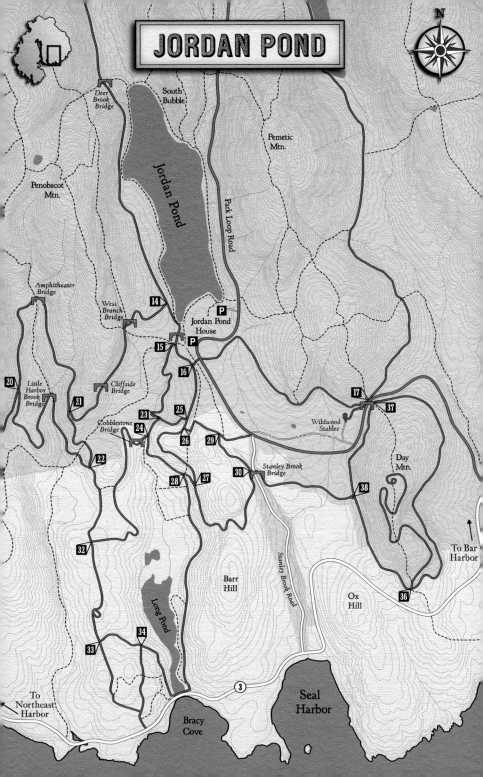

SCHOODIC PENINSULA

RUGGED, ROCKY SCHOODIC Peninsula juts into the Gulf of Maine just east of Mount Desert Island. The peninsula's 2,000 acres are the only part of Acadia National Park connected to the mainland, but Schoodic has limited bragging rights when it comes to truly dramatic scenery. There are no towering mountains, hidden lakes or sandy beaches here. What Schoodic does offer, however, is a gorgeous glimpse of undeveloped coastal Maine.

The peninsula's relatively remote location shelters it from the swarms of tourists that descend on Mount Desert Island each summer. As a result, Schoodic has a more subtle, peaceful charm. If crowded roads and screaming children are fraying your nerves, Schoodic might be the scenic Valium you need.

Although Schoodic Peninsula lies just five miles east of Mount Desert Island, it's about 40 miles by road along Route 1. You can also get to Schoodic via the Bar Harbor Ferry (207-288-298, barharborferry.com), which runs a water taxi between Bar Harbor and Winter Harbor, a small fishing village near the peninsula. From late June to Labor Day the Island Explorer Shuttle (exploreacadia.com) offers a Schoodic route that loops through Winter Harbor, Schoodic Peninsula and Prospect Harbor.

The one-way Schoodic Loop Road circumnavigates the peninsula. The start and finish are connected by Route 186. Unlike Mount Desert Island's crowded Park Loop Road, the Schoodic Loop Road is relatively free of traffic, making it great for biking. There are also about eight miles of dedicated bike paths through the Schoodic Woods area. The Bar Harbor Ferry lets you bring a bike for an extra $5, or you can rent bikes from Seascape (p.207) in Winter Harbor.

Schoodic Peninsula was added to Acadia National Park in 1929. Prior to the addition, Acadia was known as Lafayette National Park, a name chosen in 1919 to reflect America's pro-French sentiment in the wake of World War I. But Schoodic Peninsula was donated by three Anglophile sisters on the condition that the name of the park be changed to something less French. George Dorr, the park's first superintendant, suggested the name Acadia based on an early name for the region. Apparently unknown to the sisters, "Acadia" was based on *L'Acadie*, a name given by—*sacre bleu!*—the French.

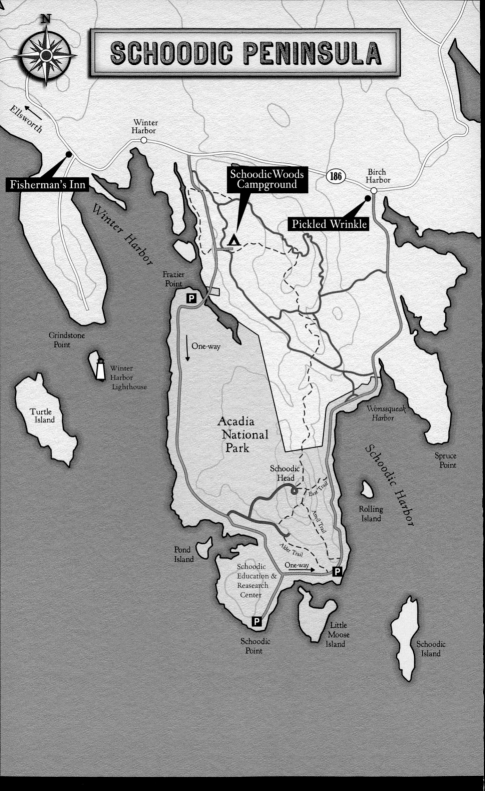

Lodging & Camping

There are about a dozen hotels in Winter Harbor and the surrounding towns. The new Schoodic Woods Campground is also located adjacent to the park. For detailed lodging and camping info visit jameskaiser.com

Restaurants

★ RAVEN'S NEST $$$ (Lnch, Din)

Winter Harbor's most upscale restaurant serves local seafood, meats and vegetables with an Italian touch. Nice wine and cocktails. Wood-fired pizza Thurs-Sun. (207-963-2234, ravensnestrestaurant.com)

★ J.M. GERRISH $ (Brk, Lnch)

This popular café and ice cream parlour serves tasty breakfasts (eggs, baked goods) and lunches (sandwiches, burgers, chowder) in a charming retro atmosphere. Great coffee. (352 Main Street, 207-963-7000, jmgerrish.com)

THE PICKLED WRINKLE $$ (Lnch, Din)

Named after a seasonably available local delicacy (p.48), this casual bar/restaurant serves quality food (sandwiches, burgers, salads, pizza) at reasonable prices. (9 East Schoodic Drive, 207-963-7916, thepickledwrinkle.com)

THE FISHERMAN'S INN $$ (Din)

This classic Winter Harbor restaurant has been serving fresh seafood since 1947, and they've got the nautical decor to prove it. Casual fine dining with an emphasis on local food. (7 Newman Street, 207-963-5585, fishermansinnmaine.com)

Winter Harbor

Named for it's well-protected harbor, which offers shelter to boats during fierce winter storms, this small fishing village (pop. 516) offers a classic slice of Downeast Maine. It's home to lobstermen, artists and wealthy summer folk whose giant mansions dot the shores of Grindstone Neck, the small peninsula at the eastern end of the harbor. After you've explored Downtown Winter Harbor, head to the tip of Grindstone Neck, where there's a granite bench with nice views and a short hiking trail that parallels the rocky shore. Seasonal events include the Winter Harbor Lobster Festival, held the second Saturday in August, and the week-long Winter Harbor Music Festival in late August (winterharbormusicfestival.com).

SEASCAPE KAYAK & BIKE

The coast around Schoodic is stunning, but it can be hard to fully enjoy the scenery from a car. Seascape offers guided kayak tours, kayak rentals and bike rentals. (8 Duck Pond Road, seascapekayaking.com)

Frazer Point

Schoodic Peninsula

The road to Schoodic Peninsula is located just east of Winter Harbor off Route 186. Turn south on Schoodic Loop Road and follow the signs to the 6-mile one-way road that wraps around the peninsula. Parking is not permitted on the right hand side of the road, but there are several pullouts along the way. Visit in the fall and you'll be treated to spectacular foliage.

FRAZER POINT PICNIC AREA

This pretty point has about a dozen picnic tables scattered around a grassy knoll that gently slopes to the shore. A small, wooden footbridge juts into the cove, offering nice views of the surroundings. Fire rings, restrooms and drinking water are also available. Bicyclists arriving by car can park here and ride to the end of the one-way road, where a car-free bike path loops back to Frazer Point.

WINTER HARBOR LIGHTHOUSE

As you continue along Schoodic Loop Road, you'll pass several clearings with views of rocky shores and cobblestone beaches. Across the harbor on Mark Island is Winter Harbor Lighthouse. Built in 1856, the 19-foot tower was faithfully lit by nine keepers and their families until 1933, when the light was discontinued and replaced by a lighted buoy. The lighthouse, which is now private property, has attracted a steady stream of literary types. Since 1933, no fewer than five writers have lived in the lighthouse.

SCHOODIC HEAD

At 440 feet, Schoodic Head is the highest point on Schoodic Peninsula. The views from the top are somewhat obscured by vegetation, but it's an interesting side trip nonetheless. To get there, head about 2.5 miles past Frazer Point, then turn left on an unpaved road. Continue about one mile to a small parking area. Four-wheel drive and high clearance are recommended. Random tree fact: Schoodic Head is home to one of the only stands of jack pine in Maine.

SCHOODIC EDUCATION RESEARCH CENTER (SERC)

This cluster of buildings is home to a scientific research center focused on ecology and natural history. Stop by the visitor center in beautiful Rockefeller Hall for a nice overview of SERC and the Schoodic Peninsula. Inside you'll find displays about the region's natural history and the building's fascinating 70-year history as a top-secret naval base. (schoodicinstitute.org)

SCHOODIC POINT

After passing the turnoff for SERC, continue south to the multi-tiered parking area at Schoodic Point. This is the tip of Schoodic Peninsula, providing sweeping views of the Gulf of Maine and Mount Desert Island to the west. Because Schoodic Point is fully exposed to the Gulf of Maine, its rocky shore gets pounded by powerful waves when storms kick up huge swells. On days with big waves, the surf can be spectacular. But be extremely careful: rouge waves have swept spectators off the rocks.

Schoodic Point

LITTLE MOOSE ISLAND

Continue east on Schoodic Loop Road and you'll soon see Little Moose Island on your right. This pretty little island is accessible by foot at low tide, but don't wander over without consulting a tide chart. It's easy to get stranded on the island during high tide.

BLUEBERRY HILL PARKING AREA

This tiny parking area, which offers nice views of Little Moose Island and Schoodic Island, is a great place to escape the crowds at Schoodic Point.

ANVIL TRAIL

This moderate hiking trail, which starts just north of the Blueberry Hill Parking Area, heads 1.1 miles to Schoodic Head. From Schoodic Head, loop back to the Blueberry Hill Parking Area via the Schoodic Head Trail (0.6 miles) and the Alder Trail (0.6 miles).

SCHOODIC HARBOR & WONSQUEAK HARBOR

Continuing along the eastern edge of Schoodic Peninsula, you'll pass Schoodic Harbor and tiny Wonsqueak Harbor before exiting the park. Continue on the two-way road until you reach Birch Harbor, which intersects with Route 186. If you're hungry or thirsty, swing by The Pickled Wrinkle, which serves beer, burgers and carnivorous sea snails (p.207).

Schoodic Mountain

Other Attractions

DONNEL POND PUBLIC RESERVED LAND

This 15,000-acre protected area is one of the region's best-kept secrets. In addition to pristine Donnel Pond, which is great for swimming, paddling and fishing, there are several miles of hiking trails. The most spectacular hike heads to the top of Schoodic Mountain, which rises 1,069 feet above sea level. From the peak you'll enjoy stunning panoramas of Downeast Maine, including dramatic views of Mount Desert Island. The 2.8-mile loop up Schoodic Mountain starts at the Schoodic Beach parking area. After hiking to the top, head down to Schoodic Beach for a refreshing swim, then walk a half-mile back to the parking area.

To get to Donnel Pond Public Reserve, follow Route 1 to the town of Sullivan, then turn northeast onto Route 183. Drive about 4.5 miles, then turn left at the dark Donnel Pond sign (which can be a bit hard to see). Follow Schoodic Beach Road about five minutes to the trailhead. Visit maine.gov for more info.

PETIT MANAN WILDLIFE REFUGE

Located in the town of Steuben, Petit Manan Wildlife Refuge is one of the top birding destinations in Maine. Over 300 bird species have been spotted in the refuge, which protects over 6,000 acres of habitat. There are several miles of hiking trails, including the Hollingsworth Trail (1.8 miles round-trip), which offers views of 123-foot tall Petit Manan Lighthouse (p.113) on clear days.

ISLE AU HAUT

LOCATED 15 MILES southwest of Mount Desert Island, Isle au Haut is Acadia's most far-flung parcel of property. While Mount Desert Island is defined by tourism, Isle au Haut is a genuine working Maine island where fishing has been the primary occupation for over 200 years. Today about 70 people live year-round on the six-mile long by two-mile wide island. Roughly half of Isle au Haut belongs to Acadia National Park—representing arguably the most pristine coastal landscape in Maine. If "rugged," "remote," and "rock-bound" are some of your favorite words, it's time to add "Isle au Haut" to your vocabulary.

Isle au Haut ("High Island") was named by the French explorer Samuel Champlain in 1604. Although Champlain traveled up and down the coast of Maine on his voyage of discovery, he named very few places along the way. But Isle au Haut, with its tallest mountain rising 543 feet above the water, was simply too obvious a landmark to remain anonymous. Not surprisingly, Isle au Haut great for hiking. Over 18 miles of rugged trails crisscross the park. But other than hiking, relaxing, and soaking in the scenery, there's not much else to do on Isle au Haut—which is exactly why some people love it.

Now the hard part: getting to Isle au Haut, which reaches farther into the Atlantic (15 miles) than any other large island in Maine. The first step is to drive to Deer Isle, an island six miles north of Isle au Haut that's connected to the mainland by a bridge. At the southern tip of Deer Isle is the town of Stonington (a two-hour drive from Bar Harbor) where you can catch the mailboat/passenger ferry to Isle au Haut. Schedules vary depending on the season, but from mid-June to early September (except Sundays) the ferry also stops at Duck Harbor, located near the southern tip of the island. Contact the Isle au Haut Boat Company for current schedules and fares (207-367-5193, isleauhaut.com). Another option is Old Quarry Adventures, which offers hiking, biking and kayaking day trips to Isle au Haut on the *Nigh Duck* (207-367-8977, oldquarry.com).

Day tripping to Isle au Haut (catching the morning and evening ferry) gives you about seven hours on the island. But it takes enough effort to get here that you might as well spend the night, giving you plenty of time to explore the island. There are two lodging options on Isle au Haut: cozy, expensive inns near the town landing, or rugged, inexpensive lean-to shelters at the park's Duck Harbor Campground. If you'd like to stay at an inn, visit jameskaiser.com for up-to-date hotel information. If you'd like to stay in a lean-to, follow the instructions on the following page.

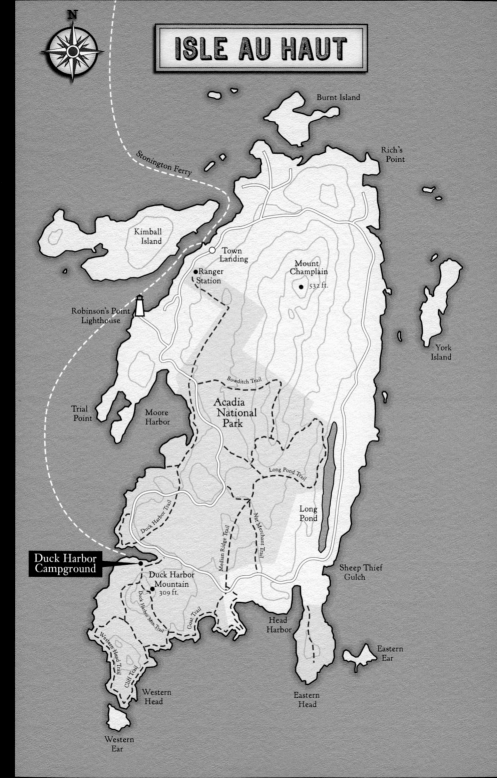

Before Isle au Haut was settled by whites, Wabanaki Indians paddled to the island to gather sweetgrass and hunt ducks by driving them into the island's narrow harbor (now named Duck Harbor). The first white settler arrived in 1772, and fifty years later there were roughly 200 people living on Isle au Haut, most of them fishermen who benefitted from the island's close proximity to offshore fishing grounds. In 1860 a lobster cannery opened on the island, and by the 1880s roughly 300 people lived here. But when gas-powered engines arrived in the early 1900s, fishermen could commute from the mainland and Isle au Haut's population fell dramatically. Electricity didn't arrive until 1970, and phone service came in 1988. Today there are roughly 65 year-round residents on Isle au Haut, including author Linda Greenlaw, the female swordfish captain chronicled in *The Perfect Storm*.

TOWN LANDING
Isle au Haut's small town landing is the social hub of the island and the best place to experience the slow pace of Maine island life. Just up the road is the Isle au Haut General Store (207-335-5211, theislandstore.net), which sells snacks and basic goods. Just down the road is Acadia's Isle au Haut ranger station (207-335-5551).

BLACK DINAH CHOCOLATIERS $ (Brk, Lnch)
Located about a half-mile west of Town Landing, this unique cafe offers breakfast and lunch paninis, plus the decadent chocolates for which they are famous. Sample flavors like blueberry-black pepper and strawberry-balsamic. (207-335-5010, blackdinahchocolatiers.com)

DUCK HARBOR CAMPGROUND
This small campground, operated by Acadia National Park, is home to five lean-to shelters that offer the only camping on Isle au Haut. Each 8-foot by 12-foot lean-to sleeps up to six people. Facilities include a fire ring, picnic table, and pit toilet. The campground is open from May 15 to October 15, and reservations are required prior to arrival. Contact the park for a reservation request form (207-288-3338) or go online at nps.gov/acad. One reservation covers camping for up to six people with a maximum stay of three to five nights. From Mon–Sat during peak season, the mailboat ferry stops at the landing in Duck Harbor, about a quarter mile from the campsite. Off season you'll have to hike five miles from the town landing to reach Duck Harbor Campground.

HIKING ON ISLE AU HAUT
Isle au Haut's best hiking trails are concentrated at the southern tip of the island, not far from Duck Harbor Campground. Among the most popular: Duck Harbor Mountain (Strenuous, 2.4 miles round-trip) which rises 300 feet above Duck Harbor. Another good option is connecting the Cliff Trail and Western Head Trail (Moderate, 2 miles one-way) which will take you in and out of dark spruce forests along Western Head. Note: The trails on Isle au Haut are often rugged and overgrown, so be sure to pay attention when you're hiking.

Isle au Haut & Kimball Island

NORTH ISLAND

FOR DECADES THE northern part of Mount Desert Island was a beautiful but unexciting place. Yes, there were some great oceanfront campgrounds, plenty of budget motels, and the wonderful Bar Harbor Oceanarium, but the real action was further south. These days, however, there are enough great attractions along Route 3 and Route 102 to warrant their own section. Because this area includes both western Bar Harbor and the village of Town Hill, I've decided to call it simply "North Island."

★ MOUNT DESERT OCEANARIUM
Located nine miles northwest of downtown Bar Harbor, this is the place to go if you're interested in the fascinating ecology of coastal Maine. The Oceanarium features a lobster museum and lobster hatchery, where thousands of baby lobsters are nurtured from birth to be released into Maine waters. There are also marine exhibits and an outdoor salt marsh walk. Open Mon–Sat, 9am–5pm, mid-May to late October. Admission: $12 adults, $7 children. (1351 Route 3, 207-288-5005, theoceanarium.com)

★ GREAT MAINE LUMBERJACK SHOW
This highly entertaining lumberjack show is actually located in Trenton (on the mainland), but it deserves to be somewhere in this guide, so I'm putting it here. The Great Maine Lumberjack Show brings Maine's rich logging history to life. It features modern-day lumberjacks sawing, chopping, tree climbing, ax throwing and log rolling. (127 Bar Harbor Road, 207-667-0067, mainelumberjack.com)

★ ATLANTIC BREWING COMPANY
If you're into craft beer, swing by the oldest and most famous brewery on Mount Desert Island. Tours are offered daily at 2pm, 3pm and 4pm. All of their many beers are sold in the brewery store, plus hats, T-shirts and other swag. (15 Knox Road, 207-288-2337, atlanticbrewing.com)

BAR HARBOR CELLARS
Run by the same folks behind Atlantic Brewing Company, Bar Harbor Cellars makes wine from grapes harvested in Italy and California. Their tasting room, located in a beautiful barn built in the 1850s, offers samples throughout the day. (Route 3, 207-288-3907, barharborcellars.com)

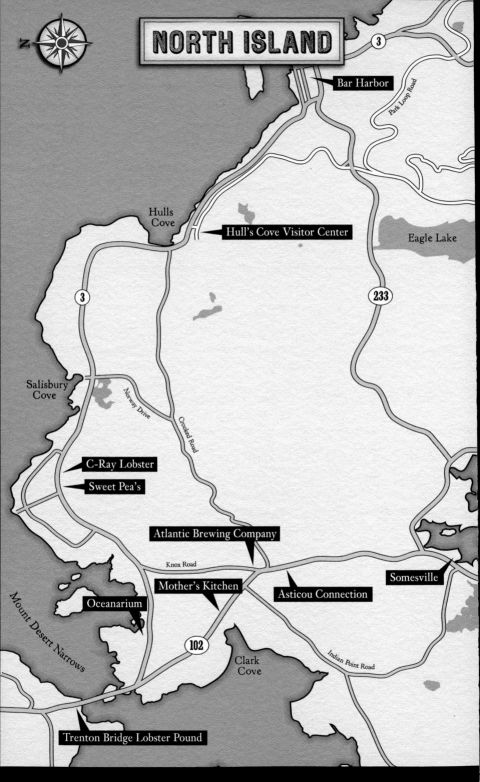

ASTICOU CONNECTION

This charming gallery showcases high-quality paintings, furniture and crafts from local artists, including Ken Savage's beautiful wood carvings. (1302 State Hwy 102, 207-288-2400, asticouconnection.com)

TRIPLE CHICK FARM

For farm-fresh free-range eggs and certified organic vegetables, swing by this quaint roadside stand. Open Weds–Sat, 10–4. Sat only off season. (Route 102, 207-288-2888, triplechickfarm.com)

RAT'S CLAMS

For some real local flavor, swing by Rat's house, where he and his wife sell fresh clams, mussels and lobsters out of their garage. Look for the rustic wooden sign just past Triple Chick Farm on the opposite side of the road.

Restaurants

★ TRENTON BRIDGE LOBSTER POUND $$ (Lnch, Din)

Perched next to the Trenton Bridge (yes, technically it's on the mainland) this legendary lobster shack—family owned and operated for three generations—is famous for fresh lobster, nice views and old-school devotion to wood-fired boilers. (1237 Bar Harbor Rd, 207-667-2977, trentonbridgelobster.com)

★ SWEET PEA'S CAFE $$ (Brk, Lnch, Din)

Sitting on Sweet Pea's back patio, looking out over the lovely farm, you'll feel a world away from the traffic on Route 3. Wood-fired pizzas, farm-fresh specials and wines from the adjacent Bar Harbor Cellars. (854 State Hwy 3, 207-801-9078)

★ MOTHER'S KITCHEN $ (Brk, Lnch)

It doesn't look like much from the outside, but this simple shack sells the best sandwiches on Mount Desert Island. Everything's delicious, including vegan-friendly tofu and tempeh. Carnivores love the meatloaf sandwich. Baked goods and ice cream also available. (Located next to Salisbury Hardware, 207-288-4403, motherskitchenfoods.com)

★ C-RAY LOBSTER $$ (Lnch, Din)

This unassuming restaurant, located behind a residential house, is a terrific place for fresh, reasonably-priced lobster and shellfish. Owner Joshua is one of three licenced clammers on the island, and his wife bakes tasty desserts. (882 State Highway 3, 207-288-4855, c-raylobster.com)

MAINELY MEAT BBQ $$ (Lnch, Din)

Ribs, pulled pork, chicken, sausage—it's all good washed down with fresh beer from the adjacent Atlantic Brewing Company. Veggie burgers and kids menu also available. (207-288-2337, 15 Knox Road)

BAR HARBOR

FILLED WITH MORE shops, restaurants and hotels than all other towns on the island combined, Bar Harbor is the unofficial capital of Mount Desert Island. Its narrow streets and ramshackle buildings, perched on a gentle hill overlooking the harbor, make it the quintessential Maine Coastal Town. Ice cream shops, trinket stores, and the smell of fresh seafood round out the effect. To some it's a tourist trap. To others it's a vibrant slice of Downeast Maine. No matter what your take, chances are you'll end up in Bar Harbor at some point on your trip.

The heart of Bar Harbor is the T-intersection of Main Street and Cottage Street, located just uphill from the town pier. Both streets are sardine-packed with shops and restaurants that offer a true study in contrasts: upscale galleries sell pricey artwork near novelty stores selling plastic lobsters; gourmet restaurants compete with greasy spoons; a Christmas store is located steps away from a biker shop selling bowie knives and ninja stars. It's hard to put your finger on the retail pulse of Bar Harbor, which means there's something for everyone here.

Equally incongruous is the social fabric of Bar Harbor. Fannypacked retirees, ragged hippies, Gore-tex clad outdoor buffs, casual fleece millionaires—all find fertile ground in Bar Harbor. There are also plenty of hard working locals, college party kids, and seasonal workers from foreign countries.

Although famous for its shops and restaurants, Bar Harbor is also the jumping off point for many of the island's most popular outdoor adventures—sea kayaking, whale watching, sailing cruises, etc. And if you want to explore Acadia's carriage roads, you can rent bikes in Bar Harbor and catch the free Island Explorer shuttle to Eagle Lake during peak season. The Bar Harbor Village Green, located in the center of town at the intersection of Main Street and Mount Desert Street, is the transportation hub for nearly all Island Explorer shuttles, which can take you just about anywhere on the island. And when rain puts the lid on outdoor fun, Bar Harbor's two movie theaters, multiple museums, and half dozen bars will keep you—and the rest of the island—entertained for hours.

During peak season in July and August, Bar Harbor is flooded with visitors—especially when cruise ships are in town. These days over 100 cruise ships call to port in Bar Harbor, up from 30 in 2000. Today Bar Harbor is the most popular port of call in Maine. On days when cruise ships disgorge hundreds of passengers onto the town's busy streets, long lines often form at popular shops and restaurants. If you happen to visit Bar Harbor when one (or two) enormous ships are in port, consider heading elsewhere and exploring Bar Harbor another day.

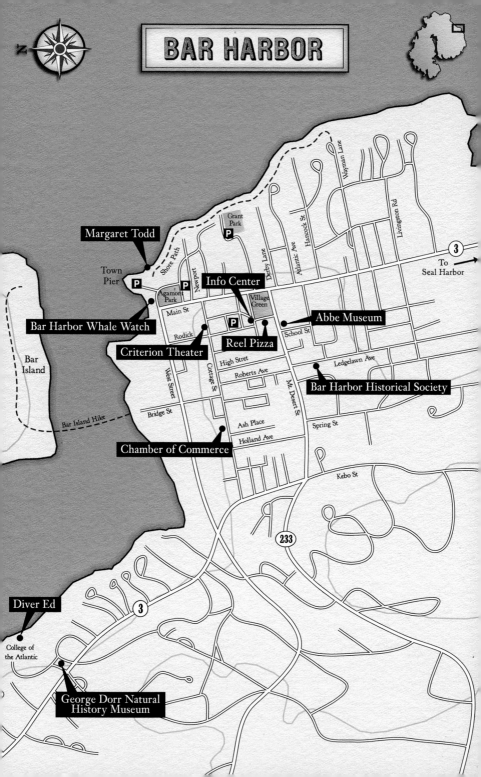

BAR HARBOR

N

To Seal Harbor

3

Margaret Todd

Grant Park

P

Town Pier

P

Shore Path

Agamont Park

Newport

Info Center

Village Green

Derby Lane

Atlantic Ave

Hancock St

Wayman Lane

Livingston Rd

Main St

P

Abbe Museum

Bar Harbor Whale Watch

Rodick

School St

Reel Pizza

Criterion Theater

High Stret

Roberts Ave

Ledgelawn Ave

Bar Island

West Street

Cottage St.

Mt. Desert St.

Bar Harbor Historical Society

Bar Island Hike

Bridge St.

Ash Place

Holland Ave

Spring St.

Chamber of Commerce

Kebo St

233

Diver Ed

3

College of the Atlantic

George Dorr Natural History Museum

Bar Harbor Sights

★ BAR HARBOR SHOREPATH

This easy, ¾-mile path wraps around the eastern tip of Bar Harbor, offering terrific views of Frenchman Bay and the Porcupine Islands. (Note that sections of the Shore Path pass over private property, so please be respectful.) Start your stroll at the Bar Harbor town pier, and follow the paved path towards the Bar Harbor Inn. To your right you'll see two cannons, which were once stationed on Egg Rock Island to guard Frenchman Bay. Past the cannons lies the Bar Harbor Inn, which started out as the Reading Room Clubhouse in 1887. At the time, the Reading Room was a private, all-male "literary club" where "most of the reading was done through the bottom of a cocktail glass." Continue down the Shorepath and you'll see Balance Rock, a large, precariously balanced boulder that was carried here by glaciers during the last Ice Age. When the glaciers melted, Balance Rock settled into its unlikely position. Grant Park, a bit farther down on the left, is a nice place for a picnic, and near the end of the Shore Path you'll see the Bar Harbor breakwater, a man-made stone wall that shelters Bar Harbor from large offshore waves. Local lore claims the breakwater was financed by J.P. Morgan so large waves wouldn't spill cocktails on his yacht. When you reach the end of the Shorepath, you can retrace your steps back to the Town Pier, or turn right and follow Wayman Lane up to Main Street, where lots of shops and restaurants await.

Bar Island

No visit to Bar Harbor is complete without a visit to the town's namesake island. Twice a day when the tide goes out, an underwater sandbar is exposed that temporarily connects Bar Harbor to Bar Island. The sandbar starts at the end of Bridge Street, about a half mile west of the Bar Harbor town pier. There's roughly a three-hour window (90 minutes before and after low tide) when you can walk across the sand bar and explore Bar Island. A 0.5-mile path on the island heads to an overlook 120-feet above sea level that offers terrific views of Bar Harbor. The path starts at the southern tip of Bar Island, continues past a large field, then bears left on the way towards the overlook. (Plan on a 15 to 20 minute walk from the Sand Bar to the overlook). Be sure to check local papers for tide schedules before walking across to Bar Island.

Bar Island Sand Bar

Agamont Park

AGAMONT PARK

This popular park, set on a gentle hill overlooking the shore, offers gorgeous views of Bar Harbor, the Porcupine Islands, and Frenchman Bay. The park's fountain was brought from Italy and dates to around 1600. If you're here on the Fourth of July, Agamont Park offers the best views in town of the fireworks.

VILLAGE GREEN

This large, central park hosts art and music festivals throughout the summer. On Mondays and Thursdays in July and August, the Bar Harbor Town Band offers free concerts at 8pm. The west side of the Village Green serves as the hub for the Island Explorer shuttle system (p.30).

WEST STREET

West Street is great for a short stroll if you'd like to see some of Bar Harbor's grand old mansions, many of which have been converted to inns. Follow West Street away from the Bar Harbor Pier and you'll pass the elegant Bar Harbor Club, which is over 100 years old and was fully restored in 2008 after falling into disrepair for several decades. Continue past Bridge Street—which leads down to Bar Island—and follow West Street to the Maine Sea Coast Mission. This Christian organization offers free social services to Mainers who live year-round on eight offshore islands. The elegant brick building that serves as their headquarters was previously owned by the heirs to the Campbell Soup fortune.

Visitor Information
ACADIA NATIONAL PARK INFORMATION CENTER
This small brick building next to the Village Green is staffed with experts ready to answer questions about Acadia National Park and the Island Explorer shuttle system. You can also purchase park passes and pick up free park publications.

Museums
★ABBE MUSEUM
This large, impressive museum is devoted to native cultures and traditions in Maine. The museum layout follows a reverse timeline, which starts in the present and goes backwards in time. Tools, crafts, and other cultural artifacts are displayed, as well as modern artwork by native artists. A small museum shop sells beautiful native baskets, traditional crafts, and a large selection of books. Educational programs, craft workshops, and archaeological field schools are also offered. Open daily, admission: $6 adults, $2 children. (26 Mount Desert Street, 207-288-3519, abbemuseum.org)

★ GEORGE B. DORR NATURAL HISTORY MUSEUM
Located on the campus of the College of the Atlantic (half a mile north of downtown Bar Harbor on Route 3), this small museum is devoted to the natural history of Mount Desert Island. The museum has exhibits on local animals and a touch tank filled with crabs, starfish, sea cucumbers, and other intertidal creatures. The museum is open Tues–Sat, 10am–5pm, mid-June to Labor Day. Admission: $3.50 adults, $1 children. (105 Eden Street, Route 3, 207-288-5395, coamuseum.org)

BAR HARBOR HISTORICAL SOCIETY
A great place to learn more about Bar Harbor's opulent Cottage Era. Historic photos are the real draw, but the museum also offers a wealth of information on Bar Harbor. Open mid-June to mid-October, Monday–Saturday, 1pm–4pm. Free admission. (33 Ledgelawn Ave., 207-288-0000, barharborhistorical.org)

What's That Sound?
Every day at noon and 9pm, a booming sound blasts through the streets of Bar Harbor, momentarily frightening and confusing anyone near the Village Green. The sound comes from a powerful air horn located on top of the Bar Harbor Fire Station, next to the Village Green. A century ago the noon blast allowed people to synchronize their clocks, and the 9 pm blast alerted minors of a citywide curfew. Today it's mostly a tradition, although the horn is still used to notify villagers of school closures in the winter due to snow.

Boat Tours

No visit to Mount Desert Island is complete without a boat tour, and some of the best tours depart from Bar Harbor.

★ STARFISH ENTERPRISE

Diver Ed's "Dive-In Theater" (p.26) is justifiably famous. After putting on a drysuit, Diver Ed jumps overboard with an HD video camera and sends a live feed of the seafloor back to a TV onboard. Ed then resurfaces with a bag full of sea creatures for a fascinating show-and-tell. Adults $40, seniors $35, kids $30. (207-288-3483, divered.com)

★ BAR HARBOR WHALE WATCH COMPANY

Bar Harbor Whale Watch offers several great trips. Their most popular is whale watching on the *Friendship V* (p.26). Other cruises include Nature and Sightseeing, Lobster Fishing and Seal Watching, and a Lighthouse Tour that visits five local lighthouses. Adults $60, kids $25. (207-288-2386, barharborwhales.com)

★ MARGARET TODD

This 151-foot schooner—the only four-masted schooner to work New England's waters in over 50 years—offers two-hour cruises around Frenchman Bay and the Porcupine Islands. The *Margaret Todd* (p.27) sails three times daily (10 am, 2 pm, sunset). All trips depart from the Bar Harbor Inn pier, where tickets are available. Adults $40, children $30. (207-288-4585 , downeastwindjammer.com)

★ LULU

Want to learn about lobstering? Climb aboard the 42-foot *Lulu*, where Captain John Nicolai hauls up lobster traps, pulls out live lobsters, and spouts off fascinating facts. The tour also includes seal watching at Egg Rock and plenty of local history. (207-963-2341, lululobsterboat.com)

MISS SAMANTHA

The 56-foot *Miss Samantha* offers naturalist-guided tours of Baker Island, the most remote of the Cranberry Isles (p.271). On the way to Baker Island you'll pass the spectacular eastern shore of Mount Desert Island, which boasts dramatic cliffs and beautiful mansions. (207-288-5374, barharborwhales.com)

ISLANDER

The 67-foot *Islander* offers four-hour fishing trips in Frenchman Bay. Cod, harbor pollock and mackerel are some of the species you might catch. The crew can help with every step of the process—setting the line, landing the fish, filleting the catch. Great for kids and beginners. 40 passengers max. Adults $46, kids $32. (207-801-2300, barharborboattours.com)

Bus Tours

OLI'S TROLLEY

Oli's offers four narrated trolly tours: Cadillac Mountain (1 hour), Acadia National Park (2.5 hours), Downtown Bar Harbor (30 mins), and Town of Mount Desert (2.5 hours). Adults $10–30, kids $7–16. Tickets available in the Oli's Trolley store at 1 West Street. (866-987-6553, acadiaislandtours.com)

ACADIA NATIONAL PARK TOURS

Acadia National Park Tours offers a 2.5-hour naturalist-narrated bus tour of Bar Harbor and Acadia National Park. Trips depart downtown Bar Harbor at 10am and 2pm, May–October. Adults $30, kids $18. Tickets available at Testa's Restaurant, 53 Main Street. (207-288-0300, acadiatours.com)

Bike Rentals

BAR HARBOR BICYCLE SHOP

Since 1977 the Bar Harbor Bicycle Shop has been catering to casual tourists and hardcore bike enthusiasts. Open from March through December. (141 Cottage Street, 207-288-3886, barharborbike.com)

ACADIA BIKE AND CANOE

In addition to renting bikes, Acadia Bike and Canoe offers organized biking trips on Mount Desert Island, Schoodic Peninsula, and Swan's Island. Multi-day bicycle tours are also available. (48 Cottage Street, 207-288-9605, acadiabike.com)

Sea Kayaking

Bar Harbor is the most popular departure point for sea kayaking trips (p.19). The following outfitters are all recommended.

AQUATERRA ADVENTURES

Launching directly from the Bar Harbor Pier, Aquaterra Adventures specializes in trips around the Porcupine Islands. Their Family Discovery Trip is great for young children. (1 West Street, 207-288-0007, aquaterra-adventures.com)

COASTAL KAYAKING TOURS

Coastal Kayaking offers half-day and full day tours, plus sunset paddles and multi-day camping trips. (48 Cottage Street, 207-288-9605, acadiafun.com)

NATIONAL PARK SEA KAYAK

This eco-oriented outfitter offers tours on the western side of Mount Desert Island, which is calmer than Frenchman Bay and has lots of terrific wildlife. (39 Cottage Street, 800-347-0940, acadiakayak.com)

Scenic Flights

Nothing puts Acadia's stunning, glacially-sculpted landscape in perspective like the view from the air. Two companies offer scenic flights departing from the Bar Harbor Airport (p.28).

SCENIC FLIGHTS OF ACADIA

These Cesna flights offer the best value. Their office is located in a small building next to the airport runway just south of the Trenton Market on Route 1A. (207-667-6527, scenicflightsofacadia.com)

ACADIA AIR TOURS

For a truly unique experience, fly around the island in a yellow Biplane (built in the late 1990s) or soar on an engine-less glider. Acadia Air Tours has two offices: one in Bar Harbor at 1 West Street, and one near the airport just north of the Trenton Market. (207-667-7627, acadiaairtours.com)

Notable Shops

SHERMAN'S BOOKSTORE

The best bookstore for miles, with a terrific selection of books on Acadia and Downeast Maine. (56 Main Street, 207-288-3161, shermans.com)

CADILLAC MOUNTAIN SPORTS

This local outfitter, founded in 1989, has the best selection of outdoor gear on Mount Desert Island. (26 Cottage Street, 207-288-4532, cadillacsports.com)

Entertainment

In addition to the attractions listed below, there are a number of seasonal events and festivals held throughout the summer and fall (p.40).

CRITERION THEATER

This historic art-deco theater, open since 1932, plays Hollywood movies and often features live shows. Operated as a non-profit, the theater was renovated in 2015. Local tip: the balcony seats upstairs are definitely worth the extra dollar. (35 Cottage Street, 207-288-3441, criteriontheater.org)

REEL PIZZA

This two-screen theater shows a mix of Hollywood hits and small independent and foreign films. There are couches and reclining chairs, and they sell fresh pizza and beer. (33 Kennebec Place, 207-288-3811, reelpizza.com)

IMPROVACADIA

This improv comedy troupe, founded by the former music director of Chicago's legendary Second City, performs nightly. It's improv, so performances vary, but every time I've gone it's been worth the price of admission. (15 Cottage Street, 2nd Floor, 207-288-2503, improvacadia.com)

Drinks & Nightlife

Bar Harbor has the liveliest nightlife on the island. The town is home to about half a dozen popular bars, all with a laid-back, casual vibe. The **Thirsty Whale** (40 Cottage St.) gets my vote for Bar Harbor's most classic watering hole, popular with locals and tourists alike. Around the corner, the **Lompoc Cafe** (36 Rodick St.) attracts a lively crowd of scruffy millennials. Further up the street you'll find the **Dog and Pony** (4 Rodick Place), famous for its open-air porch that draws thirsty crowds on hot summer nights. **Leary's Landing** (2 Mount Desert St.) is the town's best Irish Pub. Back on Cottage Street is the tiny but popular **Cottage Street Pub** (21 Cottage St.) and the charming **Finback Alehouse** (30 Cottage St). Craft beer lovers can head to **Blaze** (198 Main St), where over two dozen Maine microbrews are served on tap. Down by the waterfront, **Geddy's** (19 Main St.) has been serving adult beverages amid kitschy nautical decor since the 1970s. And if you're looking for a sports bar filled with plenty of big screen TVs, head to **Little Anthony's** (131 Cottage St).

Groceries

The largest grocery store in town is **Hannaford** (86 Cottage Street, 207-288-5680). There's also the natural food store **A&B Naturals** (101 Cottage Street, 207-288-8480) and you can buy farm-fresh food at the weekly **Bar Harbor Farmer's Market**, held every Sunday 10am–2pm in the YMCA parking lot (21 Park Street)

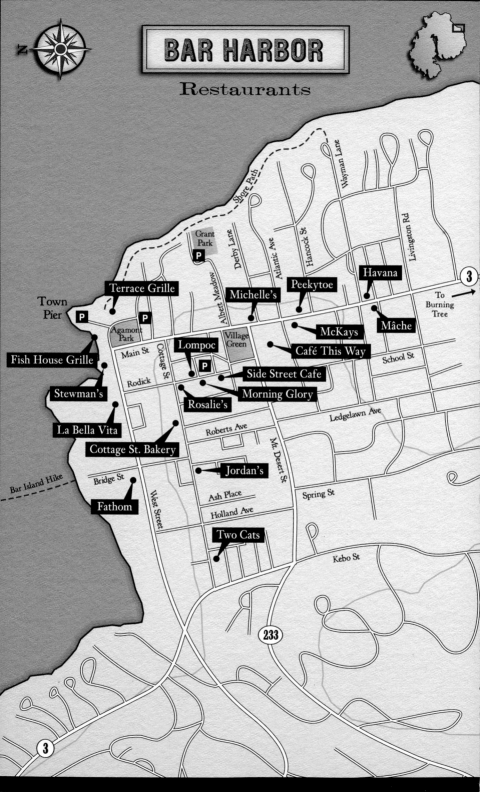

Bar Harbor Restaurants

★ THE BURNING TREE $$$ (Din)

Famous for exceptional seafood. The Burning Tree's creative menu combines flavors from around the world with plenty of local ingredients (many of the herbs and vegetables come from their own garden). The cozy, charming restaurant is located five miles south of Bar Harbor on Route 3. Closed Tuesdays. (69 Otter Creek Drive, 207-288-9331)

★ MÂCHE $$$ (Din)

This elegant French/Mediterranean bistro is one of the best restaurants in Bar Harbor. The menu changes frequently, but you can often expect lamb, quail, duck and a wide variety of local seafood prepared with the highest quality seasonal ingredients. The atmosphere is sophisticated, the wine list is superb, the desserts are decadent. Closed Sunday and Monday. (321 Main Street, 207-288-0447, machebistro.com)

★ FATHOM $$$ (Din)

Tucked away off Bridge Street, Fathom is easy to miss, but the menu is one of the best in Bar Harbor. Continental classics (Chateaubriand style filet, seared duck breast, halibut baked in parchment), some prepared with international flourishes (kimchi, chimichurri, coconut milk). The seafood shines, as do the wine and cocktails. (Bridge Street, 207-288-9664, fathombarharbor.com)

★ CAFE THIS WAY $/$$ (Brk, Din)

Creative, hip cuisine in a laid-back atmosphere. Hearty breakfasts offer all the classics, plus tasty benedicts and homemade corned beef hash. Dinners run the gamut from pecan crusted halibut to roasted duck breast to zucchini "noodles." Good wine list and creative cocktails. (14 1/2 Mount Desert Street, 207-288-4483, cafethisway.com)

SIDE STREET CAFE $$ (Lnch, Din)

This charming cafe is a local favorite for its combination of delicious, reasonably-priced food, upscale drinks and cozy ambiance. Sandwiches, wraps, salads, burgers, plus great lobster dishes, including one of the best lobster rolls on the island. Open year-round. (49 Rodick Street, 207-801-2591, sidestreetbarharbor.com)

LA BELLA VITA $$$ (Brk, Lnch, Din)

Located in the elegant Harborside Hotel, La Bella Vita offers delicious Italian food with nice waterfront views. Lunch and dinner feature Italian classics like veal scallopini and chicken piccata, plus pastas, wood-fired pizzas and paninis. Breakfast items are prepared with an Italian touch. (55 West Street, 207-288-5033, labellavitaristorante.com)

MICHELLE'S FINE DINING $$$ (Brk, Din)

Traditional French cuisine with New England flair. Located in the beautiful Ivy Manor Inn, Michelle's is formal and elegant. Old-school classics served with an expert touch. Perfect for a romantic meal or a special occasion. (194 Main Street, 207-288-2138, michellesfinedining.com)

PEEKYTOE PROVISIONS $$ (Lnch, Din)

Seafood lovers should head straight to this upscale market, where everything's fresh and local. Fish, lobster, oysters, chowder, seaweed salad, plus Maine-made specialty products. (244 Main Street, 207-801-9161, peekytoeprovisions.com)

HAVANA $$$ (Din)

Local food prepared with Latin flair: lobster moqueca, conchinita pibil, empanadas, paella. Good wine list, plus mojitos, caiparinas, pisco sours and other great Latin American cocktails. (318 Main Street, 207-288-2822, havanamaine.com)

TWO CATS $ (Brk)

One of the best breakfasts in town. Famous for their eggs Benedict, served on homemade biscuits. Located in a renovated home, the interior is bright and welcoming. There's almost always a wait, but reservations are accepted. Open until 1pm daily. (130 Cottage Street, 207-288-2808, 2catsbarharbor.com)

MCKAY'S PUBLIC HOUSE $$ (Din)

This upscale pub/bistro serves a range of hearty favorites, from steak and seafood to gourmet burgers. Quality food that won't break the bank. Great wine and beer selection. The open-air seating is delightful on a warm summer night. (231 Main Street, 207-288-2002, mckayspublichouse.com)

ROSALIE'S PIZZA $ (Din)

The best pizza on Mount Desert Island. In a town where it's easy to spend $100 on dinner for two, Rosalie's is a superb value, especially for families. Fresh ingredients and homemade dough make all the difference. They also offer subs, calzones, stuffed slices and salads. (46 Cottage Street, 207-288-5666, rosaliespizza.com)

Best of Bar Harbor

Best Breakfast: Cafe This Way, Two Cats
Best Dinner: Mâche, Burning Tree
Best Lobster Roll: Side Street Cafe
Best Seafood: Burning Tree, Peekytoe
Best Value: Jordan's, Rosalie's

LOMPOC CAFE $$ (Lnch, Din)

This casual bar/restaurant serves upscale comfort food with a great selection of local craft beers. Their outdoor patio and bocce court are always popular with the 20-something hipster crowd. (36 Rodick Street, 207-288-9392, lompoccafe.com)

JORDAN'S $ (Brk, Lnch)

Eating at this classic diner feels like stepping into a Norman Rockwell painting. It's where locals go to meet up with friends, catch up on gossip, and fill up on delicious blueberry pancakes. Open 5am–1pm, every day. (80 Cottage Street, 207-288-3586, jordanswildblueberry.com)

MORNING GLORY BAKERY $ (Brk, Lnch)

Hippies flock to this tasty bakery for breads, sandwiches, soups, baked goods and desserts. (39 Rodick Street, 207-288-3041, morningglorybakery.com)

COTTAGE STREET BAKERY $$ (Brk, Lnch, Din)

Terrific baked goods, plus sandwiches, burgers, seafood and steaks. Famous for their homemade blueberry pie. (59 Cottage Street, 207-288-3010)

MDI ICE CREAM $

Best ice cream in Bar Harbor. "Fearless Flavor" is their motto, and they mean it. Two locations: 7 Firefly Lane, 325 Main Street. (207-801-4007, mdiic.com)

Lobster In Bar Harbor

There are several classic lobster shacks on MDI (p.46), but none are located in Bar Harbor. Here are the town's best waterfront options.

STEWMAN'S LOBSTER POUND $$ (Lnch, Din)

The largest and most popular place for lobster in Bar Harbor. Terrific waterfront location. If the Walt Disney Co. wanted to design a Classic Maine Lobster Shack, it would look just like Stewman's. (207-288-9723)

THE FISH HOUSE GRILLE $$ (Lnch, Din)

This classic seafood joint, situated next to the Bar Harbor Pier, serves all the old-school classics—baked seafood, fried seafood, seafood rolls, homemade clam chowder—plus a raw bar. (1 West Street, 207-288-3070)

TERRACE GRILLE $$ (Lnch, Din)

Situated in front of the beautiful, historic Bar Harbor Inn, the open-air Terrace Grille combines upscale food with fabulous waterfront views. (7 Newport Drive, 207-288-3351)

SEAL HARBOR

SEAL HARBOR IS a tiny village with few tourist attractions—and its ultra-wealthy residents would like to keep it that way. Ox Hill, which rises above the eastern shore of Seal Harbor, is home to some of the most expensive homes in New England. But drive along its twisty roads and all you'll see are tiny wooden signs (painted in patented "Seal Harbor Green") proclaiming the oddly elegant names of the mansions lying at the ends of the long, long driveways. *Felsmere*, *Keewaydin*, *Glengariff*—when it comes to Seal Harbor mansion names, the more *Lord of the Rings* the better. Meanwhile, down on Main Street, high-priced shops and boutiques are conspicuously absent from a town that boasts a greater net worth than some developing countries. And such tourist-luring establishments are unlikely to arrive anytime soon.

Although Seal Harbor is one of the wealthiest summer colonies in America, it remains relatively unknown because its residents come here to *escape* the spotlight. Seal Harbor is about getting back to nature—albeit from the comfort of 30-room mansions and 60-foot yachts. And therein lies the old-school, Old Money ethos of the town. Despite the throngs of private servants, private garden-ers, and private assistants roaming Ox Hill in the summer, your average Seal Harbor millionaire is as apt to ramble on about native plants and migrating birds as hedge funds and currency swaps. This attitude is perhaps best embodied by the Rockefellers, who are actively involved with local charities and land conservation efforts.

But while Seal Harbor is known (or not known) for its stealth wealth, the town's otherwise low profile was thrust into the limelight with the arrival of Martha Stewart in 1997. After purchasing *Skylands*, a sprawling hilltop estate once owned by the Ford family, Martha dazzled her fans with glossy magazine spreads of her new summer hideaway. Suddenly, domestic divas everywhere knew that Seal Harbor was the *real* place to be in Maine. But despite the tem-porary commotion, the horsey-set residents simply hunkered down and let the commotion pass, and today the tiny village remains as charming and lackluster as ever.

In fact, Seal Harbor is probably the most under-appreciated town on the island. Most visitors simply drive by with little more than a passing glimpse of the picture-perfect harbor filled with expensive yachts. But Seal Harbor's tiny town green and jewel-like beach are great places to avoid the crowds and soak in the scenery. And Little Long Pond, just west of town, is a great place to stroll around and enjoy some dramatic mountain views.

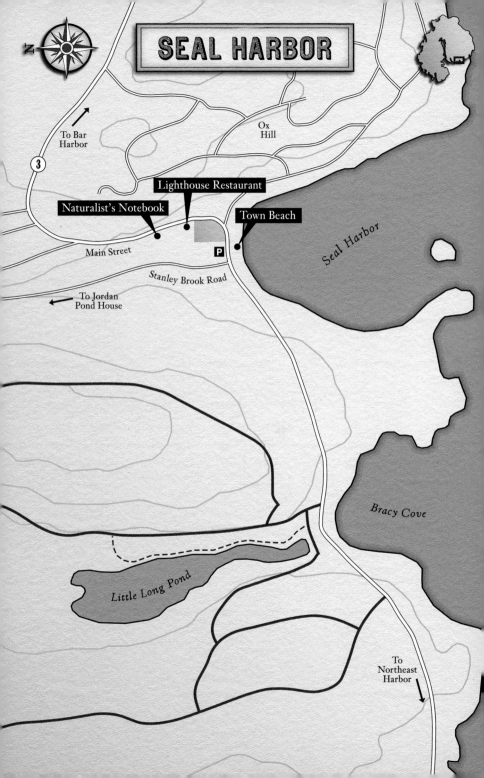

★ SEAL HARBOR TOWN BEACH

This small public beach is one of only two natural sand beaches on the island (the other is Sand Beach on the Park Loop Road). But while Sand Beach is often swarming with crowds on hot summer days, the Seal Harbor Town Beach is generally quiet and relaxed. Even better, the ocean water in this shallow harbor is slightly—*slightly*—warmer than the water at Sand Beach.

★ NATURALIST'S NOTEBOOK

This charming store/museum is a nature-lover's dream come true. Inside you'll find books, photos, specimens, art displays, and ecologically friendly products spread across three floors. Open 10–5 daily. Special events listed on their website. (16 Main Street, 207-801-2777, naturalistsnote.wordpress.com)

LIGHTHOUSE RESTAURANT $$ (Lnch, Din)

Seal Harbor's only restaurant boasts old-school nautical decor and a menu to match, with lots of seafood options. (12 Main Street, 207-276-3958)

THE COFFEE SHOP

This small cafe, located next to the Lighthouse Restaurant, sells coffee and espresso drinks, plus breakfast burritos and homemade pastries. Open 6am–4pm.

LITTLE LONG POND

This gorgeous pond lies just west of "downtown" along Route 3. The low-key setting is a great place to kick back, relax, and soak in the mountain views.

NORTHEAST HARBOR

IF SEAL HARBOR is a town of stealth wealth, Northeast Harbor is becoming a town of wealth on prominent display—to the consternation of the Old Money families that have summered here for generations. Once upon a time the Rockefellers, Astors and Fords drove around Northeast Harbor in beat-up automobiles, hobnobbed with locals, wore tattered clothes, and pretended that they were not, in fact, worth millions of dollars. But in the past few decades, New Money has slowly crept in, bringing bigger yachts, fancier cars, and other forms of conspicuous wealth to prove that they are, in fact, worth millions of dollars.

Some Northeast Harbor residents worry their Old Money hideaway is becoming "trendy." The thought of Mount Desert Island ever becoming the next Martha's Vineyard or, worse, *The Hamptons*, had many blue bloods coughing up cheap grilled cheese sandwiches at the ultra-exclusive Northeast Harbor Swim Club (where the food served is soooo not New Money). But to date, the Kardashians have yet to motor into the harbor with a phalanx of cameramen in tow. And despite the unsavory influx of a few billionaires who actually earned their money, Northeast Harbor appears to be hanging on to its relatively low-key profile just fine. Old Money types still spend their days thumbing through the prestigious "Redbook"—a tiny, secretive directory listing the winter and summer addresses of the Northeast Harbor/Seal Harbor elite—and private clubs still have decades-long "waiting lists" for new members wishing to apply.

But despite the private drives, private clubs, and other private enclaves, Northeast Harbor remains a fabulous place to visit. And some of its top attractions are—hold your breath—free! But don't leave your credit card at home. Main Street is filled with pricey art galleries and other high-end shops catering to gourmet tastes, so plan accordingly.

Ironically, Northeast Harbor was born of rather humble circumstances. In the early 1800s it was home to farmers and fishermen. The first summer visitors consisted of artists, clergymen, and intellectuals. When a wealthy New York banker offered to buy a Northeast Harbor farmer's property in the late 1800s, the farmer responded, "We have some very fine people in Northeast Harbor, including a Bishop and three college Presidents. We don't want any Wall Street riffraff!

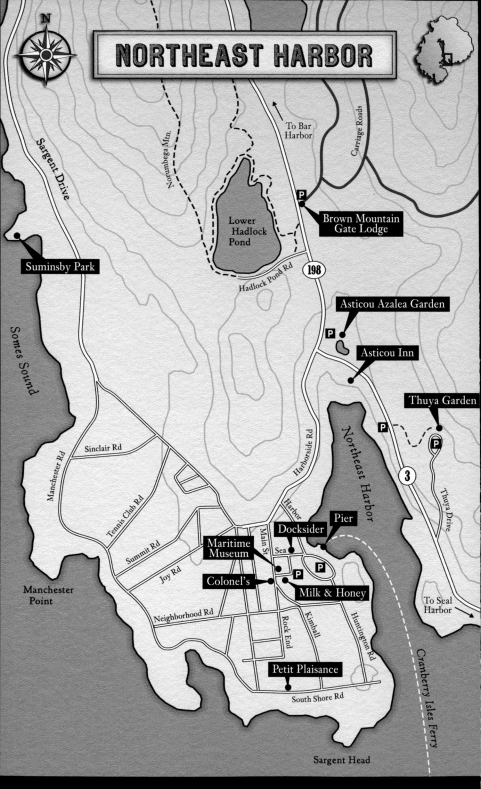

Northeast Harbor Sights

★ THUYA GARDEN & LODGE

Perched on a hill above Northeast Harbor, Thuya Garden is one of the most beautiful gardens on Mount Desert Island. You can drive to the garden via Thuya Drive, but I prefer hiking the moderate, ¼-mile trail that starts by the parking area just south of the Asticou Inn. The trail rises through a shady, pine-scented forest with views of the boat-filled harbor below. Thuya Garden is a late summer garden that features spectacular blooms in August. Adjacent to the garden is Thuya Lodge, the former summer home of Joseph Curtis. The lodge has been kept exactly as Curtis left it, offering a rare glimpse into the lifestyles of early summer residents who, though wealthy, preferred the rustic life, thus earning them the name "Rusticators." (207-276-3727, gardenpreserve.org)

★ SARGENT DRIVE

Twisting along the eastern edge of Somes Sound, Sargent Drive is one of the most beautiful drives on the island. Stretches are comparable to the Park Loop Road. If you're heading to/from Bar Harbor or western MDI, take beautiful Sargent Drive instead of boring Route 198. From downtown Northeast Harbor, drive to South Shore Road, cut across to Sargent Drive and drive north past the grand mansions. About two miles north of the golf club (one mile south of Route 198), turn onto Suminsby Road, bear right and drive down the hill to Suminsby Park. This beautiful public park has picnic tables, grills and fire pits. Try to grab the picnic table at the water's edge, which offers panoramic views of Somes Sound.

ASTICOU AZALEA GARDEN

This small, impeccably maintained garden features over 70 varieties of azaleas, laurels, and rhododendrons. Different flowers bloom between late May and July, but the most impressive blooms generally happen in the first two weeks of June. The garden, designed by Northeast Harbor resident Charles K. Savage in 1956 and funded by John D. Rockefeller, Jr., is styled after a Japanese stroll garden. It even has a rock garden complete with raked sand. Open from May to November, sunrise to sunset. A small parking area is located off Route 198, just north of the intersection with Route 3.

BOAT TOURS

A small booth next to the harbormaster's office sells tickets and provides info for boat tours departing from Northeast Harbor, including ferry service to the Cranberry Isles. The *Sea Princess* offers nature cruises, historic cruises, and evening trips to the Islesford Dock Restaurant (207-276-5352, barharborcruises.com). Downeast Friendship Sloop (sailacadia.com) offers sailboat trips for up to six people on the elegant Friendship Sloop *Helen Brooks*.

NOTABLE SHOPS

Northeast Harbor is home to some of the best art galleries on the island, plus a handful of great bookstores. Start at one end of Main Street and pop in wherever strikes your fancy. Among the highlights: Shaw Contemporary Jewelry, Artemis Gallery, Island Artisans, Redfield Artisans, The Naturalist's Notebook, Wilkhegan Old Books, and McGrath's.

NORTHEAST HARBOR TOWN DOCK

If you like sailboats and yachts, a stroll past the town dock is a must. This is one of the best places in the world to see a Hinckley (p.261) in its native habitat. The collection of yachts in the harbor is most impressive in July and August, before most have been put in storage or shipped down to Florida.

GREAT HARBOR MARITIME MUSEUM

With so many boat buffs in Northeast Harbor, it's no surprise that the town has the island's best maritime museum. Although the space is small, the changing exhibits are always interesting. Open Tues–Sat, 10–5, late June to mid-September. (125 Main Street, 207-276-5262)

THE OLD SCHOOL HOUSE & MUSEUM

This small museum, located a short drive from Northeast Harbor on Route 198, is run by the Mount Desert Island Historical Society. Exhibits change, but they always focus on interesting aspects of Mount Desert Island's history. The yellow building, originally built as a schoolhouse in 1892, was restored by the Historical Society in 1999. (373 Sound Drive, 207-276-9323)

PETITE PLAISANCE

Petit Plaisance is the former home of French novelist Marguerite Yourcenar, the first woman inducted as an "immortal" into the Academie Francaise (the highest honor a writer can receive in France). When World War II broke out, Yourcenar fled to Northeast Harbor, and once here she decided she could never live anywhere else. Free tours in English or French are given by appointment between June 15–August 31. (South Shore Road, 207-276-3940)

NORTHEAST HARBOR GOLF CLUB

This 18-hole golf course, located just north of town, is open to visitors. Some of the holes have views of Somes Sound. Ask about the time Bob Flynn got a hole-in-one. (15 Golf Club Road, 207-276-5335, nehgc.com)

Northeast Harbor Restaurants

★PEABODY'S AT THE ASTICOU $$ (Brk, Lnch, Din)

Located in the historic Asticou Inn—the oldest hotel on the island (1883)—Peabody's offers the most upscale dining experience in Northeast Harbor. If you're looking to soak in a bit of Yankee elegance, there's no better place. Try the popovers. (15 Peabody Drive, 207-276-3344, asticou.com)

★MILK & HONEY $$ (Brk, Lnch)

Tucked away behind the Great Harbor Museum, this charming cafe is the best deal in Northeast Harbor. Milk & Honey serves delicious baked goods, sandwiches, salads and sides. Lots of local ingredients. Great for take-out. (3 Old Firehouse Lane, 207-276-4003, milkandhoneykitchen.com)

★ABEL'S LOBSTER POUND $$$ (Lnch, Din)

This waterfront restaurant, perched just above Somes Sound, is the most upscale of all the island's authentic lobster restaurants. Since 1939 Abel's has been serving fresh lobster cooked in traditional wood-fired boilers. There are plenty of indoor tables with great views, but if it's nice you should try to sit outside. Dinner reservations required. (207-276-5827, abelslobsterpound.com)

COLONEL'S RESTAURANT $$ (Brk, Lnch, Din)

This casual restaurant serves seafood entrees, burgers, sandwiches, soups and salads. A full bar offers several beers on tap, and the attached bakery sells breads and pastries. (143 Main Street, 207-276-5147, colonelsrestaurant.com)

THE DOCKSIDER $$ (Lnch, Din)

For over 30 years, the ramshackle Docksider has been serving lobster rolls overflowing with meat, plus burgers, sandwiches, seafood dinners and ice cream. (14 Sea Street, 207-276-3965)

Bear Island Lighthouse

This picturesque lighthouse, located on tiny Bear Island just off Northeast Harbor, first went into operation in 1839. The 31-foot tall brick tower is situated on the island's highest point and the beacon can be seen up to 10 miles away. Sadly, in the early 1980s the lighthouse was decommissioned and fell into disrepair. In 1987 Acadia National Park acquired the island, and in 1989 Friends of Acadia refurbished the lighthouse and the beacon was relit. To help pay for the upkeep of the lighthouse, the park service leases the island to a private individual who has a house on the far side of the island.

SOMESVILLE

SOMESVILLE IS SO quaint it hurts. The white clapboard houses, leafy sidewalks, consistently friendly citizens, and impeccably well-tended flower beds seem to have sprung forth from a Norman Rockwell painting. But this is the real deal, complete with a Strawberry Festival in July, a Blueberry Festival in August, and Wednesday morning pie sales at the Somesville Union Meeting House. Simply put, Somesville is the kind of town where even thinking about swearing as you walk down the street makes you feel guilty.

Driving down Route 102, traveling at the posted speed limit of 35 mph, you can pass through Somesville in a little under a minute. Blink and you might miss it. But you'll know you're here when you see a gorgeous arched footbridge on the right side of the road—one of the most famous landmarks on the island. Almost all of the town's attractions are located within walking distance of the footbridge, so look for parking as soon as you see it (or use the Island Explorer shuttle, which will stop in Somesville on its way to Southwest Harbor if you ask).

Somesville was the first permanent town on Mount Desert Island. In 1761, 22-year-old Abraham Somes sailed north from Gloucester, Massachusetts, and built a log cabin on the shore of this well-protected harbor. The location offered plenty of oak trees (perfect for lumber), several nearby streams (perfect for hydropower), and a saltwater marsh (perfect for hay). The following year Somes returned with his wife and three daughters and named the town "Betwixt the Hills." Before long, several other families had joined them. By the 1830s Somesville had grown by leaps and bounds. According to one early report, it had "one small store, one blacksmith shop, one shoemaker's shop, one tan-yard, two shipyards, one bark mill, one saw mill, one lath mill, one shingle mill, one grist mill, and one schoolhouse."

Two decades later, the town played a critical role in establishing Mount Desert Island as a major tourist destination. In the summer of 1855, Somesville hosted a large group of early tourists who spent a month at a local tavern. One of the tourists was Frederic Church, a famous artist whose paintings of Mount Desert Island catapulted the island to national fame. But within a few decades, Somesville was no longer the most important town on Mount Desert Island. Bar Harbor and Southwest Harbor, which lay closer to coastal shipping routes, had become the island's new power centers, leaving Somesville high and dry. Development in Somesville ground to a halt, pickling the town in a colonial time warp that's perfect for modern-day sightseers.

(Note: This section also includes information on the nearby towns of Town Hill, Pretty Marsh, and Seal Cove.)

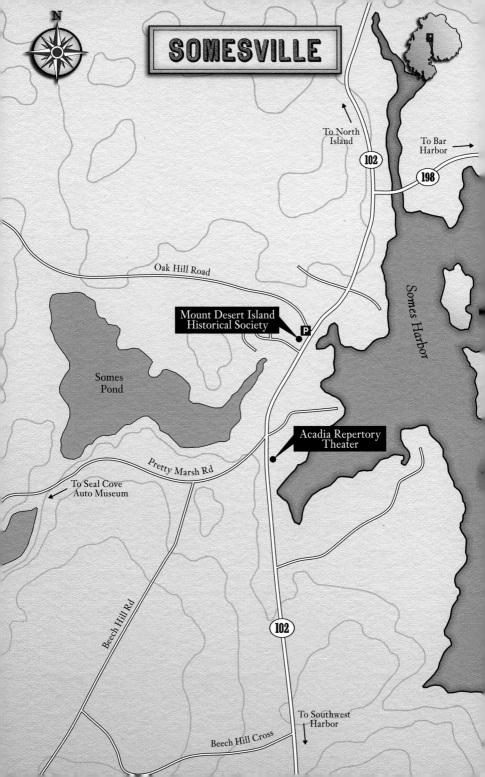

★SEAL COVE AUTO MUSEUM

This out-of-the-way museum shows of the stunning antique car collection of summer resident Richard Paine, who inherited a fortune and spent much of it on cars. There are five Model Ts, as well as Cadillacs, Buicks, and Benzes over 100 years old. (1414 Tremont Road, 207-244-9242, sealcoveautomuseum.org)

FOOTBRIDGE AND MDI HISTORICAL SOCIETY

Somesville's footbridge is one of the most famous sights on the island, and the adjacent museum features changing exhibits on local history. There's also an heirloom garden that blooms late May to October. (207-276-9323, mdihistory.org)

LONG POND

The largest lake on Mount Desert Island. Can swim at the beach near the northern tip.

ACADIA REPERTORY THEATER

Between July and September this local theater company performs a mix of comedies, dramas, children's plays and Agatha Christie murder mysteries in Somesville's Masonic Hall. (207-244-7260, acadiarep.com)

BEECH HILL FARM STAND

This organic farm offers produce and locally-produced goods such as honey, preserves, meat, eggs, dairy products, baked goods, berries, juice and specialty foods. Open 9am–4pm, Tues–Sat, June –October. (207-244-5204, 171 Beech Hill Road)

SOUTHWEST HARBOR

SOUTHWEST HARBOR IS the largest town on the western "quiet" side of Mount Desert Island. Centered around a beautiful working harbor, it's a delightful mix of the island's three common human species: modest fishermen (mostly found in Bass Harbor), rich summer folk (mostly huddled together in Northeast and Seal Harbor), and vacationing tourists (drawn to Bar Harbor like moths to a flame). As such, you won't be hit over the head with an abundance of tourist options in Southwest Harbor, but that's exactly why people like it.

That said, there's still plenty here to keep a tourist occupied. Several boat tours depart from the harbor, and some of the island's best hikes are just a short drive away. Southwest Harbor is also home to some great B&Bs and some truly terrific restaurants. If you don't mind being a 30-minute drive away from the famous eastern side of the island—or you aren't thrilled about the crowds you'll encounter there in July and August—this is the place for you.

Due to its physical separation from the rest of the island, Southwest Harbor has always had a different vibe. It was the first town on the island to lift the famous automobile ban imposed by summer residents in the early 1900s, and today it revels in being more laid back than its exclusive neighbors across Somes Sound. The island's boozy Oktoberfest, which features over 20 Maine microbreweries, is held here each year, and the town's annual Flamingo Parade revels in lowbrow absurdity. The pink plastic flamingo-themed parade is presided over by Don Featherstone, the real-life inventor of the pink plastic flamingo, who makes the pilgrimage north from Massachusetts every year. Following the parade is a cocktail party sponsored by the town's fictional "Yacht and Polo Club."

Despite its occasional antics, Southwest Harbor remains a genuine working harbor filled with lobster boats and surrounded by boatyards. But upward pressure on real estate prices has caused some changes in recent years. As more and more "summer folks" buy homes on this side of the island, property taxes have spiraled upward, putting pressure on locals and local businesses. Hinckley Yacht Company moved its boatbuilding operations to the mainland years ago, and Ralph Stanley Boatbuilders was forced to abandon its waterfront facility in 2009. Whether or not Southwest Harbor will become completely gentrified remains to be seen, but for now it remains one of the most diverse towns on the island.

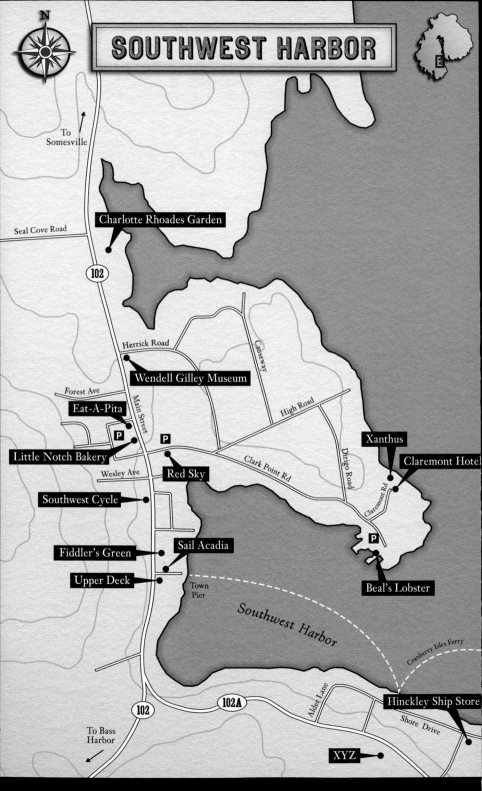

★ CLAREMONT HOTEL

Perched on a hill overlooking Somes Sound, this is one of the most historic hotels on the island. The prices are steep, but you don't have to be a guest to enjoy it. In July and August their waterfront boathouse is the best place in town for a cocktail between 5pm and 9pm, and the hotel offers a free lecture series on Thursday evenings (check the local paper for details). The hotel also features three exquisitely manicured croquet courts, and the Claremont hosts a Croquet Classic each year in early August. (22 Claremont Road, 800-244-5036, theclaremonthotel.com)

★ ECHO LAKE

Three miles north of town is Echo Lake, the island's most popular swimming hole. At the southern end of the lake is a popular man-made beach that has changing rooms and water fountains. To get to the beach, look for the "Acadia National Park, Echo Lake Entrance" sign south of Echo Lake on Route 102. Farther north along Route 102 are Echo Lake Ledges, reached via a short, wooded path from the Acadia Mountain parking area. These small, rocky ledges are a local favorite because they're almost always less crowded than the beach.

WENDELL GILLEY MUSEUM

Birders love this small museum, which displays the fabulous wooden bird carvings of local legend Wendell Gilley. In addition to the permanent collection, the museum features special exhibits, bird carving demonstrations, and bird carving workshops. (4 Herrick Road, 207-244-7555, wendellgilleymuseum.org)

CHARLOTTE RHOADES PARK BUTTERFLY GARDEN
This public flower garden is a great place to escape the crowds and enjoy the ocean views. There are several shaded picnic tables overlooking Norwood Cove.

CARROLL HOMESTEAD
This small house, built in 1825, offers a glimpse into the hardscrabble lives of early island settlers. On Tuesdays in July and August the park service opens the house to the public. Located off Route 102 south of Echo Lake.

MAINE GRANITE INDUSTRY HISTORICAL SOCIETY
Located in a lawn mower shop, this tiny museum has old photos and historic info. (62 Beech Hill Crossroad, 207-244-0175)

SOUTHWEST CYCLE
The only bike rental shop on the western side of the island, perfect if you're heading to the Cranberry Isles or Swan's Island (p.279). (370 Main Street, 207-244-5856, southwestcycle.com)

Boats, Boating & Sea Kayaking

★ SAIL ACADIA
Terrific sailing trips on the beautiful *Alice E.* (p.27), plus a lobster tour that includes hauling up traps. (11 Apple Lane, 207-266-5210, sailacadia.com)

DOWNEAST SAILING ADVENTURES
Offers tours on the 33-foot Friendship Sloop *Surprise* and lobster fishing tours on the 47-foot wooden boat *Hurricane*. (207-288-2216, downeastsail.com)

ACADIA DEEP SEA FISHING
The 43-foot *Vagabond* offers half-day and full-day fishing trips in search of cod, mackerel, bluefish and more. Lobster traps are hauled for each passenger, and any legal sized lobsters are yours to keep. (207-244-5385, acadiafishingtours.com)

MAINE STATE SEA KAYAKING
The Quiet Side's only sea kayak outfitter offers tours of Blue Hill Bay, Western Bay, and Somes Sound. The four-hour trips are limited to 12 people maximum. (254 Main Street, 207-244-9500, mainestateseakayak.com)

HINCKLEY SHIP STORE
Even if you can't afford a Hinckley (p.261), you can load up on shirts, hats and other Hinckley-branded gear at the official store. (130 Shore Road, 207-244-7100)

MANSELL BOAT RENTAL
Sailboat and motorboat rentals. Daily and weekly rates are available on boats from 14 to 31 feet. (207-244-5625, mansellboatrentals.com)

Restaurants

★ RED SKY $$$ (Din)

The best restaurant in town, offering exquisite meals in an atmosphere the owner describes as "unstuffy elegance." Everything from the homemade pasta to the hand-cut meats is delicious, but the seafood really shines. Terrific wine list, decadent desserts. (14 Clark Point Road, 207-244-0476, redskyrestaurant.com)

★ FIDDLERS' GREEN $$ (Din)

This casually refined restaurant has an eclectic menu that ranges from great steaks to inspired seafood dishes. Large beer and wine list, plus great cocktails. Closed Monday. (411 Main Street, 207-244-9416, fiddlersgreenrestaurant.com)

★ XANTHUS $$$ (Din)

Located in the Claremont Hotel, this is the most formal restaurant in Southwest Harbor. (For over a century they required jackets and ties; now it's no T-shirts or shorts.) The setting is classy and elegant, the food is excellent. (22 Claremont Road, 207-244-5036, theclaremonthotel.com)

★ XYZ $$$ (Din)

This upscale Mexican restaurant features authentic flavors from Xalapa, Yucatán, and Zacatecas. Despite the out-of-the-way location, it's always packed. The food is tasty, the homemade margaritas are great, and the XYZ pie is legendary. Closed Sundays. (80 Seawall Road, 207-244-5221, xyzmaine.com)

★ CAPTAIN'S GALLEY AT BEAL'S $$ (Lnch, Din)

This classic lobster shack at Beal's Lobster Pier has a rough-around-the-edges charm—picnic tables, paper plates, and salt water tanks where you can pick your lobster. (182 Clark Point Road, 207-244-3202, bealslobster.com)

EAT-A-PITA/CAFE 2 $/$$ (Brk, Lnch, Din)

Healthy Eat-A-Pita offers pitas stuffed so full of veggies they come with a fork. At night Eat-A-Pita becomes Cafe 2, which offers quality food in a laid-back atmosphere. Perfect if you've got kids in tow. (326 Main Street, 207-244-4344, eatapitasouthwestharbor.com)

LITTLE NOTCH BAKERY $ (Lnch, Din)

This delightful bakery/sandwich shop also offers soups, salads, pizzas, pastries and paninis. (340 Main Street, 207-244-4043)

UPPER DECK $$ (Lnch, Din)

Perched high above the marina with great views of the harbor, this is the place to be if you love looking at a boat-filled harbor. Seafood, burgers, sandwiches, salads. (433 Main Street, 207-244-8113, upperdeckdining.com)

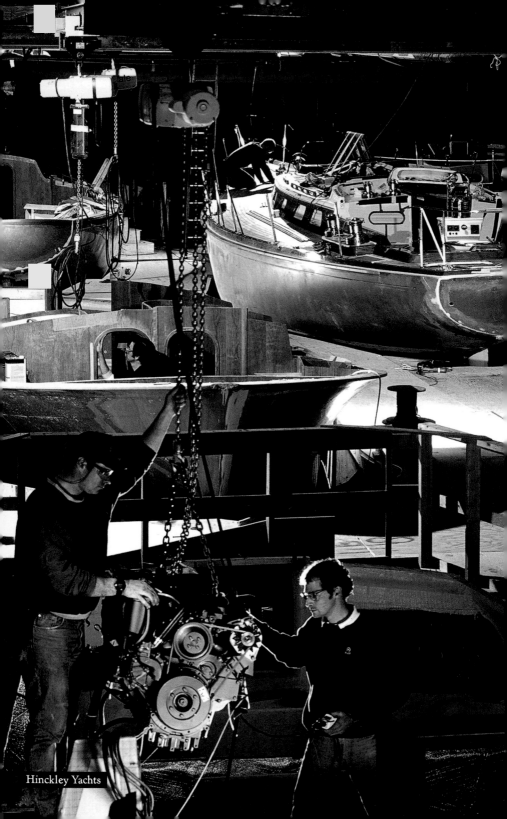

Hinckley Yachts

Boat Building on Mount Desert Island

BOATS AND BOAT BUILDING have played a vital role on Mount Desert Island for centuries. From the Wabanaki, who plied the waters in birchbark canoes, to the first settlers, who came in search of raw sailboat materials, islanders have always depended on the sea. Not surprisingly, local boat building knowledge is second to none.

The most renowned MDI boat builder is Hinckley (hinckleyyachts.com), which is famous for its high-tech luxury yachts. Want advanced soundproofing materials built into the Kevlar/carbon hull? Comes standard. Need a wine rack for slightly wider bottles from Burgundy? They do that. What started in 1928 as a boatyard for local fishermen morphed into a sailboat company devoted to pleasure craft. In the 1950s Hinckley was an early adopter of fiberglass, thrusting them to the forefront of the high-tech, luxury sailing world. In 1994, the company introduced the elegant, jet-propelled "picnic" boat, which reimagined classic Maine lobsterboats as stylish, luxury cruisers. Picnic boats, which start around $400,000 and head well into the millions, now make up the majority of their sales.

Morris Yachts (morrisyachts.com) started making high-end sailboats in 1972, and sailing remains their primary focus. Their boats are the first choice of many sailors. What's the difference between a Hinckley and a Morris? Martha Stewart owns a Hinckley, Jimmy Buffett owns a Morris.

Want a smaller sailboat? The Classic Boat Shop (classicboatshop.com) custom builds elegant, 21-foot daysailers. Still can't find the Mount Desert Island boat of your dreams? Ellis Boat Company (ellisboat.com) and John Williams (jwboatco.com) offer customized boats based on traditional Downeast designs. Wilbur Yachts (wilburyachts.com) specializes in highly customized designs. Want a jacuzzi or a baby grand piano on board? Wilbur Yachts does that.

Starting in the 1950s, most boat builders switched from wood to fiberglass, but one Southwest Harbor resident proudly bucked the trend. Born in 1929, Ralph Stanley learned the boat building craft at a time when all boats were made of wood. Despite the time and money savings fiberglass offered, Stanley never abandoned wood. As he once told a group of local schoolchildren, "If God wanted fiberglass boats, he'd have made fiberglass trees." In 1999 Stanley was chosen as one of 12 National Heritage Fellows, and he has been named "Boat builder Laureate of the Maine Coast."

BASS HARBOR

PERHAPS THE BEST way to describe Bass Harbor is to describe what it's not. Located near the southwestern tip of Mount Desert Island, Bass Harbor is about as far away from Bar Harbor—both physically and metaphorically—as possible. There are no cruise ships, T-shirt shops, or tourist swarms here. Instead, Bass Harbor remains a traditional Downeast fishing village with a lobster boat-filled harbor surrounded by old wooden piers. Pickup trucks vastly outnumber SUVs, and local lawns are piled high with lobster traps and colorful buoys. On an inherently touristy island, Bass Harbor can be a breath of fresh air.

Bass Harbor is one of my favorite places on Mount Desert Island—a relaxing mix of unpretentious summer folk and hard-working locals happily removed from the crowds. And yet there's just enough to do here so you won't get bored. The area around Bass Harbor is home to Mount Desert Island's only lighthouse, two easy hiking trails, a terrific boat tour, and the island's best lobster shack. And if Bass Harbor still isn't remote enough for your taste, you can catch a ferry to Swan's Island (p.279) or Frenchboro (p.277), two small offshore islands home to traditional fishing villages.

Today Bass Harbor is home to roughly 80 lobsterboats, one of the largest fleets in Maine. But not that long ago, sardines were king. Underwood Wharf, the large brick building on the eastern side of the harbor, was once the largest sardine cannery in the state. In the 1950s there were roughly 50 sardine canneries in Maine, and they employed more people than any other industry. Back then spotter planes would find schools of herring (sardines) offshore and alert local fishermen. When herring populations dwindled in the 1960s, Underwood Wharf switched to canning blueberries, and in 1977 the cannery closed for good. Today the historic brick building has been converted into luxury condos.

Mindful that important local industries can be lost, the town has taken steps to preserve the lobster industry that still thrives here. In 2009 the family-owned Davis Wharf in Goose Cove became permanently protected for commercial fishing purposes. Today less than 20 miles of Maine's 3,000 mile coast is classified as "working waterfront" where fishermen can unload their catch. Hopefully, with proper planning, Bass Harbor can retain its traditional character for years to come.

Note: Technically, the village of Bass Harbor lies on the eastern side of Bass Harbor, the village of Bernard lies on the western side of Bass Harbor, and both are part of the town of Tremont. If you continue north on Route 102, you'll pass the tiny communities of Goose Cove and Seal Cove before reaching Pretty Marsh.

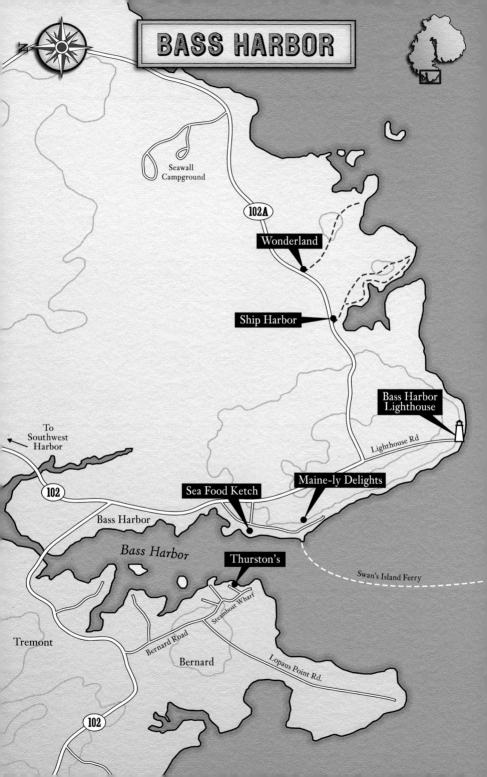

★ BASS HARBOR LIGHTHOUSE

The Bass Harbor Light (p.266), the only lighthouse on Mount Desert Island, is Bass Harbor's must-see destination. Wooden steps lead from the parking area to the rocky shore below. Open from sunrise to sunset.

★ ISLAND CRUISES

The fascinating cruises aboard the R.L. Gott (p.27) explore the islands south of Bass Harbor, which are filled with amazing wildlife and history. (207-244-5785, bassharborcruises.com)

SHIP HARBOR NATURE TRAIL

This 1.3-mile round-trip trail is my favorite hike near Bass Harbor. The trail wanders through the woods and along the peaceful shores of Ship Harbor. Try to arrive during low tide, when you can check out some fantastic tide pools.

WONDERLAND

This easy 1.4-mile trail heads through the woods to a nice cobblestone beach, then loops around the tip of a small, rocky peninsula. Try to visit at low tide, when several large tide pools are exposed at the edge of the peninsula.

BERNARD ROAD

This small, quiet road is home to a handful of eclectic antique shops and art galleries. Just head down the road, keep your eyes open for signs, and stop wherever strikes your fancy.

Restaurants

★ THURSTON'S $$ (Lnch, Din)

In my opinion, Thurston's is the best place for lobster on the island. The screened-in porch offers stunning views of the harbor and the adjacent pier, where lobsterboats unload fresh lobster throughout the day. The recently-added bar is gorgeous. Burgers, sandwiches and tasty chowders are also available. (Steamboat Wharf Road, 207-244-7600, thurstonslobster.com)

SEA FOOD KETCH $$ (Lnch, Din)

This waterfront restaurant combines spectacular harbor and mountain views with traditional seafood classics. The menu offers plenty of surf and turf, and one of my favorite lobster rolls on the island. The outdoor patio is the real draw, but indoor seating is also available. (47 Shore Road, 207-244-7463, seafoodketch.com)

MAINE-LY DELIGHTS $ (Lnch, Din)

Located across from the Swan's Island Ferry, this classic seafood shack offers tasty lobster rolls, crab rolls, sandwiches and more. (48 Granville Rd, 207-669-211, mainelydelights.com)

Bass Harbor Lighthouse

Since 1858 the Bass Harbor Lighthouse has been faithfully guarding the entrance to Bass Harbor and Blue Hill Bay. The beacon, originally lit by whale oil, is now powered by electricity and fully automated. All lighthouse beacons have a specific flash pattern, called a signature, which is listed on maritime charts. The red Bass Harbor beacon flashes every four seconds, and on a clear day it can be seen up to 13 miles at sea. In 1897 a 4,000-pound bronze bell was installed next to the lighthouse, but it was later replaced by offshore bell buoys. Listen closely and you'll notice that each bell buoy has a distinct pitch, which further aides in navigation on foggy days.

OFFSHORE ISLANDS

THE COAST OF MAINE is home to roughly 3,000 offshore islands—one of the highest concentrations of islands anywhere in the world. These rugged jewels—as small as a few square feet and as large as 100 square miles—add to the region's mystique and provide important habitat for nesting seabirds. In addition, five offshore islands near Mount Desert Island are home to small villages with year-round populations. These islands, physically cut off from much of the modern world and centered around the lobster industry, are some of the most culturally unique places in America.

Today four of these islands are accessible by ferry from Mount Desert Island. Just south of Mount Desert Island lie the Cranberry Isles (p.271), five small islands named after the cranberry bogs that once flourished here. The two largest islands, Islesford and Great Cranberry Island, have year-round communities and are accessible by ferry from Northeast Harbor and Southwest Harbor. A few miles to the southwest of the Cranberry Isles lies Frenchboro (p.277) and Swan's Island (p.279), two remote islands accessible by ferry from Bass Harbor. A fifth year-round island, Isle au Haut (p.213), is accessible via the town of Stonington on the mainland.

Though largely forgotten today, Maine's offshore islands once played a starring role in the history of North America. Long before colonists landed at Jamestown, thousands of Europeans fished the rich waters of the Gulf of Maine. Arriving in the spring, they hauled up mind-boggling numbers of cod, which played a major role in providing cheap, nutritious protein to rapidly growing populations in Europe. In the late 1700s, when settlers first arrived in the region, offshore islands were considered the best places to live due to their proximity to fishing grounds and coastal shipping routes. By the late 1800s, over 300 Maine islands were populated with year-round residents. But when railroads and trucks displaced ships as the most important forms of transportation, islanders found themselves cut off from much of the modern world.

Over the past century, most of Maine's offshore islands have been abandoned as greater economic opportunities have presented themselves on the mainland. Today only 15 Maine islands have year-round populations. And though many are struggling, opportunities offered by new technologies such as the internet and wind turbines offer economic hope. Modern technology may have robbed the islands of their lifeblood a century ago, but it may yet breath new life into them.

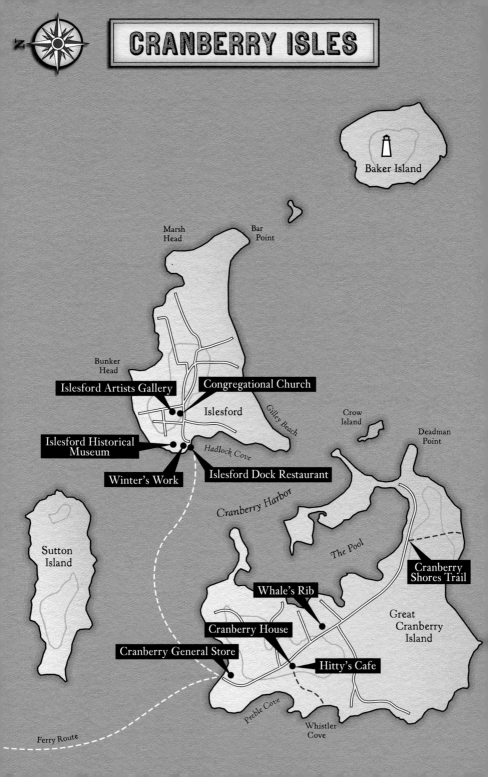

CRANBERRY ISLES

THESE FIVE OFFSHORE islands—Great Cranberry, Islesford, Sutton Island, Baker Island, Bear Island—lie just south of the eastern tip of Mount Desert Island. Originally settled in the late 1700s, the islands were named for the wild cranberries that grow here. A century ago, all five islands were occupied year-round, but today only Great Cranberry and Islesford have year-round populations. Sutton Island has only summer residents, while Baker Island and Bear Island are owned by Acadia National Park. The combined year-round population of Islesford and Great Cranberry is roughly 140 people.

Both Great Cranberry and Islesford are well worth a visit. The islands' intriguing mix of fishermen, artists and wealthy summer folks, combined with spectacular views of Mount Desert Island, makes for a great day trip. Far removed from traffic and crowds, the pace of island life on the Cranberry Isles is distinctly relaxed. Don't be alarmed if strangers wave as you walk past.

Passenger ferries (below) make round-trip journeys among the islands, so you can visit Great Cranberry and Islesford on a single ticket. I like to visit one in the morning and the other in the afternoon. Both can be explored on foot, but the paved roads are also great for biking.

At their peak nearly 100 years ago, both Great Cranberry and Islesford had booming shipyards, multiple schools and vibrant fishing fleets. But over the past century, as populations have dwindled, island life has dramatically changed. Today the median age on the Cranberry Isles is 48, and fewer than 30 people are younger than 18. The economic pulse of the islands still revolves around the sea, however, with lobstering and boatbuilding as the primary occupations.

Getting to the Cranberry Isles

Beal & Bunker - The official mailboat to the Cranberry Isles, in service since 1950, departs year-round from Northeast Harbor. (207-244-3575)

Cranberry Cove Ferry - From Memorial Day through September, the *Island Queen* offers daily shuttles between Southwest Harbor and the Cranberry Isles. (207-244-5882, cranberrycoveferry.com)

Sea Princess - Departing daily from Northeast Harbor, the Sea Princess offers nature cruises through the Cranberry Isles, including a visit to Islesford. (207-276-5352, barharborcruises.com)

The Delight - This 6-person water taxi offers service to the Cranberry Isles from Northeast Harbor, Seal Harbor or Southwest Harbor. You can also book private sunset cruises to the Islesford Dock Restaurant. (207-244-5724)

Islesford

Islesford, aka "Little Cranberry Island," is the most populated of the Cranberry Isles, with roughly 200 summer residents and 65 year-round residents. It's also the most popular island to visit due to its dockside restaurant, historical museum and art galleries. You can bring a bike, but it's easy enough to walk around the island, which only has a handful of paved roads. After exploring Islesford, you can check out the economic heart of the Cranberry Islands at the Islesford Lobster Co-op, located next to the town pier. Throughout the day, lobstermen unload their catch and buy bait at the Co-op. For more information visit islesford.com

★ ISLESFORD HISTORICAL MUSEUM

This small museum, founded in 1919 and currently operated by Acadia National Park, features exhibits and artifacts relating to life on Islesford. There's a permanent collection, plus temporary exhibits that change each year. Open daily late-June through September. (207-288-3338)

★ ISLESFORD DOCK RESTAURANT $$ (Lnch, Din)

Perched on a 200-year-old coal dock overlooking the harbor, this waterfront restaurant offers tasty food and stunning views of Mount Desert Island. The menu offers plenty of fresh seafood and creative entrees, plus burgers, salads and sandwiches. Open for lunch and dinner, Weds–Sunday, mid-June to early-Sept. *The Delight* (p.271) offers sunset dinner cruises to the restaurant from Northeast Harbor. (207-244-7494, islesforddock.info)

★ ART GALLERIES

The Islesford Dock is home to Winter's Work (207-244-3500, winterswork.com), Islesford Pottery (207-244-9108) and the Islesford Dock Gallery. Just up the road is Islesford Artists (Mosswood Road, islesfordartists.com), a wonderful gallery founded by lobsterman/artist Dan Fernald, which showcases the work of local artists. A bit further up the road you'll find signs pointing you to Island Girl Seaglass, which features folksy seaglass jewelry.

Art lovers should also visit the Islesford Congregational Church, which features beautiful seaglass windows by the island's most famous artist: Ashley Bryan. For more on Ashley visit ashleybryancenter.org

LOBSTER BOAT TOUR

Islesford resident Stefanie Alley offers 90-minute tours on her lobster boat. During the tour she hauls traps and explains the lobstering process. (207-244-7466)

LITTLE CRANBERRY LOBSTER

This small, tidy shack near the pier sells fresh seafood, snacks, cold drinks and branded gifts. They also ship live lobster anywhere in the country. (844-494-2529, littlecranberrylobster.com)

Great Cranberry Island

At 1,000 acres, Great Cranberry is the largest of the Cranberry Isles. Its year-round population is just 40 people, but its summer population swells to about 250. A two-mile road heads from the town dock to the eastern tip of the island. It's possible to explore the island on foot or bike, but another great option is the Great Cranberry Explorer, an 8-person golf cart that makes regular runs up and down the road. The narrated Explorer, which is driven by volunteers from the Historical Society, is free to ride, but donations are appreciated. I like riding the Explorer to the tip of the island, hiking the Whistler Cove Trail, then flagging the Explorer down for a ride to Cranberry House.

★CRANBERRY HOUSE

Home to the Preble-Marr Museum, which explores the history of Great Cranberry Island. Above the museum is the Art Center, a gathering place for classes, movies and lectures. (207-244-7800, gcihs.org)

★ HITTY'S CAFE $ (Lnch)

This lovely cafe, located in Cranberry House, serves delicious sandwiches, soups, salads and baked goods. Free wifi. (207-244-7845)

WHISTLER COVE TRAIL

Behind Cranberry House is an easy, well-marked trail leads to a beautiful cobblestone beach at Whistler Cove. The trail takes about 30 minutes round-trip.

CRANBERRY SHORES TRAIL

Located near the eastern tip of the island, this half-mile trail offers an easy stroll through the forest to the rocky shoreline. About 20 minutes round-trip.

CRANBERRY GENERAL STORE (Brk, Lnch)

This small market next to the dock sells basic food and supplies. Inside you'll also find the Seawich Café, which sells burgers and sandwiches. (207-244-0622)

WHALE'S RIB

The only thing more charming than this gift shop is owner Polly Bunker, who has run the Whale's Rib for over 40 years. (207-244-5153)

Baker Island

Baker Island, the most remote of the Cranberry Islands, was settled two centuries ago by William and Hannah Gilley. The Gilleys and their 12 children raised cows, chickens and roughly 50 sheep on the 123-acre island. In 1828 a 26-foot lighthouse was built, and in 1855 the original lighthouse was replaced with the current 43-foot tall tower. Today the island is owned by Acadia National Park. Ranger-guided boat tours of Baker Island are offered on the *Miss Samantha* (p.230).

Islesford & Mount Desert Island

Frenchboro

ISLANDS SOUTH OF BASS HARBOR

Frenchboro

This 1,500-acre island, home to a year-round population of roughly 40 people, is officially called Long Island. But because there are several Long Islands in Maine, locals call it Frenchboro, the name of the island's one tiny village. The island was first settled in 1813, and in 1910 the population peaked at 197. Since then a steady stream of islanders have left for the mainland. Today the local economy revolves entirely around lobsters and lobstering. Despite the small population, nearly a dozen children attend K-7 in the island's one-room schoolhouse. The Frenchboro Library and Historical Society (207-334-2924) is a great place to learn more about this rugged island's history.

Frenchboro is famous for its annual Lobster Festival, held the second Saturday of August. The festival is the biggest party of the year, attracting over 500 people who arrive by lobster boat, private yacht or a special ferry that departs from Bass Harbor in the morning. If you miss the festival, you can still enjoy fresh lobster at Lunt's Dockside Deli (207-334-2922, luntsdeli.com) in July and August. Unless you have your own boat, the best way to visit Frenchboro is with Island Cruises (p.265), which offers day trips to Frenchboro from Bass Harbor.

Placentia

Located halfway between Mount Desert Island and Swan's Island, Placentia has one of the region's most fascinating 20th century histories. In 1948 two 36-year-olds, Arthur and Nancy Kellam, purchased this 552-acre island for $7,500. For the next 35 years the couple lived on Placentia in near total seclusion. There was no running water or electricity, they chopped their own wood and grew their own vegetables, and when they needed supplies such as kerosene or batteries they rowed two miles to Bass Harbor in a wooden dory.

Art was a Cornell-educated engineer who had worked on military aircraft for the Lockheed Corporation. Nan had graduated from the University of Wisconsin. During WWII the couple lived in Southern California, and following the war they decided to abandon modern life. After a nationwide search for a remote island, the Kellams bought Placentia. According to Nan's journal: "At 3 o' clock on the 23rd of May, Art cashed his last salary check, then we made a little round of calls, paying respects to civilization before turning our backs on it ... we hoped to build a simple house and a simple life, to learn to appreciate fundamental things."

In 1985 Art died of pneumonia, and his ashes were spread on the island. After three summers and one winter on Placentia by herself, Nan moved to Bass Harbor. Following her death in 2001, Placentia was donated to the Nature Conservancy. The story of the Kellams is chronicled in the book *We Were An Island*.

Swan's Island

Lying six miles southwest of Mount Desert Island, Swan's Island features 7,000 acres of classic coastal scenery and one of the prettiest harbors in Maine. Home to roughly 350 year-round residents, visiting Swan's Island feels a bit like stepping back in time. Other than satellite TV and the internet, little has changed over the past several decades, and the island's tight-knit community continues to live a life that revolves almost entirely around the sea. If you're looking for the salt of the earth, it doesn't get much saltier than Swan's Island.

Swan's Island also boasts one of the most colorful histories of any Maine island. When French explorer Samuel Champlain first set eyes on the island in 1604, he named it *Brûlé Côté*, "Burnt Coast"—presumably because wildfires had recently burned the island. Over the years, Brule Cote's pronunciation and spelling was twisted and mangled to "Burnt Coat," which is now the official name of Swan's Island's most famous harbor. Even today, Swan's Island continues to engage in linguistic lawlessness. Since 1986 island residents have made a deliberate attempt to restore the historically accurate apostrophe to Swan's Island—in defiance of nautical charts and the U.S. Postal Service.

Swan's Island's first white settler was Thomas Kench, who fled here after going AWOL during the Revolutionary War. For over a decade Kench lived on the island as a hermit. Then one morning he awoke to find settlers arriving by boat. He must have been horrified to learn that the island had been purchased by his former Revolutionary War commander: Colonel James Swan. Apparently tensions between Swan and Kench had eased considerably by then, for Kench lived on the island an additional 10 years before moving to the mainland.

To populate his new island, Colonel Swan offered 100 acres to any homesteader who promised to stay at least seven years. The first man to accept this offer was David Smith, who arrived here from New Hampshire in 1791. Over the course of his life, Smith fathered 27 children by three wives, earning him the local nickname "King David." (Today many Swan's Island residents can still trace their family lineage back to King David.)

At its peak in the late 1800s, Swan's Island boasted a population of over 700 and its fishermen were consistently ranked first or second in Maine in terms of annual catch. During the 1900s, when gas-powered engines made offshore fishing from the mainland possible, the island lost over half of its year-round population.

For up-to-date information on Swan's Island visit jameskaiser.com

GETTING TO SWAN'S ISLAND

Swan's Island is accessible via a 30-minute ferry that departs Bass Harbor several times daily (schedules posted at maine.gov/mdot/ferry/swansisland). Tickets are available at the ferry terminal in Bass Harbor (207-244-3254). Note: I do not recommend taking your car during the busy summer months, when space on return trips is limited. Better to rent bikes in Southwest Harbor (p.255) and enjoy them on Swan's Island's 20 miles of paved, uncrowded roads.

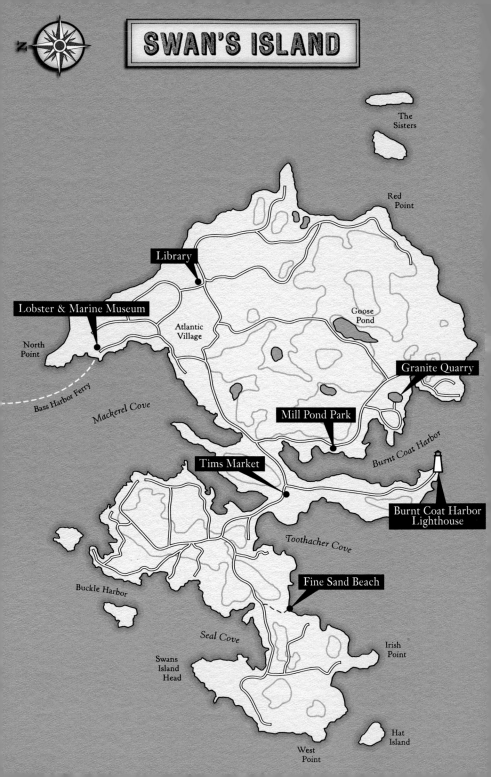

★ BURNT COAT HARBOR LIGHTHOUSE

Built in 1872 and automated in 1975, this classic lighthouse is home to history and art exhibits. The tower, which is about 35 feet high, boasts tremendous views. There are also 1.8 miles of nearby hiking trails, including the Long Point Beach Trail, which offers great views of the surrounding islands on clear days. The lighthouse is located at the tip of Hockamock Head, about 4.2 miles from the ferry terminal. (burntcoatharborlight.com)

★ FINE SAND BEACH

One of the most beautiful beaches in Maine. On a hot summer day, there's no better place to swim and soak in the sun. The beach is accessible via a short hiking trail through the woods.

★ LOBSTER & MARINE MUSEUM

Located near the ferry terminal, this small museum offers a fascinating glimpse into the human history of Swan's Island, from native times to the present day. There are several rooms of fishing and nautical artifacts, plus a display on natural history. (207-526-4423, swansislandlobsterandmarinemuseum.org)

TIMS ISLAND MARKET & TAKEOUT $

This tiny market and food trailer is the social hub of Swan's Island. Check out the flyers by the door to find out what's happening on the island. Basic food and supplies are available in the market, and the adjacent trailer serves seafood rolls, burgers, sandwiches and pizza. (207-526-4410)

SWAN'S ISLAND LIBRARY

Books, wifi and rotating historical exhibits. (451 Atlantic Road, 207-526-4330)

MILL POND PARK

Located just down the hill from the Mill Pond Health Center, this lovely park has picnic tables, grills and terrific views of Burnt Coat Harbor.

GRANITE QUARRY

The island's old granite quarry is now used as a swimming hole. Even if you don't go swimming, the road to the quarry offers classic views of the harbor, lighthouse and piers full of lobster traps and colorful buoys.

SATURN PRESS

Since 1986 this high-end print shop has been making stationary and greeting cards using antique letterpresses. (463 Atlantic Road)

SWEET CHARIOT MUSIC FESTIVAL

In early August Swan's Island plays host to a three-night music festival, which is very popular with boaters. (sweetchariotmusicfestival.com)

JAMES SWAN

The remarkable story of James Swan, the first owner of Swan's Island, is almost beyond belief. In 1675, when Swan was just 11 years old, he arrived in America from Scotland. By age 17 the ambitious self-taught youngster had written a book arguing against the Slave Trade, making him one of America's earliest Abolitionists. Later he joined the Sons of Liberty, participated in the Boston Tea Party, and fought at Bunker Hill. Following the war, he was elected to the Massachusetts State Legislature, and shortly thereafter he inherited a large fortune from a wealthy Scotsman who, though not related to Swan, admired the young man's ambition. Swan used the money to purchase and sell confiscated Tory property, multiplying his inheritance several times over.

Armed with newfound wealth, Swan led an increasingly flamboyant lifestyle. He speculated in risky investments, fought and won a duel, and boasted of owning the most luxurious horse-drawn carriage in America. In 1786 Swan purchased Swan's Island and most of the small islands surrounding it. He referred to this property as his "Island Empire" and built a grand mansion on Swan's Island where he entertained guests in lavish style. But just one year after purchasing Swan's Island, many of his risky investments turned sour. To make up for his losses, he invested in even riskier ventures. When trace amounts of gold were discovered on Swan's Island, Swan spent huge sums of money establishing a full scale mining operation. Three years later, the mining operation had produced enough gold to make "one good sized wedding ring."

As Swan's debts compounded, he was forced to flee to Paris to escape his creditors and try to rebuild his fortune. Using aristocratic connections, Swan landed several lucrative contracts with the French Army, but the contracts fell apart with the onset of the French Revolution. Although Swan escaped the guillotine, he was later arrested by French authorities for an alleged debt of two million francs. Although Swan had the money, he insisted that he did not owe it and he refused to pay—a noble stance that landed him in prison for the next 22 years. While incarcerated, Swan paid off many of the debts of his fellow inmates, but he refused to even speak with the man who claimed he was owed two million francs.

By the time Swan was finally released from French prison, he was 76 years old. His wife and most of his friends had passed away. Having nowhere to go, Swan returned to prison and pleaded to become an inmate again. His offer was refused, and three years later Swan died alone on a Paris street.

Fine Sand Beach

Swan's Island

Over 150,000 copies sold

Travel tips, hotel info, updates and more

jameskaiser.com